STUDIES IN IMPERIALISM

CW00823138

general editor John M. MacKenzie

When the 'Studies in Imperialism' series was founded more than twenty-five years ago, emphasis was laid upon the conviction that 'imperialism as a cultural phenomenon had as significant an effect on the dominant as on the subordinate societies'. With more than ninety books published, this remains the prime concern of the series. Cross-disciplinary work has indeed appeared covering the full spectrum of cultural phenomena, as well as examining aspects of gender and sex, frontiers and law, science and the environment, language and literature, migration and patriotic societies, and much else. Moreover, the series has always wished to present comparative work on European and American imperialism, and particularly welcomes the submission of books in these areas. The fascination with imperialism, in all its aspects, shows no sign of abating, and this series will continue to lead the way in encouraging the widest possible range of studies in the field. 'Studies in Imperialism' is fully organic in its development, always seeking to be at the cutting edge, responding to the latest interests of scholars and the needs of this ever-expanding area of scholarship.

Empire careers

MANCHESTER 1824

Manchester University Press

Empire careers

WORKING FOR THE CHINESE CUSTOMS SERVICE, 1854–1949

Catherine Ladds

MANCHESTER
UNIVERSITY PRESS

The right of Catherine Ladds to be identified as the author of this work has been asserted by her in accordance with the Copyright, Designs and Patents Act 1988.

Published by Manchester University Press
Altrincham Street, Manchester M1 7JA, UK
www.manchesteruniversitypress.co.uk

British Library Cataloguing-in-Publication Data is available

Library of Congress Cataloging-in-Publication Data is available

ISBN 978 1 7849 9370 2 *paperback*

First published by Manchester University Press in hardback 2013

This edition first published 2016

The publisher has no responsibility for the persistence or accuracy of URLs for any external or third-party internet websites referred to in this book, and does not guarantee that any content on such websites is, or will remain, accurate or appropriate.

Printed by Lightning Source

For Dave and Elaine Ladds

CONTENTS

LIST OF TABLES

LIST OF FIGURES

Cover image Customs fourth assistants R. F. C. Hedgeland (left) and
P. P. P. M. Krèmer (right), Nanjing, c. 1899–1903

All photographs are from the Hedgeland Collection, School of
Oriental & African Studies and are reproduced courtesy of SOAS
Library.

ACKNOWLEDGEMENTS

I owe a great deal to several institutions and people who provided intellectual and practical assistance in the researching and writing of *Empire Careers*. First and foremost, I owe a debt of gratitude to Robert Bickers at the University of Bristol who guided this project in its early stages, providing much-needed advice and criticism. For his very useful observations on an early version of this manuscript, I am thankful to Rana Mitter. Various institutions funded the research on which this book is based. The Arts and Humanities Research Council and the British Academy supported several research trips to China, to the United States and to various archives in the UK. I owe a great deal to the European Studies Center at Nanjing University where I spent three months as a visiting scholar in the summer of 2007, thus enabling me to carry out extra research in the Customs archives. Several libraries and archives provided invaluable assistance, particularly the employees of the Second Historical Archives of China in Nanjing and Susannah Rayner at SOAS Library.

Many individuals gave much-needed moral support during the research and writing of this book. I am grateful to Weipin Tsai and Federica Ferlanti for their companionship and help while navigating the archives in Nanjing, 2004–5, and to Deborah Yalen at Colorado State University who has listened to me talk about this book with patience and good humour over the past two years. Lastly, I would like to thank Justin, for his unfailing encouragement in addition to his proof-reading skills, and my parents and grandparents for their support.

LIST OF ABBREVIATIONS

CAS   Colonial Administrative Service
CCS   Chinese Customs Service
ICS   Indian Civil Service
IG   Inspector General
NRS   Non-Resident Secretary
SMC   Shanghai Municipal Council
SMP   Shanghai Municipal Police

GENERAL EDITOR'S INTRODUCTION

In 1872 the Rev. Anthony Stocker Aglen arrived in the village of Alyth, Perthshire, to take up his post as the rector of St Ninian's Episcopal Church. He brought with him his wife Margaret Elizabeth, née Mackenzie and a young son Francis Arthur, born in 1869 when his father was curate in Scarborough. Young Francis must have played in the garden of the parsonage in Cambridge Street, Alyth, and explored the village as he got older. His holidays from Marlborough School (then a school for the sons of clergymen) were naturally spent in Alyth and when he came to look for work he had a stroke of luck. The Venerable Archdeacon Aglen (as he became) had been to a preparatory school with one Robert Hart. They had become friends and corresponded with each other all their lives. Hart had become the second Inspector General of the Chinese Maritime Customs and is often regarded as one of the most influential figures in late nineteenth-century China. He was notorious for placing relatives and the sons of friends in that service. The Venerable Archdeacon must have written to him and Francis duly went to China in 1888 when he was barely nineteen. The younger Aglen's rise in the customs service was rapid. From 1897, still under thirty, he held the rank of Commissioner and was in charge of the major customs houses in Tientsin (Tianjin), Nanking (Nanjing) and Shanghai. During the Boxer siege of the legations in Peking (Beijing), he actually deputised for Hart while the latter was trapped (and like the others in the legation found himself reading his own *Times* obituary). Hart seems to have rewarded him by making him his chief secretary at the headquarters of the customs service in Beijing. Aglen duly succeeded Hart in 1910 and was appointed substantive Inspector General in 1911.

In 1906 Francis Aglen married Isabel Marion (generally known as Senga), the daughter of the distinguished Edinburgh botanist Sir Isaac Bayley Balfour. They had three sons and two daughters, but she prematurely died at sea travelling from China in 1925. Aglen subsequently married, in 1927, Anna Moore, the daughter of a Scottish shipping agent, Murray Ritchie of Leith, who worked in Santiago, Chile. She seems to have been the governess of the Aglen children for some years and regularly travelled back and forth between China and Britain with them. Aglen's period as Inspector General was a highly turbulent one, so much so that, after the fall of the Qing dynasty in 1911, the Chinese administration was in sufficient disarray that he began to bank the very considerable customs revenue in European banks under his own name.

He then proceeded to service the Chinese foreign loans and occasionally doled out money to pay for the police or for building flood dykes.
He was, by default, the treasurer of China. No wonder he himself
referred to the customs service as an 'imperium in imperio'.[1] Moreover,
according to the account of Paul King, one of the customs commissioners, Aglen seems to have been better liked than his predecessor.[2]
He and his wife had been particularly concerned about members of the
customs service fighting in the First World War. In addition, he made
strenuous attempts to put recruitment and training on a more sound
footing.

Aglen was dismissed from the service in 1927 because he had refused
to follow the order of the Beiyang government to collect surtaxes which
had not yet been approved by the Western powers.[3] Many, including
western representatives in Beijing, regretted his departure, although
he was given the consolation prize of a year on full pay. After a period
of living in London he returned to Alyth and bought a house called
Burnside on the edge of the village. By now he was garlanded not only
with British honours, including the GCMG, but also the highest orders
of China, Japan, France, Italy, Denmark, Belgium and Norway. Many
countries were grateful to him for struggling to keep the Chinese
finances on some sort of even keel. The Aglens duly continued to
interact socially with well-to-do local families such as the Kinlochs,
the Rattrays, the Tennants and the Ramsays. Indeed one of his sons,
Edward, married Persis Clerk-Rattray of Craighall, a few miles away.
Paul Ramsay of Bamff, near Alyth, knew this aunt and uncle well and
also remembers Aglen's widow, apparently known to all as Cheech,
who moved from Burnside to a smaller house in that same Cambridge
Street where her husband had spent his childhood. She was by all
reports a highly colourful and eccentric, even fearsome, figure and used
to recount tales of her time in China. She was surrounded by many
Chinese memorabilia brought back from the Far East by Aglen and
herself. Her former housekeeper still lives in Alyth.

Clearly this is relevant to this book, but the reason I relate this
intriguing story is that I too live in that same Perthshire village of Alyth
in retirement. I know the present owner of Burnside House and I am
well acquainted with Sir Francis Aglen's distant relative by marriage,
Paul Ramsay. It all reflects the ways in which micro- and macro-history
can interact. The village of Alyth (which has other notable connections
with empire that I have explored) acts as a sort of crossroads where the
local and global intersect, where people move away into a wider world
and become mixed up in remarkable events. Sometimes, as in the case
of Francis Aglen, they even return to Alyth. Such local and personal
connections (which can probably be found almost anywhere) open

windows on that world and, by a curious coincidence, I had just begun to put all this story together at exactly the time that Catherine Ladds's notable book on the Chinese customs service arrived on my desk for inclusion in the MUP 'Studies in Imperialism' series.

As she recounts, the Chinese customs service was the means whereby the Western powers set about what they regarded as the necessary modernisation of China. It constituted the principal financial apparatus whereby the Chinese funds could be placed on a sound footing, such that western loans and indemnities could be safely serviced. It was thus the key pivot between Chinese and foreign interests. Although these events seem relatively recent, they all seem a far cry from Eurozone crises of today and from the vision of a Eurozone debt commissioner going to China cap in hand to attempt to secure the financial support of a country of vast wealth, the economy of which is in considerable surplus and seems to have experienced few of the checks suffered by those in the West. The transformation of China in just the past fifteen to twenty years has been truly staggering, even reflected in such statistics as the extent of car and mobile phone ownership. China is now the major player in a globalised world.

The Chinese customs service was highly significant in this process of globalisation. Its personnel was extraordinarily international in its composition – as reflected in the range of orders received by Francis Aglen – and led one commentator to refer to it as the Foreign Legion of the East. Its operations were staggeringly diverse, involving not only the raising of the customs revenue (the most secure and extensive revenue of China in the period) but also the organisation of coastal lighthouses, harbour maintenance, quarantine arrangements, anti-piracy patrols and aspects of the postal service, as well as the collection of both meteorological information and statistics. The service was thus in the business of knowledge collection, the process that underpins all power. Given its maritime business, the customs also had its own fleet of cruisers and lighthouse tenders.[4] Its customs houses were to be found in no fewer than forty-six ports, the really significant ones being the treaty ports where western powers had taken from a weakened China not only trading rights but also aspects of legal and administrative extraterritoriality which made them in effect international imperial enclaves. In such ports, the very architecture of the customs office invariably reflected the intrusive power of the West (just as the grand customs houses of British ports seemed to reflect the grandeur of the state's presence).

This book strikingly complements the work of Brunero, which offered a political overview of the service and concentrated on the 1920s and 1930s. The author covers a longer period and is particularly interested in the personnel of the service, the large number of foreign officers who ran its affairs (there were also of course many Chinese). Using an impressive array of sources in China, Europe and America, she demonstrates that they were not always the supremely self-confident, romantic figures of imperial lore. They were often fallible and vulnerable. They sometimes became mixed up in corruption.[5] They were invariably ill, suffering not only from physical diseases but also from the psychological problems of living in remote outposts and socially overheated contexts. Their social and working lives reflected the inviolable racial and class hierarchies of the imperial condition everywhere. She also examines the manner in which they were recruited (Aglen is a classic example), the qualities they were supposed to display and their working lives as well as their activities in sport, play and the clubs.[6] She looks at their record of success and failure, their origins, their experiences, and the manner in which they departed. The service survived through strikingly turbulent times, but in the end was consumed in the joint fires of war and of Communist revolution. It all seems a far cry from a peaceful Perthshire village that was, nonetheless, distantly plugged into these global events.

John M. MacKenzie

Acknowledgments: I am grateful to Irene Robertson of the Alyth Family History Project, to Michael Long of Burnside House, to Paul Ramsay of Bamff House and to the resources of the National Library of Scotland for information that contributed to the writing of this general editor's introduction. As it happens, it is the hundredth I have written for the 'Studies in Imperialism' series, which perhaps justifies the fact that it is the longest.

John M. MacKenzie

Notes

1 Quoted in Donna Brunero, *Britain's Imperial Cornerstone in China: The Chinese Maritime Customs Service, 1854–1949* (Abingdon: Roneledge, 2006), p. 31.
2 Paul King, *In the Chinese Customs Service: A personal record of forty-seven years* (London: T. F. Unwin, 1924), pp. 232, 295, 303.
3 This incident is fully described in Brunero's book (note 1). The situation was further complicated by the splits in the Chinese administration between Beijing in the north and Guangdong in the south.
4 Some of these vessels are illustrated and all are listed in the Greenwich National Maritime Museum monograph by B. Foster Hall, *The Chinese Maritime Customs: An international service 1854–1950* (London: National Maritime Museum, 1977). Hall was himself Commissioner of Customs in Hankow and Canton (Guangdong) in the 1930s. His photograph of the staff at the latter in 1939 shows 82 men, ten of them Indoor (without uniforms) and the rest in uniform. This distinction is fully explained by Catherine Ladds in the course of this book. The customs ships were inevitably used for senior staff social events, as illustrated in Brunero's book.

5   The probate of Aglen's will, indicating that he left £57,000 in 1932 seems to suggest that, although he had many opportunities for corruption, he avoided all such temptation. His salary was of course a considerable one.

6   These are reflected in the photographs that have come down to us. Cathy Ladds has herself arranged an exhibition of these photographs which was shown in Bristol. She was also involved in a project to digitise such images, showing customs officials, Aglen among them. These reveal them both in formal poses and settings and in more informal surroundings as at the Peking Club, at dinners, and at musical evenings. Some of these can be seen in the Hart collection deposited at Queen's University Belfast and in the Hedgeland collection at the School of Oriental and African Studies in London, available on line at http://chp.vcea.net/Collection_China_Maritime_Content.php?CF=8. I am grateful to Cathy Ladds for this information and for transmitting those images in which Aglen appears.

CHAPTER ONE

Introduction: the Customs, China and the empire world

Much is being written these days about co-operation among the United Nations, and the necessity for men of various nationalities to learn to work together during and after the war. The 90 years' history of the Chinese Customs Service demonstrates that men of all nationalities, with the most varied racial, educational, social and religious backgrounds, can work together harmoniously and efficiently. There have been as many as 23 different nationalities represented in the Chinese Customs staff, and this cosmopolitan personnel was moulded into a united, well-disciplined group whose *esprit de corps* and loyalty to China are proverbial.[1]

These words were written by Lester Knox Little, the last foreign Inspector General (IG) of the Chinese Maritime Customs Service (CCS), in 1944 as part of a brief history of the institution to which he had devoted thirty years of labour.[2] There is more than a hint of nostalgia for the past glories of the Service in Little's reiteration of timeworn truisms about the model of cosmopolitan co-operation supposedly pioneered by the foreign Customs staff. By 1944 the combined onslaught of Chinese nationalism and Japanese aggression had dismembered the Customs, stripped it of many of its powers and dramatically reduced the foreign staff, reducing the institution to a shadow of its former self. In a time when the days of the Foreign Inspectorate were clearly numbered, Little and the handful of other foreigners still in the Chinese government's employ took comfort in their Service's noble past traditions. What is more, Little was writing from the beleaguered wartime capital of Chongqing, where the Customs' example of international co-operation seemed particularly enviable in the face of Japanese bombing raids. In the context of global discussions about the urgent need to establish a transnational organisation capable of preventing and mediating future conflicts, Customs cosmopolitanism seemed remarkably prescient.

The Customs had its roots in a provisional system of administering foreign trade at Shanghai devised by the British, French and American consuls in 1853 as an emergency measure in response to the disruption caused by the Small Swords Uprising in September that year.[3] The permanent Foreign Inspectorate of Customs, which replaced the 'provisional system' on 12 July 1854, stayed true to its multinational beginnings.[4] Headed by a British Inspector General until the American L. K. Little took over in 1943 and employing a large cosmopolitan staff, the Customs was nonetheless an organ of the Chinese state, ostensibly answerable to the highest levels of the Chinese government. Always much more than a revenue-collecting agency, the Foreign Inspectorate's responsibilities soon grew to be far-reaching. After Sir Robert Hart took over the helm from the first IG, Horatio Nelson Lay, in 1863 the Customs began to be fashioned into a powerful and efficient bureaucracy. Hart's political connections with influential officials in the Qing state ensured that his expansionist and modernising impetus was practically granted a free rein by the Zongli Yamen (Bureau of Foreign Affairs), under whose jurisdiction the Customs operated after 1861.[5] The Customs Marine Department pioneered the lighting of the China coast, the printing press of the Statistical Department produced publications and reports on countless China-related topics, China's post office was founded (1896) under the auspices of the Customs and prominent personalities in the foreign staff sometimes assumed diplomatic functions.[6] Over the century of its existence the Customs employed 11,270 service-listed Chinese and approximately 11,000 foreigners of around twenty-five nationalities. This international personnel became the hallmark of the Foreign Inspectorate, emblematic of its uniqueness in an era of imperialist competition.

Imperial networks, the Customs and China

Empire Careers explores the life and work experiences of the Customs' multinational staff, asking how expatriates were personally and professionally changed by a career overseas. Its chapters consider the professional triumphs and tribulations of the Customs' foreign personnel, the social activities they engaged in, the personal and family lives they fashioned, their physical and mental illnesses and how all of these factors were influenced by the changing political context in China and abroad. Above all, this book considers how the life trajectories of European and American expatriates were shaped by the ideas, ideologies and structures of the broader imperial world, thus contributing to a recent intellectual shift towards thinking about imperial history in global terms. Several ambitious works have situated imperial history within large-scale, transnational processes, exploring how the ebb and flow of global geo-politics, cultural change and economic systems impinged upon the British Empire.[7] While *Empire Careers* makes no pretensions to being global in scope, it does enhance this recent broadening of the historical imagination in important ways. Through a case study of Customs' personnel it sheds light upon China's connections with the West and East Asia's integration into the migratory pathways that criss-crossed the globe during the age of empire.

A steadily growing segment of this literature has attempted to recast modern empire-building as a form of proto-globalisation. In the 1990s the term 'globalisation' entered common usage as a way of encapsulating the contemporary prominence of transnational processes and the intensification of connections between different regions. Most commentators in the social sciences and popular media tend to portray globalisation as a very contemporary product of the digital age, an assumption that has prompted other scholars to excavate its deep historical roots. Modern empire-building, which required and facilitated the formation of long-distance connections, seems to present a logical focus for exploring its antecedents.[8] While welcoming this corrective to the ahistoricity of much globalisation scholarship, a growing number of sceptics have cautioned against projecting this very contemporary concept on to the past. Frederick Cooper, for instance, has criticised globalisation's paucity as an analytical tool for understanding either the past or the present.[9] According to its critics, the very idea of globalisation, which purportedly encompasses a vast range of phenomena, suffers from a frustrating imprecision and falls into the trap of labelling all large-scale transnational processes as global, thereby neglecting careful consideration of the specificity and limitations of long-distance connections. Furthermore, both those who laud and those who lament globalisation's effects presume a gradual and inexorable intensification of global interconnectedness over time. Yet, as Cooper observes, 'Historical analysis does not present a contrast between a past of territorial boundedness and a present of interconnection and fragmentation, but rather a back-and-forth, varied combination of territorializing and deterritorializing tendencies.'[10]

Examining the specific nature and precise mechanisms of different types of long-distance connections presents a more fruitful approach to understanding the transnational forces of empire than the catchall concept of globalisation. Recent work on the 'British world', for instance, emphasises how multiple communities across the globe were connected through a shared identification with 'Britishness' during the age of empire.[11] By the late nineteenth century the dispersal of migrants from the British Isles around the world had fostered the construction of a global identity, which transcended the narrow boundaries of the nation-state. Acceptance into the British world was determined through cultural ties, shared principles and 'whiteness', although it must be remembered that many non-white people also sought to adopt a British identity and met with varying degrees of acceptance.[12] The idea of a 'British world', whose boundaries were not easily pinned down, articulates a broader and more flexible way of thinking about imperial connections than that of empire.

This literature is intimately linked to scholarship advocating a 'networked' approach to imperial history, reimagining empires as held together by numerous points of cultural, economic, social and professional connection.[13] Rather than picturing colonial connections as simply radiating out from the 'metropole' to the colonies, imperial space is visualised as weblike, thus helping to conceptualise reciprocal links *between* colonies. Much of this work has focused on how knowledge and ideologies were transported through these channels. Tony Ballantyne, for example, has argued that networks enabled 'cultural traffic' to flow between different sites of empire.[14] In a similar vein Alan Lester's *Imperial Networks: Creating identities in nineteenth-century South Africa and Britain* explores how three interacting and conflicting colonial discourses – governmental, settler and humanitarian – were forged through networks. In their efforts to influence public and official opinion in Britain, both settlers and humanitarians collected supporting case studies from the broader imperial world, knowledge of which was transmitted through intercolonial channels in letters and newspapers. In the course of this political battle settler and humanitarian identities solidified and, crucially, empire-wide discursive networks were developed. In this analysis imperial networks are envisaged as multiple, competing, changeable and largely informal.[15]

Colonial networks were not, however, only discursive in nature. Real goods, people and capital travelled through these pathways. What is more, the personal nature of imperial connections cannot be overestimated. Zoë Laidlaw, for instance, demonstrates how professional, friendship and kinship ties were relentlessly tapped by colonial elites in the hope of gaining access to patronage holders at the Colonial Office in the early nineteenth century. In this period, 'Imperial networks connected people first, places second'.[16] Networks were forged in the first place by the migrations of people around the globe, who formed economic, political and cultural connections in the course of their journeys.[17] Furthermore, as Gary Magee and Andrew Thompson have shown in their exploration of the 'British world economy', migrant efforts to maintain cultural links to Britain also had material implications, shaping consumer habits and the character of economic activity in the colonies.[18] Networks, then, were based on several different types of long-distance connection between individuals and groups of people, some of which were firmer and more enduring than others. The strongest and most intimate were based on bonds of family and friendship. Professional connections and membership of organisations such as scientific societies or Masonic lodges created semi-official links between individuals across the globe. National or regional affiliations could also exert a powerful umbilical pull, especially for expatriates in China where men and women of multiple nationalities jostled for position. Other types of connection were less personal, such as those forged by shipping companies, banks and newspapers, yet they nonetheless created a weblike infrastructure through which goods, knowledge, money and communications could flow.

Although the concept of a networked British world provides a useful way of thinking about cross-empire connections, not least in that it encourages consideration of 'metropole' and colony within the same analytical framework, the existing literature is not without limitations.[19] The overwhelming focus has so far been on Anglophone groups in the British Dominions, while other destinations of migration and settlement have been mostly neglected.[20] The vastness of British migration to the Dominions and the United States partly explains this omission. Of the 22.6 million people who left the British Isles, either voluntarily or involuntarily, between 1815 and 1914, the overwhelming majority ended up in the Antipodes or North America.[21] The 'neo-Britains' that resulted from this massive dispersal thus formed the backbone of the British world. Yet there remains the question of the approximately 674,000 individuals who left the British Isles between 1853 and 1920 for destinations other than the USA, Canada, Australasia and South Africa.[22] Where did they go, what did they do overseas and how long did they stay? Furthermore, did non-Anglophone travellers and migrants also make use of imperial networks? Perhaps most importantly, to what extent did all of these migrants belong to the 'British world'?

This book partially answers these questions by considering the extent to which China was part of a networked empire world. Since at least the early nineteenth century China had been a key hub in the 'triangular' trade in tea and opium that linked together Bengal, London and Guangzhou. It was only in the 1860s, however, after the Opium War (1839–42) and the Arrow War (1856–60) forcibly 'opened' more Chinese ports to foreign trade and residence, that Britons – along with Americans and other Europeans – began sojourning and settling in China in larger numbers. These men and women came to China to work as missionaries, to take advantage of new commercial opportunities, to enter the burgeoning consular service and to staff new institutions such as the Customs. This case study of the Customs, which employed by far the largest foreign personnel of all the political and commercial organisations operating in China by the late nineteenth century, helps us to visualise how people ended up in China after navigating the various 'circuits of empire'.[23] Some, for example, joined after journeying to China with the merchant marine while others gained access to the Inspector General's patronage by exploiting a family connection to the Service. A networked analysis encourages better understanding of the role that institutions such as the Customs played in producing knowledge about China and presenting it to audiences in Europe and beyond. What is more, networks are a useful conceptual tool for understanding why people went where they did after leaving the Customs, whether elsewhere in China, home or to another site of empire.

By placing the Customs' claims to cosmopolitanism at centre stage, *Empire Careers* also considers the extent to which non-Britons were able to utilise imperial circuits. The political exigencies of competition and co-operation between multiple imperial interests in China meant that the Customs' personnel contained an eclectic mix of nationalities. The case of the Chinese Customs Service, then, demonstrates the limits of a national approach to exploring imperial networks. Men and women of multiple nationalities, who did not necessarily identify with 'Britishness', used the pathways forged by the British Empire to seek out professional and personal opportunities overseas and to propel their movements around the world. Neither should we, as David Lambert and Alan Lester have cautioned, fall into the trap of viewing transnational networks as a British invention. Although their exploration is beyond the scope of this book, it must be remembered that the networks of modern imperial powers were predated by long-established webs of commerce and cultural exchange in Asia and the Middle East.[24] Furthermore, in the modern era nations and empires other than the British forged their own transnational pathways. *Empire Careers* provides a glimpse into the personal and professional connections maintained by Scandinavians, Russians and others, which were given strength through national allegiance.

While *Empire Careers* emphasises how a broad range of people – British and non-British, elite and non-elite – could potentially gain access to imperial networks, it simultaneously underscores their undemocratic nature. Characterising imperial networks as informal, fluid and multilayered encourages us to think of these connections as open and democratic. Yet, although some networks were reasonably open, such as those established by seamen, others were more exclusive than inclusive.[25] This was especially true in the empire world, where

[6]

inequality – particularly that based on race – was interwoven into the very fabric of political, economic and social institutions and structures. Admittance to imperial networks was granted or restricted according to one's race, class, gender and nationality. In a world where the British Empire dominated, British elites were granted privileged access to professional and economic networks. Thus, they were usually more effortlessly mobile than non-elites and non-Britons. Its cosmopolitan staff profile notwithstanding, the Customs was an unabashedly Anglophone institution until the 1930s. Furthermore, prospective employees in the elite administrative arm of the Service were expected to fit the profile of an *English* colonial administrator, whatever their national origins. Access to imperial webs, then, was always deliberately bounded.

Ultimately, this book shows that China *was* incorporated into imperial circuits in crucial ways, yet its significance to these networks was nonetheless circumscribed. The fact that China's sovereignty was never fully extinguished checked the spread of foreign power somewhat, which was reflected in the relatively small foreign population. Even at its height in the mid-1920s, the total number of British residents in China (excluding Hong Kong) stood only at 15,247, as compared with approximately 320,000 foreign residents of other nationalities.[26] They therefore lacked the political, cultural and economic heft of settlers in the Dominions, and were thus less influential in shaping the British world. Yet they nevertheless strove to sustain connections with friends and family at 'home', sought out personal and professional links wider afield throughout the empire and contributed to flows of goods, ideas and ideologies around the world. *Empire Careers* also underscores the role of institutions in making, maintaining and limiting long-distance connections. As an organisation that regulated China's overseas trade, the Customs oversaw China's integration into global trading networks. Furthermore, the Inspectorate energetically pursued connections with the broader empire world through its overseas recruitment practices, by establishing a London office, and by participating in international exhibitions. Indeed the Inspectorate actively sought recognition as a vital institution of the British world by, for example, modelling itself on the English civil service and colonial administrative services. Lastly, the Customs' multinational personnel encourages us to imagine China not as an isolated 'outpost' of empire but rather as a place where multiple imperial trajectories converged, overlapped and pushed up against one another.

Overseas careers in the empire world

Empire Careers is particularly concerned with understanding the professional migrations of people to China and around the empire world, thereby augmenting a rich body of literature on imperial migrations.[27] As a multinational organisation that employed both elites and non-elites, the Customs is a fecund source of examples of how nationality and socio-economic status influenced migration experiences. A recurrent cast of characters dramatises these themes. Their life stories interlace with quantitative data about career trajectories to shed light upon how people experienced working for the Customs. These personal histories reveal the diverse career paths followed by Europeans and Americans overseas. So far histories of the Foreign Inspectorate have largely been dominated by the enigmatic figure of Sir Robert Hart (1835–1911), the indefatigable nineteenth-century IG (1863–1908) credited with transforming the Customs into an efficient, multipronged and internationally renowned service. An Ulsterman born to a middling Portadown family, Hart travelled to China to become a student interpreter in the British consular service in 1854 after graduating from Queen's University Belfast. In 1859 he resigned to join the Customs and his subsequent rise in the Service was meteoric; after just four years he was promoted to the top job. Hart has captivated the imaginations of generations of historians because of his inimitable style of leadership, his closeness to certain Qing statesmen and the rapid expansion of the Customs' responsibilities under his tutelage.[28] Widely recognised as the most influential foreigner in nineteenth-century China, Hart received numerous honours from both the Chinese and British governments, including a baronetcy. He was a true servant of China, working tirelessly to promote the Service's interests until he finally left his adopted country in 1908.

The fascination with Hart's story, while understandable given his importance, overshadows the thousands of other life histories that were to some extent shaped by the Customs. Hart's life was, of course, atypical. Far more common were those who, rather than devoting a lifetime of work to China, stayed in the Customs for a brief sojourn before moving on to greener pastures. Edwin C. Denby, an American from Evansville, Indiana, whose father was minister to China 1885–98, gained a Customs appointment on the strength of his family connections in 1887. Unlike Hart, however, Denby intended the Customs to be only a temporary billet and he returned to the US in 1894 to become a lawyer. After practising law for several years he was elected to Congress as a Republican in 1905, later gaining renown as Secretary of the Navy (1921–24). The Briton J. O. P. Bland, in the Customs 1888–96, also saw his appointment as a springboard to more lucrative opportunities. An occupational chameleon, Bland parlayed his Customs experience into numerous other positions on the China coast, including Secretary of the Shanghai Municipal Council, representative for the British and Chinese corporation, journalist, popular historian and polemicist. No servant of China, Bland was increasingly derisive of his former service, which he considered too conciliatory towards China's interests.[29] Others stumbled into the Customs almost accidentally, especially those who worked for the low-status Outdoor and Coast Staffs. The Norwegian sailor A. H. Rasmussen arrived in China on a merchant ship in 1905 and impulsively decided to stay for a while. The Customs was by then a well-known source of stopgap employment for seamen at a loose end in the treaty ports and Rasmussen duly joined in Shanghai. The slow pace of promotion, lack of prospects and monotony of the Customs meant, however, that he leapt at the chance to leave for a better opportunity working for the China coast firm Arnold, Karberg and Co. in 1920.[30]

Although most had no desire to stay in the Customs for ever, there were always numerous men who anticipated a long career in the Service, who joined at the age of eighteen or nineteen and stayed until retirement or death – whichever came first. The heads of the custom houses in each port, the Commissioners, generally fell into this category. This career trajectory was most common in the Indoor Staff, the Service's executive arm, which offered decent pay and benefits and a measure of stability. Many young, middle-class men who could not afford to attend university and lacked the qualifications to enter a more elite overseas service chose this career route. Alfred E. Hippisley, in the Customs 1867–1910, applied for an appointment while still studying at Bristol Grammar School. He travelled to China in 1867, and after less than ten years of hard work was promoted to a series of senior posts in the Inspectorate General in Beijing, including Statistical Secretary and Chinese Secretary. Well-informed about Chinese politics, which he commented on extensively in his diary, Hippisley performed his work diligently and expertly.[31] Similarly the high-flier Kishimoto Hirokichi was one of the first Japanese appointed to the Indoor Staff in 1905. By 1927 he was second-in-command, holding the coveted post of Chief Secretary, and was widely tipped to become the next IG. His Customs career ended somewhat ignominiously, however; after the Foreign Inspectorate was taken over by the Japanese in 1941 he served as IG under the puppet regime in occupied China and was dismissed, along with all other Japanese employees, at the end of the war. Hippisley and Kishimoto were archetypical career administrators who were successful at forging long careers overseas, yet others were not so lucky. The archives are replete with stories of failures and missteps. F. Kleinwächter, a relative of Prince Bismarck appointed to the Indoor Staff in 1863, was too hot-headed for a life of pen-pushing. Initially a favourite of Hart who reached the position of Commissioner after only four years, Kleinwächter soon became embroiled in disputes with local Chinese and foreign officials. 'He's an awfully quarrelsome, pigheaded fellow', wrote an exasperated Hart in 1869. Eventually Kleinwächter's temper got the better of him when he resigned in anger in 1889 after the Zongli Yamen refused to take his advice on the matter of the silk trade.[32] The Briton Oliver Hall followed a very different career path in the Customs, yet his exit was similarly discomfiting. Hall reached the senior position of chief examiner in the Shanghai Outdoor Staff after twenty-eight years of service and probably intended to settle in China. Instead he found himself expelled from the Customs in 1938 after he was accused of taking bribes from a Chinese merchant. Hall, his wife and their eight children were left destitute.[33]

In focusing on the life histories of these individuals, and many others like them, *Empire Careers* contributes to a recent revival of historical biography. Unlike life stories written in the age of imperialism, usually lionising accounts of illustrious colonial governors, martyred missionaries and famous adventurers, this new wave of colonial life histories has a fundamentally different agenda. Books such as Gregor Muller's *Colonial Cambodia's 'Bad Frenchmen'* and Robert Bickers's *Empire Made Me* have selected otherwise obscure individuals as their subjects and seek to explain how broader economic, cultural and political processes impinged upon their life trajectories.[34] Other works, such as Miles Ogborn's *Global Lives: Britain and the world, 1550–1800*, have positioned their subjects within the broad sweep of global forces, exploring how lives were shaped by early globalisation and how individuals in turn propelled globalising processes, by, for example, forging connections between colonies.[35] By focusing on the diverse life stories shaped by the Customs, this book addresses a broad agenda of reassessing common colonial caricatures of upper-class Englishmen, errant adventurers and dipsomaniac thugs.[36] Charismatic individuals, such as aristocratic governors who coolly bent colonised peoples to their will and intrepid heroes, animated colonial projects for people at home during the age of imperialism.[37] Even today these characters retain an enduring allure. But tales of mastery and adventure are only one part of the colonial experience. Beneath these stereotypes are thousands of personal and individual stories and dramas of fortunes made and lost, relationships forged and broken, of loyalties cast away and built anew, as the experiences of the Customs' lower-level staff show. As such, *Empire Careers* enhances a growing body of scholarship developed over the past two decades that seeks to reincorporate settler cultures and communities into colonial narratives.

'Colonisers' barely featured in post-independence histories of the imperial age. Postcolonial scholars instead concerned themselves with constructing national histories and with writing the experiences of the colonised into the historical record, thereby providing a much-needed corrective to decades of scholarship that ignored the agency of colonised peoples and instead focused on the intricacies of imperial rule and the exploits of colonial governors. Colonisers were, however, often caricatured in the process. Although European and American settlers, sojourners and expatriates are still uneasily regarded as dubious scholarly subjects, there is now a broad consensus that both coloniser and colonised were central to shaping colonial cultures and societies.[38] Recent studies have highlighted the heterogeneous character of colonial communities, in which a broad range of projects and ideologies competed.[39] Furthermore, although entrenched and institutionalised inequalities demarcated along racial lines were central to the colonial experience, white Europeans and Americans did not exercise untrammelled power. Indeed many singularly failed to exploit the enhanced opportunities available to white men and women in the empire world, which were circumscribed by nationality, class and personal blunders. In their study of the letters of two settlers in the South Sea Islands, for example, Richard Eves and Nicholas Thomas draw attention to the frequent *failure* of personal colonial projects, which were often marked by disappointment and fraught with self-doubt.[40] Over the past fifteen years, these themes have also been explored with regard to China's foreign communities.[41] In the treaty ports, where no single colonial power ruled, an even greater multiplicity of life trajectories met, intersected and sometimes conflicted.

This was especially true with regard to national identity. In developing a transnational history of imperialism in East Asia, *Empire Careers* shows how individuals of diverse nationalities oscillated between co-operation and competition in colonial spaces where no single foreign power held sway. Although nationally bounded perspectives on empire must be interrogated, especially on the heterogeneous edges of empire such as China, it is equally true that, in the words of Stuart Ward, 'the idea of nationalism has had a profound influence on the ways in which people have made sense of the imperial experience'.[42] Many European and American expatriates saw themselves as furthering their home country's prestige, power and prosperity abroad. National identity could be sharpened in the colonial context both in an effort to create distance from indigenous communities and to counter the dislocating experience of migration by fostering a shared sense of national belonging.[43] Yet the case of the Customs raises the issue of how, at the same time as nation-states were assuming a much more rigid shape, in terms of the citizenship regimes and national identities they promoted, the structures of an increasingly interconnected world worked to part-fragment national loyalties by pulling out men and women from Europe, North America and Japan to staff the institutions of empire. In the empire world national allegiances competed and coexisted with local and global identities. Robert Bickers, for example, has observed how British settlers in Shanghai incorporated three main strands into their identity: 'British, imperialist, local'.[44] Furthermore, like the contributors to the collection of essays edited by David Lambert and Alan Lester, *Colonial Lives across the British Empire*, this book sheds light on how colonial identities were deconstructed and reconstituted over the course of a career overseas in the process of moving between imperial spaces.

The strong organisational cultures cultivated by imperial institutions such as the Customs add another component to this complex mix of identities. Increasing interest in the contours of colonial communities has also given rise to a number of studies of colonial administrative and policing services.[45] As organisations that drew labour and talent – both putative and real – from Britain, from elsewhere in Europe and, in the case of the Customs, from America and Japan, they provide an unparalleled insight into the heterogeneity of colonial societies. The personnel of these organisations, comprised of both marginals and elites, shed light upon the complex hierarchies determined by race, class and nationality that criss-crossed the colonial world. Furthermore they formed a frontline of contact between the colonial state and local communities. It is therefore important to understand the world and worldview of the countless administrators, policemen, railway engineers and soldiers who oiled the machinery of empire. The ways in which they thought about empire, colonised peoples and the organisations they worked for influenced how colonial power was deployed in a very real way. As a 'hybrid' institution that simultaneously represented the Chinese government, foreign power and cross-national co-operation, the Customs developed a distinctive identity that set its staff apart from other foreign organisations and communities in China. Professionally, foreign Customs employees were expected to act as loyal 'servants of the dragon throne', dedicated first and foremost to furthering China's interests. *Empire Careers* explores the personal and professional ramifications of working within another state's administration, demonstrating how expatriates negotiated a broad range of allegiances, experiences and identities over the course of their careers. As employees of an institution that straddled the foreign and Chinese worlds, the foreign Customs staff were able to flit opportunistically between different communities and identities with more ease than most.

[12]

China, the Customs and colonialism

Until very recently the history of colonialism in China had been largely forgotten in the West, despite the fact that in China itself 'semi-colonialism' is regarded as *the* defining theme of the modern period, 1842–1949. Although colonial enclaves such as Hong Kong, Weihaiwei and Macao existed, no foreign power particularly wanted to annex China as a formal colony, with the exceptions of Japan and possibly Russia. Instead, foreign individuals, governments and institutions exerted dominance over various aspects of China's political, economic and cultural life, by, for example, seizing control of key state organs such as the Customs. These actions were enabled and bolstered by a series of treaties – often referred to as the 'unequal treaties' – which granted privileges to foreign interest groups on unfavourable terms to China. The 'opening up' of the treaty ports to foreign trade and residence, the artificially low tariff levied on foreign trade, extraterritoriality and the right for missionaries to proselytise in the interior were all stipulated and protected by treaties, the first of which was the 1842 Treaty of Nanjing signed between Britain and China as the conclusion to the Opium War (1839–42). These treaties were extracted and reinforced by diplomatic pressures, violence threatened by the ever-present foreign gunboats that patrolled China's coast and waterways, and periodic bouts of conflict such as the Arrow War (1856–60) and Boxer War (1900–1).[46] Despite the foreign stranglehold on the Chinese state, which began to loosen its grip only in the late 1920s, imperialism in China has generally been branded as 'informal' and therefore peripheral to the 'real' story of colonialism as embodied by British India.[47]

The history of colonialism in China has also been overlooked for political reasons. The post-1949 field of Chinese studies in the West was largely developed in the United States. In the midst of Cold War politics, scholars of China's modern history and foreign relations consciously or unconsciously distanced America from the ignoble history of colonialism in China.[48] Instead China's interactions with the West between 1839 and 1949 were reframed as a partnership, which struggled to bring modernity to China's shores. 'Modernity, however defined, was a Western, not a Chinese, invention,' claimed John K. Fairbank, pioneer of Chinese studies at Harvard.[49] In Fairbank's analysis, rather than rising to the modernising challenge of the West, China sought instead to accommodate the foreign powers in the nineteenth century through the relatively harmonious joint Sino-Western administration of treaty port institutions, which he placed in a continuum of China's long-standing 'institution of *foreign participation* in its government'.[50] Fairbank's model of Sino-foreign administration – which he dubbed 'synarchy' – was embodied by the Foreign Inspectorate of Customs, 'the institution most thoroughly representative of the whole period'.[51] Thus the history of imperialism in China became the decidedly more benign history of China's foreign relations.

From the mid-1980s an over-zealous response to Paul Cohen's call for a 'China centerd history of China' eclipsed the history of China's relations with the West.[52] The profusion of studies of Chinese themes and impulses that resulted from Cohen's call to arms against Western-centricism provided a necessary counterbalance to the assumption that change in modern China was propelled by European and American actors. However, it also precluded exploration of the complexity of Western influences. Very recently China's re-emergence as a global power has prompted a new wave of interest in the troubled history of Sino-foreign relations.[53] *Empire Careers* contributes to this nascent reassessment of China's colonial past by placing the foreign presence at centre stage while also recognising the agency of Chinese forces and actors. The history of the Customs is intertwined with the broader arc of imperialism in China. While purporting to serve Chinese interests, the Customs was instrumental in enforcing the unequal treaty system by, for example, upholding the artificially low five per cent tariff on foreign trade.[54] Indeed the Foreign Inspectorate of Customs, which replaced the 'provisional system' of administering foreign trade at Shanghai on 12 July 1854, was created to ensure that China and the foreign powers fulfilled their treaty obligations of remitting and collecting the agreed duties.[55] Hart's diverse projects, ranging from harbour construction and maintenance to acting as an intermediary between the Zongli Yamen and the foreign diplomatic establishment, undoubtedly accelerated the growth of a modern industrial and bureaucratic infrastructure. Yet they also facilitated the foreign penetration of China. As Chen Xiafei, one of the editors of a four-volume edition of Hart's correspondence with his deputy in London, has concluded, Hart is best described as a 'far-sighted colonist'.[56]

Hart's successor, Sir Francis Aglen (IG 1911–27), cemented the symbiotic relationship between the Customs and the foreign powers by assuming direct control of banking the Customs revenue, which had previously been supervised by the Chinese Superintendent of Customs in each port. In the process a portion of the revenue was earmarked for repayment of foreign loans and the Boxer Indemnity, thus raising nationalist ire.[57] Come 1927 Aglen found himself dismissed by the Beijing government and, after a lengthy succession battle, succeeded as IG by Hart's nephew, Frederick Maze (IG 1929–41).[58] By the time Maze was appointed as IG the Foreign Inspectorate was working in a fundamentally changed environment. With a relatively strong central government led by Chiang Kai-shek in power and a burgeoning popular nationalist movement on the streets, Maze recognised the need to curtail foreign influence in the Customs by, for example, agreeing to the official termination of foreign recruitment in 1929.[59] However, many of his capitulations to the Guomindang, such as his much-derided willingness to swear an oath of loyalty to the new government, smacked of political and personal opportunism to many observers. During the long conflict with Japan, 1931–45, the Customs fell victim to imperialist interests once again as custom houses in occupied China were gradually seized by the Japanese authorities. After the outbreak of the Asia Pacific War in December 1941 the Foreign Inspectorate, which had been based in Shanghai since 1928, was rent in half. The Shanghai headquarters were seized by the Japanese and continued to operate as a 'bogus' Customs regime headed by former Chief Secretary Kishimoto Hirokichi under the aegis of the Wang Jingwei collaborationist government until 1945. A rival Customs establishment, headed by the Nationalists, was created from scratch in the wartime capital of Chongqing in January 1942 to administer customs revenues in free China. In 1945 the last foreign IG, Lester Knox Little (IG 1943–50), found himself in charge of a depleted Customs staff working for a financially drained government engaged in a full-blown civil war with the Communist Party. Commensurate with the dismantling of the foreign presence in China more broadly during the 1940s, the foreign character of the Customs was steadily eroded in this period. The Customs had weathered many political storms but it could not survive this one; after almost a century of existence the Chinese Communist Party's triumph in 1949 dealt the final blow to the Foreign Inspectorate.

Fairbank may have viewed the Foreign Inspectorate as the perfect embodiment of 'synarchy', but, as this brief history shows, its role and responsibilities were closely entwined with the rise and fall of imperialism in China. As a bureaucracy that was ostensibly subordinate to the Chinese state, the Customs *was* different from other colonial enterprises in China. Yet it nonetheless enacted a colonial project of a specific type. The Customs did not attempt to subjugate China with gunboats, but it did aim to construct a quintessentially British bureaucratic apparatus within the Chinese government. As will be discussed at length in Chapter 2, its raison d'être was to make China modern through a period of foreign tutelage. The very idea that China needed to change along Western lines and the accompanying conviction that only foreigners possessed the expertise and character to achieve this was a mainstay of imperialist ideologies. James Hevia has convincingly argued that colonialism in China in the nineteenth century took the form of a 'pedagogical project' to teach the Chinese government how to behave in the modern world of empires. This project oscillated between coercion, as exemplified by periodic military conflict that was usually inflicted upon China on flimsy pretexts, and tutelage, as typified by the institutions and structures of foreign power, such as the unequal treaties and the Foreign Inspectorate of Customs. These two sides of imperialism, 'hard' and 'soft', worked in tandem, enacting a double-pronged penetration of China.[60] The Customs, then, represented a less belligerent brand of imperialism, one which attempted to instruct rather than coerce and work within Chinese institutions rather than destroying them, but it was hardly 'informal'. Indeed, its activities enabled the broader expansion of the foreign presence.

In reassessing the Customs' relationship to foreign and Chinese power *Empire Careers* builds upon a small body of recent work with a similar agenda. These studies overwhelmingly focus on the high politics of this relationship, or on Robert Hart's leadership. Notable among them is Donna Brunero's *Britain's Imperial Cornerstone in China*, an exploration of the Foreign Inspectorate's political history and its relationship to British imperialism.[61] As the first book-length study of the socio-political history of the foreign staff, which makes extensive use of recently opened personnel records in the customs archive in Nanjing, *Empire Careers* both complements existing work on the Customs and considerably expands its purview. Through exploring the experiences of its lower-level staff, it refutes the common assumption that the foreign presence was of negligible importance to China's modern history.[62] Although the extent of Western economic influence in China is up for debate, exploration of the world of the Customs staff makes it plain that the foreign presence was a tangible reality for many Chinese communities. Shanghai has so far dominated histories of China's interactions with the West. The city's large foreign communities, slightly seedy glamour, well-earned reputation as a crucible of political and cultural modernity and its position as China's main commercial entrepôt have captivated generations of scholars and writers of popular histories.[63] Yet, the history of the Customs, which operated in forty-six ports ranging from large coastal treaty ports to small western border towns by 1931, reveals the sheer breadth of foreign influence. The Customs was, moreover, visually conspicuous. The imposing colonial-style architecture of Customs buildings, the uniformed ranks of its staff and the mannerisms and behaviour of the European and American employees themselves were all visibly alien, especially when placed against the backdrop of a sleepy inland backwater.

This book fills a gap in the existing literature on Sino-foreign relations by considering how the lower-level staff of the Customs enacted foreign power on a day-to-day basis. With the exception of several somewhat hagiographical life histories of eminent Sinologists and adventurers, there have been very few investigations of how ordinary people in China actually put the ideologies and policies of colonial power into practice in the course of their everyday working, social and private lives. Study of the Customs staff demonstrates how this process was mediated by broader imperial ideologies, strong institutional cultures and the personal beliefs, allegiances and experiences of individuals. To reconstruct the experience of working for the Customs and living in China, *Empire Careers* draws primarily upon the Customs Service archive lodged in the Second Historical Archives of China in Nanjing, a rich seam of personnel records and correspondence recently made accessible to researchers. The structure of this book roughly approximates the life trajectories of expatriates, from their initial journeys over the seas to the dispersal of former Customs men around the empire world after leaving the Service. Each chapter covers a broad period in order to underscore how broad processes of political and social change and continuity, both in China and internationally, altered the context in which the Foreign Inspectorate and its staff worked between 1842 and 1949. Special attention is paid to the nineteenth century, when the policies and principles of the Service were being established, and the Nanjing decade (1927–37), when Nationalist Party rule combined with the growth of popular anti-imperialist sentiment to transform the conditions of life and work.

Chapter 2 lays the foundations of the book by broadly sketching how the Customs' vision of its role and responsibilities intersected with imperialist ideologies. The treatises, statistics, commentary and histories produced by the Customs and its foreign staff provide an insight into how they viewed their adopted country and their position within it. These texts and statistical tables also shaped Western knowledge of Chinese culture, politics and society in important ways. Ultimately this chapter shows that there were multiple voices with the Customs and that its foreign employees often flitted between several interlinked perspectives and ideologies over the course of their lives. Furthermore, despite the Inspectorate's attempts to distance itself and its staff from the broader foreign establishment in China, its project to modernise China under Western tutelage was in and of itself an explicitly imperialist agenda. Chapter 3 explores the recruitment procedures followed by the Service and the global networks of patronage, family, communications and employment that propelled and enabled the international relocations of the employees of colonial institutions. In building a socio-economic profile of the foreign staff this chapter illuminates the diverse range of people for whom China spoke of opportunity, elite and non-elite. It finds that expatriates were not primarily motivated to seek work overseas because of a single-minded commitment to imperialism;

[17]

rather, family links to empire, previous employment in the empire world, a desire for adventure and, importantly, the prospect of a reliable career were more important factors.

Chapter 4 reconstructs the working environments occupied by staff in the different branches of the Service. Particular attention is paid to the dramatic changes wrought upon the Customs working world by the growth of popular anti-imperialism in the 1920s, the rise to power of Chiang Kai-shek's Nationalist Party in 1927, and the War of Resistance (1937–45). Although the Inspectorate insisted that it was a politically neutral institution, in reality its contentious hybrid status and position at a crossroads between the Chinese and foreign worlds placed it at the centre of political storms. Like the employees of other colonial institutions, the Customs staff were required to negotiate delicate power balances with other local and national powerbrokers in order to perform their work. The social and private worlds of the foreign staff are the subject of Chapter 5. Treaty port social spheres were crosshatched with complex hierarchies based on race, class and nationality, as the experiences of the Customs staff demonstrate. Furthermore, like colonial institutions elsewhere in empire, the Foreign Inspectorate was intensely concerned about the potential for the private conduct of its employees to erupt into scandal. As an organ of the Chinese state whose existence rested on the rationale that foreigners possessed the superior 'character' necessary to lead China into a new age of progress, the Customs was doubly anxious about public reputation. These anxieties reveal the fragility of colonial power formations, which, it was believed, could be undone by rumour and scandal. The final chapter examines the endpoint of a Customs career: leaving the Service. The modes by which individuals withdrew from Service, by resignation, death, retirement or dismissal, are telling of the wide range of successes and failures that characterised colonial careers. By exploring the post-Customs lives and destinations of foreign employees, this chapter considers how people were changed by the experience of working within a different state's administration. Throughout this book I refer to the multiple overlapping imperial structures and networks that crisscrossed the globe as the empire world. The empire world encompassed not only 'formal' colonies directly ruled by colonial authorities but also outposts of 'informal' empire such as China and the spaces and pathways in between these sites through which people, goods, communications and capital flowed.[64] People who worked on the edges of empire negotiated a fluid set of allegiances and identities but paramount among them was the sense of belonging to a global web of empires. Overall this book shows that, while the 'romance' of empire tells us much about imperial ideologies and individual strategies and fictions, the reality of everyday work and life tells us much more about the world of empire in the heyday of European power overseas.

Notes

1 Houghton Library, Harvard University, L. K. Little papers (hereafter Little papers), FMS Am 1999.1, 'personal correspondence, 1941–4', history of the Chinese Maritime Customs Service by L. K. Little, 6 July 1944.

2 The Foreign Inspectorate of Customs was named the Imperial Maritime Customs Service 1854–1911 and the Chinese Maritime Customs Service (CMCS) 1911–50. In this book I refer to it as the Chinese Customs Service (CCS), the Service or the Foreign Inspectorate.

3 See John K. Fairbank, *Trade and Diplomacy on the China Coast: The opening of the treaty ports, 1842–1854* (Stanford: Stanford University Press, 1969), chapters 21 and 22, for an account of the operation of the provisional system in Shanghai and the events leading up to it.

4 See John K. Fairbank, 'The Definition of the Foreign Inspector's Status (1854–55): A chapter in the early history of the Inspectorate of Customs at Shanghai', *Nankai Social and Economic Quarterly*, 9:1 (1936), 129–132. Until the appointment of H. N. Lay as Inspector General on 31 May 1855 the Customs was controlled by three inspectors appointed by the British, American and French consuls. These inspectors were Thomas Francis Wade (British vice-consul), Arthur Smith (interpreter to the French consulate) and Lewis Carr (of the American legation).

5 In the late Qing era the Inspectorate reported to the Waiwubu (Foreign Ministry). From 1906 it operated under the control of the Shuiwuju (Revenue Board) which in turn reported to the Ministry of Finance.

6 In the 1860s the Customs Post was established to carry the correspondence of the foreign Legations between the treaty ports. In 1896 this organisation became the Imperial Post Office, operating as a department of the Customs Service until it was transferred to the jurisdiction of the Ministry of Posts and Communications in 1911.

7 Some examples: C. A. Bayly, *The Birth of the Modern World 1780–1914: Global connections and comparisons* (Oxford: Blackwell, 2004); Jane Burbank and Frederick Cooper, *Empires in World History: Power and the politics of difference* (Princeton: Princeton University Press, 2010); John Darwin, *The Empire Project: The rise and fall of the British world-system, 1830–1970* (Cambridge: Cambridge University Press, 2009).

8 A. G. Hopkins, ed., *Globalization in World History* (New York: W. W. Norton & Co., 2002); Gary B. Magee and Andrew S. Thompson, *Empire and Globalisation: Networks of people, goods and capital in the British world, c. 1850–1914* (Cambridge: Cambridge University Press, 2010).

9 Frederick Cooper, *Colonialism in Question: Theory, knowledge, history* (Berkeley: University of California Press, 2005), chapter 4, 'Globalization', 91–112.

10 Cooper, *Colonialism in Question*, 92.

11 Carl Bridge and Kent Fedorowich, 'Mapping the British World', *Journal of Imperial and Commonwealth History*, 31:2 (2003), 1–15; Carl Bridge and Kent Fedorowich, *The British World: Diaspora, culture and identity* (London: F. Cass, 2003); P. Buckner and D. Francis, *Rediscovering the British World* (Calgary: University of Calgary Press, 2005).

12 Bridge and Fedorowich, *The British World*, 3.

13 Zoë Laidlaw, *Colonial Connections, 1815–45: Patronage, the information revolution and colonial government* (Manchester: Manchester University Press, 2005); Alan Lester, 'British Settler Discourse and the Circuits of Empire', *History Workshop Journal*, 54 (2002), 24–48; David Lambert and Alan Lester, eds, *Colonial Lives across the British Empire: Imperial careering in the long nineteenth century* (Cambridge: Cambridge University Press, 2006).

14   Tony Ballantyne, 'Empire, Knowledge, and Culture: From proto-globalization to modern globalization', in *Globalization in World History*, edited by A. G. Hopkins, 116–40; Tony Ballantyne, 'Rereading the Archive and Opening Up the Nation-State: Colonial knowledge in South Asia (and beyond)', in *After the Imperial Turn: Thinking with and through the nation*, edited by Antoinette Burton (Durham, N C: Duke University Press, 2003), 102–21.
15   Alan Lester, *Imperial Networks: Creating identities in nineteenth-century South Africa and Britain* (London: Routledge, 2001).
16   Laidlaw, *Colonial Connections*, 35.
17   See Lambert and Lester, *Colonial Lives*.
18   Magee and Thompson, *Globalisation and Empire*, particularly chapter 4, 117–69.
19   On considering metropole and colony in the same analytical category see Catherine Hall, *Civilising Subjects: Metropole and colony in the English imagination, 1830–1867* (Chicago: University of Chicago Press, 2002).
20   Magee and Thompson have, however, tackled the long-neglected issue of the extent to which the United States was part of the 'cultural economy' of the British world in *Globalisation and Empire*, 19. Another exception is Matthew Brown, 'Gregor Macgregor: Clansman, conquistador and coloniser on the fringes of the British Empire', in *Colonial Lives*, edited by Lambert and Lester, 32–57.
21   Figures from Marjory Harper, 'British Migrations and the Peopling of Empire', in *The Oxford History of the British Empire: The nineteenth century*, edited by Andrew Porter (Oxford: Oxford University Press, 1999), 75.
22   Figures from Magee and Thompson, *Empire and Globalisation*, 69.
23   To use Alan Lester's phrase from 'British Settler Discourse and the Circuits of Empire'.
24   Lambert and Lester, *Colonial Lives*, 12. For an example see Hans van de Ven, 'The Onrush of Modern Globalisation in China', in *Globalisation in World History*, edited by A. G. Hopkins, 167–95.
25   Magee and Thompson, *Globalisation and Empire*, 20–1; Simon J. Potter, 'Webs, Networks, and Systems: Globalization and the media in the nineteenth- and twentieth-century British Empire', *Journal of British Studies*, 46:3 (2007), 621–46.
26   Figures from Robert Bickers, *Britain in China: Community, culture and colonialism, 1900–1949* (Manchester: Manchester University Press, 1999), 13.
27   See, for example, Dudley Baines, *Emigration from Europe, 1815–1930* (Cambridge: Cambridge University Press, 1995); Stephen Constantine, 'British Emigration to the Empire-Commonwealth since 1880: From overseas settlement to diaspora?' *The Journal of Imperial and Commonwealth History*, 31:2 (2003), 16–35; Marjory Harper, *Emigrant Homecomings: The return movement of emigrants, 1600–2000* (Manchester: Manchester University Press, 2005); Marjory Harper and Stephen Constantine, *Migration and Empire* (Oxford: Oxford University Press, 2010).
28   Juliet Bredon, *Sir Robert Hart, the Romance of a Great Career: Told by his niece, Juliet Bredon* (London: Hutchinson, 1909); Katherine F. Bruner, John K. Fairbank and Richard J. Smith eds, *Robert Hart and China's Modernization: His journals, 1863–1866* (Cambridge, MA: Harvard University Press, 1991); John King Fairbank, Katherine Frost Bruner and Elizabeth MacLeod Matheson, eds, *The I. G. in Peking: Letters of Robert Hart, Chinese Maritime Customs, 1868–1907* (Cambridge, MA: Belknap Press, 1975); Richard S. Horowitz, 'Politics, Power and the Chinese Maritime Customs Service: The Qing restoration and the ascent of Robert Hart', *Modern Asian Studies*, 40:3 (2006), 549–81; Stanley Fowler Wright, *Hart and the Chinese Customs* (Belfast: W. Mullan, 1950). For Hart's role as adviser to the Qing state see Jonathan D. Spence, *To Change China: Western advisers in China, 1620–1960* (New York: Penguin, 2002. First pub. 1969), chapter 4, 93–128.
29   For Bland's own account of his life see his unpublished memoirs in the Thomas Fisher Rare Book Library, University of Toronto, MS 81, J. O. P. Bland papers, microfilm reel 19 (hereafter 'Bland papers, memoirs'). Also see Robert Bickers, 'Bland, John Otway Percy (1863–1945)', in *The Oxford Dictionary of National Biography*, edited by H. C. G. Matthew and Brian Harrison (Oxford: Oxford University Press, 2004).

30   See Rasmussen's memoir, *China Trader* (New York: Crowell, 1954).
31   See the Bodleian Library, University of Oxford, Alfred E. Hippisley papers (hereafter 'Hippisley papers'), MSS. Eng. c. 7285–98, e. 3586–7.
32   *I. G. in Peking*, vol. 1, letter Z/417, 24 Nov 1889, 771.
33   Second Historical Archives of China, Nanjing (hereafter SHAC), 679(1) 16953, 'Shanghai Fraud Case, 1938, involving Messrs. O. Hall, Senior Chief Examiner A and Chang Hsuan, Assistant Examiner A'.
34   Robert A. Bickers, *Empire Made Me: An Englishman adrift in Shanghai* (London: Allen Lane, 2003); Hall, *Civilising Subjects*; Gregor Muller, *Colonial Cambodia's 'Bad Frenchmen': The rise of French rule and the life of Thomas Caraman, 1840–1887* (London: Routledge, 2006).
35   Miles Ogborn, *Global Lives: Britain and the world, 1550–1800* (Cambridge: Cambridge University Press, 2008). Also see Lambert and Lester, *Colonial Lives*.
36   See, for example, the picture of delinquent and impoverished British aristocrats resident in Kenya's 'Happy Valley' painted in David Cannadine's *The Decline and Fall of the British Aristocracy* (New Haven: Yale University Press, 1990), 429–43.
37   See Edward Berenson, *Heroes of Empire: Five charismatic men and the conquest of Africa* (Berkeley: University of California Press, 2011).
38   See Frederick Cooper and Ann Laura Stoler's now-classic analysis, 'Between Metropole and Colony: Rethinking a research agenda', in *Tensions of Empire: Colonial cultures in a bourgeois world* edited by Cooper and Stoler (Berkeley: University of California Press, 1997). Some further examples: Robert Bickers, ed., *Settlers and Expatriates: Britons over the seas*, Oxford History of the British Empire Companion Series (Oxford: Oxford University Press, 2010); Elizabeth Buettner, *Empire Families: Britons and late imperial India* (Oxford: Oxford University Press, 2004); Catherine Hall, ed., *Cultures of Empire: Colonizers in Britain and the Empire in the nineteenth and twentieth centuries* (New York: Routledge, 2000); Dane Kennedy, *Islands of White: Settler society and culture in Kenya and Southern Rhodesia, 1890–1939* (Durham, N C: Duke University Press, 1987); Dane Kennedy, *The Magic Mountains: Hill stations and the British Raj* (Berkeley: University of California Press, 1996); Nicholas Thomas, *Colonialism's Culture: Anthropology, travel and government* (Princeton: Princeton University Press, 1994).
39   See, for example, Ann Laura Stoler, *Carnal Knowledge and Imperial Power: Race and the intimate in colonial rule* (Berkeley: University of California Press, 2002); For the case of Shanghai see Robert Bickers, 'Shanghailanders: The formation and identity of the British settler community in Shanghai, 1843–1937', *Past and Present*, 159 (1998), 161–211. Also see Nathan A. Pelcovits, *Old China Hands and the Foreign Office* (New York: Published under the auspices of the American Institute of Pacific Relations by the King's Crown Press, 1948), for the clash between the mercantile community in China and the Foreign Office.
40   Richard Eves and Nicholas Thomas, *Bad Colonists: The South Seas letters of Vernon Lee Walker and Louis Becke* (Durham, N C: Duke University Press, 1999). Also see Peter Marshall, 'The Whites of British India, 1780–1830: A failed colonial society', *International History Review*, 12:1 (1990), 26–44, and Muller, *Colonial Cambodia's 'Bad Frenchmen'*.
41   Bickers, *Britain in China* and *Empire Made Me*; Robert Bickers and Christian Henriot, eds, *New Frontiers: Imperialism's new communities in East Asia, 1842–1953* (Manchester: Manchester University Press, 2000); Joshua A. Fogel, '"Shanghai-Japan": The Japanese Residents' Association of Shanghai', *The Journal of Asian Studies*, 59:4 (2000), 927–50; Marcia Reynders Ristaino, *Port of Last Resort: The diaspora communities of Shanghai* (Stanford: Stanford University Press, 2001).
42   Stuart Ward, 'Transcending the Nation: A global imperial history?' in *After the Imperial Turn*, edited by Antoinette Burton, 44.
43   Bridge and Fedorowich, eds, *The British World*; Kathleen Paul, 'Communities of Britishness: Migration in the last gasp of empire', in *British Culture and the End of Empire*, edited by Stuart Ward (Manchester: Manchester University Press, 2001),

180–217. For the ways in which intellectuals conceptualised imperial citizenship in the British empire see Daniel Gorman, *Imperial Citizenship: Empire and the question of belonging* (Manchester: Manchester University Press, 2006).

44　Bickers, *Britain in China*, 108. Also see Bickers, 'Shanghailanders'.

45　Anthony Kirk-Greene has produced a number of monographs: *On Crown Service: A history of HM colonial and overseas civil services, 1837–1997* (London: I. B. Tauris, 1999); *Britain's Imperial Administrators, 1858–1966* (New York: St Martin's Press, 2000); *Symbol of Authority: The British district officer in Africa* (London: I. B. Tauris, 2006). On police forces see: Bickers, *Empire Made Me*; David M. Anderson and David Killingray, eds, *Policing the Empire: Government, authority and control, 1830–1940* (Manchester: Manchester University Press, 1991); Anthony Clayton and David Killingray, *Khaki and Blue: Military and police in British colonial Africa* (Athens: Ohio University Center for International Studies, 1989); David Arnold, *Police Power and Colonial Rule: Madras, 1859–1947* (Oxford: Oxford University Press, 1986); Georgina Sinclair, *At the End of the Line: Colonial policing and the imperial endgame* (Manchester: Manchester University Press, 2006). On the British consular service see: D. C. M. Platt, *The Cinderella Service: British consuls since 1825* (Harlow: Longman, 1971), 28. See also P. D. Coates, *The China Consuls: British consular officers, 1843–1943* (Oxford: Oxford University Press, 1988).

46　For the history of foreign encroachments on China in the nineteenth century see Robert Bickers, *The Scramble for China: Foreign devils in the Qing Empire, 1832–1914* (London: Allen Lane, 2011).

47　For theories of 'informal' empire in China see Britten Dean, 'British Informal Empire: The case of China', *The Journal of Imperial and Commonwealth History*, 14:1 (1976), 64–81; Jürgen Osterhammel, 'Semi-Colonialism and Informal Empire in Twentieth-Century China: Towards a framework of analysis', in *Imperialism and After: Continuities and discontinuities*, edited by Wolfgang J. Mommsen and Jürgen Osterhammel (London: HarperCollins, 1986), 290–314. Jürgen Osterhammel, 'Britain and China, 1842–1914', in *The Oxford History of the British Empire: Vol. 3, The Nineteenth Century*, edited by Andrew Porter (Oxford: Oxford University Press, 1999), 146–69.

48　See Joseph Esherick, 'Harvard on China: The apologetics of imperialism', *Bulletin of Concerned Asian Scholars*, 4 (1972): 9–16; Tani Barlow, 'Colonialism's Career in Postwar China Studies', in *Formations of Colonial Modernity in East Asia*, edited by Tani Barlow (Durham, N C: Duke University Press, 1997), 373–412.

49　Bruner et al., *Entering China's Service*, 1.

50　John K. Fairbank, 'Synarchy Under the Treaties', in Fairbank (ed.), *Chinese Thought and Institutions* (Chicago: University of Chicago Press, 1957), 205.

51　Fairbank, *Trade and Diplomacy*, 463.

52　Paul A. Cohen, *Discovering History in China: American historical writing on the recent Chinese past* (New York: Columbia University Press, 1984).

53　Bickers, *Scramble for China*; Prasenjit Duara, *Sovereignty and Authenticity: Manchukuo and the East Asian modern* (Lanham, M D: Rowman and Littlefield, 2003); James Hevia, *Cherishing Men from Afar: Qing guest ritual and the Macartney Embassy of 1793* (Durham, N C: Duke University Press, 1995); James Hevia, *English Lessons: The pedagogy of imperialism in nineteenth-century China* (Durham, N C: Duke University Press, 2003); Meng Yue, *Shanghai and the Edges of Empires* (Minneapolis: University of Minnesota Press, 2006).

54　Stephen Lyon Endicott, *Diplomacy and Enterprise: British China policy, 1933–1937* (Vancouver: University of British Columbia Press, 1975), 6.

55　Fairbank, 'Definition of the Foreign Inspector's Status'; Fairbank, *Trade and Diplomacy*, chapters 21 and 22.

56　Chen Xiafei and Han Rongfang, eds, *Archives of China's Imperial Maritime Customs: Confidential correspondence between Robert Hart and James Duncan Campbell, 1874–1907* (Beijing: Foreign Languages Press, 1990), xii.

57　For the extension of the Customs' fiscal duties under Aglen see Albert Feuerwerker, *The Foreign Establishment in China in the Twentieth Century* (Ann Arbor: Center for Chinese Studies, University of Michigan, 1976), 65. For the involvement of the Customs in securing and repaying foreign loans see Frank H. H. King, 'The Boxer Indemnity–"Nothing but Bad"', *Modern Asian Studies*, 40:3 (2006), 663–89. For the general history of the Aglen inspectorate see Jean Aitchison, 'The Chinese Maritime Customs Service in the Transition from the Ch'ing to the Nationalist Era: An examination of the relationship between a Western-style fiscal institution and the Chinese government in the period before the Manchurian Incident', unpublished PhD thesis, University of London, 1981.

58   On the succession crisis see Martyn Atkins, *Informal Empire in Crisis: British diplomacy and the Chinese Customs succession, 1927–1929* (Ithaca: East Asia Program, Cornell University, 1995).

59   For the history of the Maze inspectorate see Donna Brunero, *Britain's Imperial Cornerstone in China: The Chinese Maritime Customs Service, 1854–1949* (Abingdon: Routledge, 2006); Nicholas Clifford, 'Sir Frederick Maze and the Chinese Maritime Customs, 1937–41', *The Journal of Modern History*, 37:1 (1965), 18–34.

60   Hevia, *English Lessons*.

61   See, for example, Brunero, *Britain's Imperial Cornerstone*; Robert Bickers, 'Anglo-Japanese Relations and Treaty Port China: The case of the Chinese Maritime Customs Service', in *The International History of East Asia, 1900–1968: Trade, ideology and the quest for order*, edited by Antony Best (London: Routledge, 2010) 35–56. Also see the collection of articles on the Customs in a special edition of *Modern Asian Studies*, 40:3 (2006). The standard overview of the Foreign Inspectorate's history in Chinese is Chen Shiqi, *Zhongguo jindai haiguan shi* (History of the modern Chinese Customs) (Beijing: Zhongguo Zhanwang chubanshe, 2002).

62   See, for example, Lu Hanchao, *Beyond the Neon Lights: Everyday life in Shanghai in the early twentieth century* (Berkeley: University of California Press, 1999); Rhoads Murphey, *The Outsiders: The Western experience in India and China* (Ann Arbor: University of Michigan Press, 1977).

63   See, for example, Marie-Claire Bergère, *Shanghai: China's gateway to modernity* (Stanford: Stanford University Press, 2010); Nicholas Clifford, *Spoilt Children of Empire: Westerners in Shanghai and the Chinese revolution of the 1920s* (Hanover, N H: University Press of New England, 1991); Sherman Cochran, ed., *Inventing Nanjing Road: Commercial culture in Shanghai, 1900–1945* (Ithaca: Cornell East Asia Program, 1999); Stella Dong, *Shanghai: The rise and fall of a decadent city* (New York: William Morrow, 2000); Frederic Wakeman Jr and Wen-hsin Yeh, eds, *Shanghai Sojourners* (Berkeley: Institute of East Asian Studies, University of California, 1992); Wen-hsin Yeh, 'Shanghai Modernity: Commerce and culture in a Republican city', *The China Quarterly*, 150 (1997), 375–94.

64   Attention has, for example, recently been paid to the sea as an integral part of the British empire. See David Killingray, Margarette Lincoln and Nigel Rigby, eds, *Maritime Empires: British imperial maritime trade in the nineteenth century* (Woodbridge: Boydell Press, 2004).

CHAPTER TWO

The Customs mindset: ethos, ideologies and knowledge about China

Bertram Lenox Simpson, imperialist, China coast journalist, political adviser to the Chinese government, warlord collaborator and Imperial Maritime Customs Service employee, provides a fitting introduction to the multiple ideologies and identities that Customs men navigated over the course of a career in China. Better known by his penname Putnam Weale, the China-born Simpson followed his father into the Customs in 1896, but his career was to be short-lived; he left his post at the Beijing Inspectorate in 1901, possibly in disfavour after the British minister, Sir Claude MacDonald, tried to have him arrested for looting in the aftermath of the Boxer Uprising.[1] Freed from the stuffy environs of the Customs, Simpson tried his hand as a writer, the career that would make him famous. He worked as a correspondent for the *Daily Telegraph* 1911–14 and gained prominence on the China coast by penning articles supporting settler causes in various treaty port rags. Beyond the China coast, Simpson built a reputation as a novelist, polemicist and satirist, publishing ten books in all.[2] One of his early works, *Indiscreet Letters from Peking* (1907), which purported to be a memoir of the siege of the legations during the Boxer Uprising, caused a sensation with its undisguised send-up of the stolid Beijing diplomatic establishment.

Simpson may have been a sometime champion of settler interests, but this did not mean that he severed his connections to Chinese officialdom on leaving the Customs. As of 1916 he was once again on the Chinese government's payroll, albeit this time working for the republican government rather than the Qing, as an adviser on foreign affairs. Outspoken and deliberately courting notoriety, Simpson had always been a controversial figure but his moment of infamy indisputably came in 1930 when he conspired with the Shanxi warlord Yan Xishan to seize the Tianjin custom house. Yan's dissatisfaction with Chiang Kai-shek's regime had been brewing for some time and in 1930 he joined forces with the military commander and Nationalist politician Feng Yuxiang – widely known as the 'Christian General' – and Guangxi warlord Li Zongren in an attempt to establish a new national government in Beijing. Seizing the lucrative Tianjin revenue was central to this plan.

In then-IG Frederick Maze's opinion, Simpson was nothing more than a scurrilous hack, intent upon defaming the Service that had given him a start in China. 'Irresponsible firebrands like Putnam Weale and Woodhead [another treaty port journalist] are, naturally, seizing the opportunity to fan the fire, and accentuate difficulty by broadcasting the usual sensational reports – but the stability of the Maritime Customs will not be upset by their clap-trap propaganda!' Maze thundered in response to Simpson's lurid reporting of warlord intrigues in the north. 'Neither is now regarded seriously, either in China or abroad, and both are regarded as sensational and distrusted in Official circles in Peiping [Beijing] and London,' he concluded.[3] At this moment, however, Maze did not suspect Simpson of actual involvement in the conflict, although given his rakish reputation no one was particularly surprised when he marched on the Tianjin custom house on 16 June, accompanied by a former American postal commissioner, L. C. Arlington, who had resigned in 1905, and several Chinese officials allied with the anti-Chiang coalition. Together they presented Commissioner Hayley-Bell with an order removing him from office.[4] Simpson took over as head of the warlord-controlled customs establishment, which was decried by Maze as a rogue regime staffed by crooks. The de facto customs regime operated until the Manchurian warlord Zhang Xueliang reclaimed Shandong province for the Nationalists in October 1930. The Tianjin Commissioner Hayley-Bell was transferred to the London Office in disgrace and never served in China again. As for Simpson, his entanglement in warlord machinations eventually cost him his life. Shortly after the debacle he was murdered on a Tianjin street, presumably by the enemies he had made through his involvement in political intrigues.

Simpson was an opportunist and a renegade, happy to oscillate between different interest groups and ideological standpoints in order to further his own position. His prominence as a well-known writer and his escapades in Tianjin mark him as an adventurer, and this set him apart from his more conformist former colleagues in the Customs. Yet his life history nonetheless highlights the flexible and multifaceted identities and allegiances experienced by most Customs men over the course of a career in China, albeit in extreme form. First and foremost, his actions seem to point towards the Inspectorate's failure to cultivate a distinct institutional ethos uniformly among its foreign staff. Unshakeable commitment to the Customs and to serving China's interests, political disinterestedness and the development of a morally upright character were supposedly central tenets of this Service culture. The brevity of his career, his betrayal of the Customs in Tianjin in 1930 and the inglorious reputation he had earned on the China coast meant that Simpson failed on all three counts. He did not, however, abandon his allegiances to China on leaving the Customs; his work for the Beijing government and even his dubious pact with the northern warlord coalition indicate his enduring ability to make alliances with Chinese powerbrokers. Yet Simpson was also broadly supportive of imperialism in China, although often scathing of the slow-moving diplomatic authorities. In the end, like many foreign Customs officials, Simpson exhibited a deep ambivalence about both the foreign establishment and the extent of his commitment to Chinese interests. Finally, Simpson's post-Customs incarnation as writer Putnam Weale demonstrates how former Customs officers contributed to a growing body of English-language knowledge about China. His credentials were flimsy, but his early experiences in the Customs marked him as a 'China expert'.

This chapter explores the intersection of Customs ideologies and imperialist discourses and practices. It asks how the Inspectorate perceived its institutional culture, how foreign Customs officers saw their role and responsibilities, how they viewed China and how they influenced Western knowledge of Chinese culture, society and politics. In doing so this chapter investigates how the Customs worldview alternately contrasted and overlapped with broader ideologies of imperialism in China. To illuminate the interlinked shifts in Customs ideologies and Western perceptions of China between 1854 and 1949 this chapter follows a broadly chronological structure, beginning by exploring Robert Hart's foundational vision of the Customs' guiding principles. Customs officers played a central role in creating and mediating Western knowledge of China. The numerous texts and statistics produced by the Customs and its foreign employees provide an insight into how they viewed their adopted country, how they wished others to perceive them and how these perceptions influenced and were influenced by popular and academic Western knowledge of China. This chapter therefore considers trends in Customs knowledge-production, beginning with the contributions of nineteenth-century Customs Sinologists to the burgeoning information empire in China and the swing towards more negative portrayals of China from the 1890s onwards. In the early twentieth century the Customs' internal mechanisms for collecting information about China were extended and systematised in the face of the nationalist challenge. Finally, in a time when the Foreign Inspectorate's survival was increasingly threatened in the 1930s, the Customs self-publicity machine went into overdrive under the leadership of Sir Frederick Maze. In exploring changes in the Customs worldview and the ways in which the foreign staff viewed their role and position in China, this chapter contends that foreigners working within a different state's administration during the age of imperialism were able, like Simpson, to move fluidly between multiple allegiances and identities during and after their careers. In the case of the foreign Customs staff this was enabled by their employment in an organisation that spanned the Chinese and foreign worlds, which positioned them within at least two different interest groups.

China servants: Robert Hart's vision of the foreign staff

After Robert Hart's appointment as IG in 1863 he sought to fashion the Customs into a model civil service, supposedly staffed by men dedicated to impartial assistance of China and endowed with the special qualities needed to lead China into a new age of progress. Hart's foundational 1864 circular, entitled 'the Customs Service, the spirit that ought to animate it, the policy that ought to guide it, the duties it ought to perform', articulated his idealised vision for the institution and set down the guiding principles intended to bind the foreign staff together in service of a common purpose.[5] The basic principles outlined in this circular formed the bedrock of the Customs' institutional culture for almost a century.

As an organisation that straddled the Chinese and foreign spheres, the exact allegiances of the Foreign Inspectorate were the subject of conjecture and suspicion. Hart took over as IG just a few years after the Anglo-French forces had occupied Beijing and destroyed the imperial Summer Palace during the Arrow War (1856–60); mutual suspicion continued to colour relations between foreigners and Chinese. In this context Customs men were regarded by many other foreigners as deracinated turncoats, willing to abandon their national loyalties in order to serve a hostile, less civilised government. Many Chinese officials, on the other hand, eyed them as imposters intent upon furthering the interests of foreign powers at China's expense. In attempting to lay this matter to rest Hart's priority was to reassure the Chinese government that the foreign staff were first and foremost public servants of the Chinese state. In dealing with Chinese colleagues and the public, therefore, they must bear in mind 'that they are the brother officers of the one, and that they have, to some extent, accepted certain obligations and responsibilities by becoming, in a sense, the countrymen of the others'.[6] Unlike other foreigners in China, intent upon 'showing their superior enlightenment by riding rough-shod over prejudices', Customs men were expected to exhibit respect for, or at the very least tolerance of, Chinese culture. Adopting the mindset of a Chinese public servant was also deemed essential to navigating relations with Chinese officialdom. Sensitive to the fact that the very existence of the Foreign Inspectorate was an 'unpalatable fact' for many Chinese officials, implying as it did that they were unable to perform their jobs effectively without foreign help, Hart repeatedly reminded his senior employees that their job was to *assist, and not to ignore or displace native authority'* (original emphasis).[7]

Practically and ideologically, however, maintaining the mindset of a Chinese civil servant was easier said than done. Also, their intermediary position inevitably led to overlapping spheres of authority with Chinese and foreign power holders. The practical implications of this are discussed in detail in Chapter 4, but it is important to note here that the grey area occupied by the foreign staff led to endless tussles about jurisdiction. A large part of the problem was that no one could provide a precise and authoritative definition of the status of foreigners, who enjoyed extraterritorial protection secured by the 'unequal treaties', in the Chinese government's employ. In 1860 Horatio Nelson Lay, Hart's predecessor, even went so far as to commission several 'legal men' in London to comment on the official position of British Customs men vis-à-vis the Chinese and British authorities, none of whom could arrive at an unequivocal decision.[8] Local Chinese bureaucrats, for their part, resented the interference of a foreign-run Customs administration authorised by Beijing, especially in an era of decentralisation when officials in the provinces were increasingly wresting regional autonomy from the imperial government.[9] Besides, Hart's insistence that the foreign staff were *Chinese* public servants was somewhat disingenuous considering that Customs officials were required by treaty to perform consular functions in areas where diplomatic representation was patchy in the 1860s and 1870s.[10] In the end Hart was forced to admit that consuls and Chinese bureaucrats alike insisted on viewing Customs men as foreigners first and Chinese officials second.[11]

The nebulous status of foreign employees also increased the opportunity for both Chinese and foreign officials to co-opt Customs men in service of their economic or political interests. Hart was acutely aware of this possibility and accordingly sought to style his employees as disinterested public servants who stood aloof from the political machinations of less high-minded officials. Engaging in trade was forbidden as was receiving anything that could be construed as a bribe or patronage, such as rewards or decorations awarded by Chinese or foreign persons and organisations.[12] Hart ultimately left the decision of whether to get involved in local politics up 'to the good taste and discretion of the Commissioners individually', with the caveat that they should refrain from 'unwarranted or ill-advised interference'.[13] Furthermore, an outright ban was unrealistic in an age when the ranks of the foreign staff were filled with enterprising men intent upon making a name and fortune for themselves beyond the Customs. Gustav Detring is a case in point. In addition to presiding as Tianjin Commissioner for almost three decades (1877–1904), Detring masterminded several industrial enterprises in northern China aided by his close alliance with Li Hongzhang, one of the most influential Qing statesmen of the late nineteenth century.[14] Detring's undertakings prompted much indignation, mingled with envy, among colleagues who dutifully followed Hart's dictum of neutrality to the letter. A significant portion of the diary of Alfred Hippisley (in the Customs 1867–1909), for example, was devoted to letting off steam about Detring's underhand dealings. As a result of his involvement in mining and railway ventures Customs officers would now always be suspected of 'having axes of our own to grind', Hippisley fumed.[15] Yet the IG could not afford to alienate politically savvy men such as Detring and, moreover, alliances with influential statesman could help to establish the Foreign Inspectorate's legitimacy in an age when it was struggling to earn its stripes. Besides, Hart himself was no stranger to self-interested political manoeuvrings, carefully cultivating his relations with prominent Qing statesmen, notably the Zongli Yamen officials Wenxiang and Prince Gong, to further both the Customs' and Hart's personal influence.[16]

Hart's insistence that the foreign staff were disinterested servants of China also created a logical conundrum. For if the Customs was simply a Chinese service and if its employees were no different from other Chinese bureaucrats, sceptics might well ask why there was a need for a *foreign* inspectorate and a *foreign* staff in the first place. To deflect such criticisms Hart argued that foreign employees were 'China servants' of a special kind.[17] In doing so he played upon the common foreign assumption that China needed to learn from the West in order to progress.[18] Unlike other foreigners in China who argued that China needed a sharp shock, administered by foreign gunboats, to shake the government out of its lethargy, Hart firmly believed that modernity could be brought about under the leadership of beneficent foreigners. Although foreign Customs officers should not condescend to their Chinese counterparts, they were nonetheless 'representative of a civilisation of a progressive kind', Hart noted in his 1864 circular, and should therefore not suppress their natural inclination to proffer advice.[19] Still, Hart did not envisage the Foreign Inspectorate existing in perpetuity. After a period of tutelage from foreign experts, 'a day must come when the natural and national forces, silently but constantly in operation, will eject us from so anomalous a position'.[20] These three guiding principles – dutiful service of China, political disinterestedness and the obligation to bring progress to China – were never faithfully and consistently upheld in practice. They did, however, form the ideological heart of the Service's ethos for almost a century, and were continually reinvoked by those seeking to confer legitimacy on the Customs enterprise.

The Customs and nineteenth-century knowledge about China

The Customs' insistence that it was qualitatively different from other imperialist projects has proved remarkably tenacious. Successive biographers and historians have largely affirmed the Inspectorate's rhetoric about its embodiment of benign partnership with China.[21] It is unmistakable, however, that the Customs both grew out of and contributed to the proliferation of increasingly negative portrayals of Chinese culture and government gaining currency around the time of its establishment. Between 1700 and the mid-nineteenth century the ways in which China featured in European popular and intellectual culture went through a metamorphosis, from enthusiastic admiration to scorn. The European vogue for chinoiserie, which began in the seventeenth century and peaked in the mid-1700s, manifested itself in a broad range of phenomena, including fiction, theatre, commentary and a rococo aesthetic style, that played upon fanciful Chinese motifs. Histories and accounts produced by Jesuit missionaries and scholars, notably Jean-Baptiste du Halde's four-volume *General History of China* (1709), proved a fecund source for dramatists and essayists spellbound by this supposedly outlandish and exotic realm. In these works China was imagined as a pastoral Arcadia, ruled by a benevolent and wise monarch, where morality and learning were prized over base profit.[22]

As European imperial arrogance began to swell in the second half of the eighteenth century, the China craze waned. By the mid-Victorian period the image of Chinese government and society as a model worthy of European emulation had entirely vanished. Prominent essayists from Thomas De Quincey to Charles Dickens popularised this emergent Sinophobia.[23] Previously lauded as an example of benign despotism, the Chinese imperial edifice and its claims to international pre-eminence were ridiculed as antiquated and delusional.[24] How can we account for this sea change in attitudes? Early eighteenth-century Sinophilia was, as Peter Marshall has pointed out, anchored in an illusory China and filtered through romanticised Jesuit descriptions of Chinese society and government. The Western traders, adventurers, and envoys who travelled to China in mounting numbers from the late eighteenth century had different agendas and produced more critical accounts as a result. Yet this swing towards denigration speaks more of China's potency as a malleable symbolic counterpoint to the West than of changes in China itself. In the context of the European 'age of reason' Jesuit accounts were viewed with scepticism and China was increasingly judged by 'scientific' empirical standards.[25] Buoyed up by the technological optimism of the Industrial Revolution, Chinese 'backwardness' was compared unfavourably with European advances. 'In China, everything that is modern is ancient, and all that is ancient is modern,' declared Robert Douglas, keeper of Oriental books and manuscripts at the British Museum, in 1894.[26] The implication was that China, fettered as it was by cultural and technological inertia, needed Western guidance to avoid atrophying.

The Customs Service was both a product of and contributor to the negative turn in European and American portrayals of China. The presumption that the Chinese bureaucracy was too inept and outmoded to administer foreign trade effectively underpinned the establishment of the Foreign Inspectorate in 1854. Assumptions that China must change or perish ran through Hart's vision of Customs work. The foreign staff were envisaged as pioneers of a noble tradition of foreign assistance for China. Hart's conviction that Western-style progress was essential to China's survival propelled his other projects, such as his involvement in the Tongwenguan (Interpreters' College), established in 1862 to provide future government officials with a Western-style education, and the military and industrial reforms of the Self-Strengthening Movement (1861–95).[27]

The Western project to modernise China was concomitant with new systematic studies of Chinese culture, language and government. If Europeans and Americans were to help China progress they must first of all *know* the country and its people. As foreigners working for the Chinese government charged with opening up new treaty ports to overseas trade, the foreign Customs staff were ideally placed to produce and consume this new knowledge. The elite administrators of the nineteenth-century staff were expected to become erudite on Chinese matters. Alfred Hippisley recounted in his memoir how the Customs mess library in Beijing in the early 1870s was stocked with the most significant European works on Chinese history, culture and language to date, including Du Halde's *Description de l'Empire de la Chine*, Premare's *Chinese Grammar* and a complete set of the periodical *The Chinese Recorder*.[28] Several prominent Sinologists emerged from the Customs ranks. Thomas Francis Wade, the British consul placed in charge of the earliest permutation of the Foreign Inspectorate and, later, the first Professor of Chinese at Cambridge, authored several landmark guides to documentary Chinese and devised an innovative system of romanising the Chinese pronunciation.[29] Friedrich Hirth, a German in the Customs 1870–97 who later became Professor of Chinese at Columbia University, also produced a widely used textbook on documentary Chinese in 1888 in addition to multiple histories and tracts on Chinese art and culture.[30] Other nineteenth-century Customs officials catalogued, translated, summarised and presented Chinese culture to a Western audience. Both Hirth and Alfred Hippisley penned articles on Chinese porcelain, and the Belgian postal clerk J. A. van Aalst published an influential tract on Chinese music in 1884.[31] C. H. Brewitt-Taylor, in the Customs 1891–1920, completed a masterful English translation of the fourteenth-century Chinese novel *Romance of the Three Kingdoms*.[32]

Above and beyond the ad hoc production of new knowledge of China by a small coterie of Customs Sinologists, the Foreign Inspectorate also embarked on a much more ambitious series of projects to collect, collate and publish statistical data about China's economy, society, culture, terrain and climate. In 1873 a Statistical Department was established, headed by a Statistical Secretary, to centralise and systematise these activities. Acting as both a research institution and an archive, the Statistical Department produced a wide-ranging publications series on topics and genres as diverse as travelogues, science and Chinese commodities.[33] One of its primary duties was to publish monthly, quarterly and annual Returns of Trade, which exhaustively catalogued the volume and value of China's overseas trade at every treaty port.[34] Starting in 1871 Customs medical officers in the outports penned detailed reports on public health, which they dutifully relayed to the Statistical Department in Shanghai.[35] The lighthouses being steadily constructed along the coast provided the perfect infrastructure for collecting meteorological data. By 1932 meteorological measurements were being taken several times daily at fifty-two ports and lighthouses across China under the direction of the Marine Department, thus enabling the issuance of daily weather forecasts and storm warnings to mariners.[36] The post of Statistical Secretary, which entailed directing and processing research, provided useful training for a future academic career or a side-occupation as a Sinologist. Friedrich Hirth held the post, as did the eminent historian of China's trade and foreign relations, H. B. Morse, while Statistical Secretaries H. Kopsch and Alfred Hippisley published expositions of China's trade, currency and tariffs.[37]

Hart's statistical brainchild in China was an essential component

of the Customs' broader scheme to build a new institutional infrastructure modelled on Western lines. This project grew out of the
nineteenth-century association of modernity with science and empiri-
cism, which generated a seemingly relentless proclivity for measur-
ing, systematising and tabulating in Europe and North America.
Furthermore, the ability to amass, classify and analyse large amounts of
data about a broad range of social, economic and scientific phenomena
was increasingly identified with a modern state apparatus.[38] In the colonial context statistical and land surveys were imbued with additional
political meanings. Statistical projects to collect and collate data about
the physical conditions that, according to environmentalist theories,
supposedly affected human development lent pseudo-scientific legitimacy to suppositions about the inferiority of non-Western peoples.[39]
They were also intended to provide colonial governments with more
accurate knowledge about their subjects and territories, therefore enabling them to survey, rule and control more effectively. Even though, as
C. A. Bayly has shown in the case of northern India, European scientific
and statistical methods were a poor substitute for the indigenous data
collection and intelligence networks that had previously been co-opted
by colonial authorities in the late eighteenth and early nineteenth centuries, they were increasingly employed as ammunition to discredit
indigenous learning from the 1830s onwards.[40]

These practical and ideological uses of information gathering
in Europe and the broader empire world permeated the Foreign
Inspectorate's statistical undertakings. Faith in the merit of science
for science's sake, as a marker of progress and modernity, drove Hart's
meteorological project, which he envisaged would 'assist in throwing
light on natural laws, and in bringing within the reach of scientific
men facts and figures from a quarter of the globe, which, rich in phenomena, has heretofore yielded so few data for systematic generaliza-
tion'.[41] Long-established methods of state data collection in imperial
China were dismissed as inaccurate and disorderly by senior Customs
men and contrasted unfavourably with the meticulous and compre-
hensive records generated by the Statistical Department.[42] The Foreign
Inspectorate could claim that these projects would help to propel the
Qing into a new era of progress and modern state building and, moreover, that only Europeans and Americans familiar with Western statistical techniques were equal to the task.

The Customs' statistical initiative was a vital cog in a transnational
knowledge-producing machine that favoured European and American
interests. Customs meteorological stations transmitted their observations to twelve observatories in East and Southeast Asia, most of which
were run by European missionaries or colonial authorities. Although

the Returns of Trade were also printed in Chinese, copies were not supplied directly to the government until 1906, and most other Statistical Department publications were produced in English. The Customs put China on display in its exhibits at multiple international exhibitions, including the Vienna Exhibition of 1873, the London Fisheries (1883) and Health (1884) Exhibitions and the Paris Exhibitions of 1878 and 1900. Through these activities foreign Customs employees circulated new information about China around the globe, packaging it specifically for Western consumption. Every employee in the Customs, from the lowliest lightkeeper taking meteorological measurements at his lighthouse to eminent Sinologists such as Hirth, was implicated in the Customs knowledge-producing project. While we should not imagine that Hart and his acolytes carried out this work with the explicit intention of colonial domination, it indubitably had the effect of making China known, on Western terms, to the rest of the world.[43] The American travel writer Eliza Scidmore encapsulated the prevailing nineteenth-century Western attitude towards China: 'No one knows or ever will really know the Chinese – the heart and soul and springs of thought of the most incomprehensible, unfathomable, inscrutable, contradictory, logical, and illogical people on earth.'[44] By the time her travelogue was published in 1900, however, the Customs had opened China up epistemologically as well as commercially. The statistical tables, pamphlets and essays rolling off the Statistical Department's printing press laid China bare, reordered and made sense of its culture, economy, political systems and terrain, and held the finished product up for scrutiny. They thus indirectly aided and enabled foreign domination of China.

Memoirs and popular histories: turn-of-the-century portrayals of China

At the turn of the century Western attitudes towards China underwent another major shift. Although a few voices of support remained among the throng of China commentators, most European and American assessments of Chinese culture and politics from the 1890s onwards were deeply negative. Customs commentators contributed prominently to this debate. The upsurge in pessimistic portrayals of China was concurrent with the declining power of the Qing state and the escalation of imperialist competition. As European powers scrambled to annex territories across the globe their ambitions in China outgrew the stipulations of earlier treaties, which had been primarily confined to 'opening up' China to foreign trade and missionary proselytising. The foreign establishment increasingly sought access to China's interior, control over mineral resources, railways and communications systems, and the right to establish factories on Chinese soil to manufacture goods for the domestic market. The major tipping point was the Qing's defeat in the Sino-Japanese War (1894–95), a devastating humiliation that pushed China out of Korea, a former protectorate, and established Japan as the pre-eminent Asian power in the region. The war exposed the Qing's fallibility, prompting the Scramble for Concessions, which saw China carved into foreign spheres of influence. A few years later the anti-foreign Boxer Uprising and the ensuing invasion of China by an eight-power army triggered a wave of nationalistic anti-Chinese sentiment in Europe and North America. In the face of the foreign onslaught combined with domestic unrest, Qing power buckled.

One of the most noticeable trends in the voluminous essays, histories and biographies published about China around the turn of the century is a new fixation with politics and government. Two recurrent and interlinked themes stand out in this literature: denigration of the Qing as despotic, venal and antiquated, and ruminations on China's international relations. This shift in focus was clearly a response to the intensification of political and military incursions in China, which prompted a flurry of commentary on the 'Far Eastern question'. The Boxer Rising (1899–1900), in particular, prompted a slew of damning assessments of the Qing and those complicit with it. The American missionary Gilbert Reid, for example, impassionedly argued that foreign looting in Beijing and its environs was just comeuppance for the government's cruelty and xenophobia.[45] There were, of course, other voices in the crowd of commentators on the Boxer episode, who decried the brutality of the foreign troops and even argued that the Qing's actions were entirely understandable.[46] Robert Hart was at the forefront of this defence of China, outlining his arguments in measured tones in a collection of essays, *These from the Land of Sinim* (1901). According to Hart, the roots of the uprising could be traced to the treaty system imposed after 1842, which had left China 'wounded to the core', the chief culprits being the injustice of extraterritoriality and missionary interference in judicial and administrative systems.[47] Hart's analysis of the situation embodied his faith in the ability of the Qing to learn from the West and subsequently adapt without the threat of gunboats. By 1900, though, few would have agreed with him, even among his own staff. More and more Hart was viewed as an obdurate Sinophile who naively clung to a misguided notion that the Qing was redeemable.

J. O. P. Bland, in the Customs 1883–96, was a particularly voluble critic of Hart's faith in China's revival. In his unpublished memoir written in the 1930s Bland ridiculed his former IG's 'belief in the impending awakening and regeneration of China, which though shaken at the time by the evidence which the war had supplied of the cowardice, incompetence and corruption of her officials, had been since the days of the Burlingame Mission an article of his faith, destined to survive even the darker days of the Boxer Upheaval'.[48] Bland was a dyed in the wool imperialist who after leaving the Customs worked as secretary of the Shanghai Municipal Council (1896–1906), representative for the British and Chinese Corporation (1906–10) and Shanghai correspondent for *The Times* (1897–1907). He was also a prolific writer of China coast fiction, political polemics and histories.[49] His most widely read works, co-authored with Edmund Backhouse, were *China under the Empress Dowager* (1910), later revealed to be based on forged documents, and *Annals & Memoirs of the Court of Peking* (1914). Both these books offered up exoticised accounts of court intrigues and reinforced the prevailing view of the Qing as moribund and tyrannical. Bland's former employment in the Customs gave his accounts credibility, as did his post-Service career working for British settler and business interests. By dint of his experiences working for the Qing it was presumed that Bland *knew* China. His imperialist credentials, on the other hand, demonstrated that, unlike Robert Hart, his loyalties could be trusted.

Bland's preoccupation with recent Qing politics tapped into rising interest in the 'China question', which was plunged into the international consciousness by the Scramble for Concessions and Boxer War. A plethora of analyses of China's international relations emerged post-1900. Most sought to explain and justify the recent violence by appealing to the Qing's history of antagonistic behaviour towards the West over the past six decades. Alexander Michie's popular history, first published in 1900, is typical in its denunciation of the 'perfidy' that characterised the Qing's dealings with the foreign powers since the Opium War.[50] Customs historians confirmed these popular portrayals of Qing officials as truculent children who only responded to violence. H. B. Morse, for example, in the Customs 1874–1909, is respected as a serious scholar of China's politics and international trade who mentored John K. Fairbank.[51] Yet his three-volume history, *The International Relations of the Chinese Empire* (1910–17), reiterated – albeit in more measured tones – many of the assumptions of the hack writers who held forth on China's foreign affairs. According to Morse, foreign belligerency between 1838 and 1860 had been necessary to shock China out of its stupor and teach the Qing 'the lesson that only the mailed fist could guard their house'. Morse wrote regretfully about the deep humiliation inflicted upon China by the Boxer Protocol, yet claimed it was the inevitable outcome of decades of misrule by the corrupt Qing, which had failed to take heed of the lessons the West had attempted to impart.[52] To most commentators after 1900, Customs and non-Customs alike, Hart's paternalistic and benevolent model of foreign influence in China had failed resoundingly. As James Hevia has shown, the foreign powers oscillated between belligerency and tutelage in their attempts to teach the Qing how to be modern.[53] The Customs represented the 'soft' side of imperialism but, with opinion of the Qing at its lowest ebb, its foreign staff increasingly believed that Hart's mission to reform China through teaching alone was redundant.

The early twentieth century also saw the emergence of the treaty port sub-genre of memoirs and light fiction, which reached its heyday in the 1920s and was little interested in Chinese politics, except in caricatured form. China coast authors instead served up lurid tales of love, sex and sedition. These novels were part of a broader literary trend that played upon sensationalised Chinese themes. Thomas Burke's *Limehouse Nights* collection (1916) and Sax Rohmer's Fu Manchu series (1913–59) simultaneously outraged and titillated the British public with their salacious tales of white slavery and opium dens, playing upon Western fears of the 'yellow peril'. W. Somerset Maugham's *The Painted Veil* (1925) and his play *East of Suez* (1922) unashamedly capitalised on the contemporary fascination with expatriate life in the treaty ports, which by now had gained a reputation for decadence and debauchery.[54] Much of the literature produced by Customs men was derivative of these works. Both B. Lennox Simpson and J. O. P. Bland successfully made the crossover from political pundit to novelist. Simpson's first novel, *The Forbidden Boundary* (1908), catered to a prurient curiosity about interracial sex, as did the fiction of other popular writers such as Burke, Rohmer, Maugham and Louise Jordan Miln.[55] A. H. Rasmussen, W. F. Tyler, Paul King, George Worcester and L. C. Arlington, all of them Customs men, published memoirs about their time in the Chinese government's service.[56] A couple of former employees even decided to pen novels based on their time in the Customs: C. S. Archer's *China Servant* (1946) and Paul King's *The Commissioner's Dilemma* (1932), co-authored with his wife Veronica King. All of this literature was lowbrow and most of it is forgotten in the present day, yet it contributed enormously to the treaty port folklore passed down by 'old China hands' and pushed into the popular consciousness by novelists, dramatists and memoirists. Customs fiction and memoirs evoke the insularity and the self-importance of the China coast world. The treaty ports were imagined as more foreign than Chinese, built upon the efforts and sacrifices of European and American forebears who brought modernity to China.[57] Given that the Foreign Inspectorate's raison d'être was to reform China along Western lines using European and American expertise, Customs men had a clear stake in this version of China's modern history.

Revolution, nationalism and the Customs' information system

The level of awareness and understanding of Chinese society and politics among the foreign staff varied tremendously. Alfred Hippisley devoted a significant chunk of his diary to speculating on court machinations and China's international relations.[58] Similarly, the letters of Lancelot Lawford (in the Customs 1905–41) to his wife were filled with lengthy analyses of the vicissitudes of the nascent Chinese republic.[59] In contrast J. O. P. Bland confessed in his memoir that back in his Customs days he was not particularly concerned with 'the philosophy and necessities of my primordial yellow brother'.[60] Commissioners did, of course, need to be moderately au fait with local political events in order to perform their jobs, but it was in 1908 that the Customs' internal system for collecting political information was extended and systematised with the introduction of semi-official letters. In these communications, dutifully sent to the IG every two weeks, Commissioners were expected to report on a host of topics, including relations between the Customs and the Superintendent, the political climate, military movements, social life, disease and famine, public opinion and the behaviour of foreign officials. Some Commissioners were more verbose than others, but it is clear that this system enabled the Inspectorate to survey conditions in the outports much more comprehensively.

The refinement and expansion of the Customs' internal information system must be viewed in the context of broader trends in colonial knowledge production and widespread political and social unrest across China in the first half of the twentieth century. Various historians have demonstrated the politicised nature of colonial knowledge production, which was often intended to buttress colonial rule. The imperative to reach a deeper understanding of social and cultural formations through ethnographic study often arose after a period of crisis for the colonial state. Nicholas Dirks argues that colonial knowledge in India became 'anthropologized' after 1857 because this type of knowledge would ostensibly enable the colonial state to better understand the underlying causes of the rebellion, to detect the warning signs of unrest in the future and to rule more effectively by taking into account religion and custom. An 'ethnographic state' was produced in the process.[61] Similarly George Trumbull has shown how the anti-French uprising in Algeria in 1871 prompted a drive to produce ethnographic texts, researched and written by colonial administrators who were ideally placed to conduct fieldwork with Algerian informants. Cultural knowledge of colonised subjects 'enshrined in texts governed how French administrators governed, producing generalizations and explanations that determined practices'.[62] Customs information gathering in the twentieth century was rarely ethnographic, instead focusing largely on political, military and ecological conditions, but it was similarly expanded in light of a perceived crisis of colonialism after 1900. Although the foreign powers initially emerged jubilant from their victory in the Boxer War, the revolutionary tumult of the next three decades threatened to unseat foreign interests. The semi-official reports of Customs Commissioners reflect European and American wariness of Chinese nationalism.

Customs Commissioners usually arrived at their knowledge of local conditions through observation and conversations with regional officials and informants among the Chinese staff in the custom house. C. A. Bayly has shown how colonial authorities obtained political intelligence by manipulating indigenous information networks, resulting in vast differences between colonial knowledge systems across the empire world.[63] As an organisation that ostensibly blended together foreign and Chinese interests, the Customs was especially well positioned to take advantage of native knowledge-collecting practices. The extent to which foreign Customs officers were able to insert themselves into local information networks did, however, vary according to the Customs establishment's position and power in any given locality. Cultivating good relations with the *daotai* (Circuit Intendant), the travelling officials who mediated between provincial governors and local officials, and with other local powerbrokers through regular meetings and social engagements could make the Commissioner privy to a great deal of information. This relationship was a reciprocal one; local officials grilled Customs Commissioners about the intentions of the foreign diplomatic establishment and prevailing opinion in the English-language treaty port press. Alfred Hippisley quizzed Chinese employees in the Customs, past and present, about political intrigues.[64] Others found the intelligence networks established by Christian missionaries and their Chinese converts to be a valuable tool in gauging the political atmosphere in the rural hinterland. Successive Commissioners in Shantou, in particular, made heavy use of this avenue of information. Finally, the foreign Customs staff scrutinised the local Chinese press for useful information and to assess public opinion of the foreign presence.

All of this knowledge was, of course, constrained by how little or how much informants chose to tell and was also filtered by the Commissioner's own interpretation of events. And there was much for the Commissioner to have an opinion about. Customs houses were often caught up in the melees that accompanied the dramatic political and military events of the twentieth century. For instance its foreign character made the Customs a target of the burgeoning nationalist movement in the 1920s, and local Custom houses were often stuck in the middle of regional tussles between warlords intent on expropriating the revenue. The foreign staff's reaction to these events reveals their growing disquiet about the rise of Chinese nationalism and the movement's accompanying ambitions to oust the foreign powers from China. The 1911–12 Xinhai Revolution, which toppled the Qing and installed a nominally republican government, generated voluminous commentary within the Customs. Like most other foreigners in China, many Customs men believed the dethroning of the Qing was long overdue. Most Commissioners could not resist a jibe at local Qing officials. 'If the revolutionaries do rise here the officials will do nothing but take refuge in the For[eign]. Concessions,' scoffed the Tianjin Commissioner in October 1911.[65] 'Customs Weiyuan [Superintendent] Jui seems to be much alarmed for his own skin, and generally prefers to reside at Ch'aochoufu,' commented the Shantou Commissioner. The Shantou *daotai*, for his part, was incapable of fending off a revolutionary attack; his army amounted only to 'about 1,200 soldiers that *might* be relied upon'.[66] By portraying the official reaction to the revolutionary challenge as chaotic and cowardly, Customs Commissioners served to vindicate the long-held assumption that the entire imperial edifice was spineless, dissipated and unable to secure the loyalty of the people.

The Qing may have deserved to fall, according to most foreign commentators, but the new government was not much of an improvement. Although a few optimistically predicted that China would be propelled into an age of reform now that the most intractable obstacle to change – the Qing – had been removed, most scoffed at the idea.[67] The revolutionaries were generally portrayed as a shambolic mob by sceptical foreigners, and Customs Commissioners usually followed suit. The Shantou Commissioner eyed the ragtag revolutionary forces that had set up headquarters in the American and China Trading Company offices with distaste. On the day of the revolutionary takeover, he reported, this building 'belched forth a "Falstaff's Regiment"', which swiftly took control of all major government and financial establishments in the port. The new governing forces in the town had little to recommend them except for their 'highly ornate letter paper and round "Republican Seal"'.[68] Meanwhile in Tianjin the mutinying troops had achieved nothing constructive, unless one counted looting, burning and inflaming widespread panic, according to the postmaster.[69] Foreign opinion of the chaos endemic in Chinese politics seemed to be vindicated by the disintegration of the Beijing government's national authority. The period 1916–28 saw the emergence of several regional power bases ruled by 'warlords', who were often at war with one another. Most Commissioners prepared detailed reports on the local actions of troops and, in accordance with the Customs motto of political neutrality, many cultivated official relations with reigning 'warlords'. Yet, their low opinion of these local leaders was palpable. Two weeks after a takeover of the city by mutinying troops in March 1916, the Shantou Commissioner reported disparagingly that the rebel leader was 'engaging Triads, and yesterday forenoon a band of about 300 of the vilest ruffians from Chaoyang marched in procession past this office with banners, and the ancient Chinese war horns blowing'.[70] In the minds of the foreign staff there was very little to distinguish these 'revolutionaries' from the rebel hordes of old.

The antipathy of Customs Commissioners and other China coast commentators towards the different forces competing for power in China was partly to do with the chaos caused by these struggles. But it also pointed towards more deep-rooted fears about the potential for political change to upset the position of foreigners in China. Despite widespread mockery of the Qing, many believed that the dynasty, however decrepit, could provide a measure of stability for the 'unequal' treaty system. These concerns also explain foreign hostility towards the nationalist, anti-imperialist campaigns that began with the May Fourth movement of 1919, when student demonstrators marched en masse in Beijing to protest against the Chinese government's handling of the Versailles Treaty negotiations. Customs reports on anti-imperialist boycotts and protests will be discussed in more detail in Chapter 3, so it suffices to point out here that Commissioners routinely attempted to damage the credibility of the demonstrators by referring to them as a 'mob' or as 'Reds'.[71] As collaborators in one of the most glaring infringements on China's sovereignty, the Customs foreign staff clearly felt defensive. The potential for a strong central government to rise to power on the back of this outpouring of nationalist sentiment was unsettling. These anxieties partly explain the Customs' knowledge-producing drive in the twentieth century. Semi-official letters enabled the Inspectorate to gauge its evolving position in China and to assess the threat of these various challenges.

Frederick Maze and the birth of a Customs mythology, 1927–37

These fears were realised when Chiang-Kai-shek's Guomindang (Nationalist Party) established the National Government in Nanjing in 1927 and swiftly set about reclaiming China's sovereignty from the foreign powers; the Nationalists recovered the British concession at Hankou in 1927 and tariff autonomy in 1928–30. Nanjing also drew the Customs more decisively under the central government's control, establishing the Guanwushu (Customs Administration) to oversee the Foreign Inspectorate's work, while foreign recruitment was suspended in 1927. The Customs had always suffered from a curious preoccupation with posterity, but concern with its public reputation reached its zenith in response to these challenges to the foreign position. The Inspectorate thus embarked on a self-publicising drive, which involved the production and dissemination of new knowledge about the Customs' contribution to modern China. The IG Frederick Maze's concern with rehabilitating his personal reputation had as much to do with initiating this bout of self-promotion as did defending the Foreign Inspectorate in the face of the nationalist onslaught. Maze had fought bitterly for the post of IG after Aglen's dismissal in 1927, beating the British Legation-nominated candidate and officiating IG A. H. F. Edwardes in 1929. He was, moreover, lambasted in the foreign treaty port press for his willingness to swear an oath of loyalty to the Nationalist Government.[72] More than his predecessors, Maze desperately needed to justify his appointment to the top job and he did this by working hard to establish his own version of Customs history as the definitive one.[73]

Maze sponsored multiple projects intended to produce and preserve knowledge about the Customs in the 1930s. They were enabled by the establishment of a Customs Reference Library in Shanghai, to which all Commissioners were instructed to send pre-1902 correspondence. An eclectic range of works was produced, including a survey of China's foreign trade since the 1850s, a discussion of China's recovery of tariff autonomy and three volumes on Chinese junks prepared by the River Inspector George Worcester.[74] Commissioner Stanley Fowler Wright was at the forefront of this drive to rewrite Customs history. Maze talked Wright into delaying retirement and working as the official Service historian 1933–38. One of his main tasks was to trawl the Customs archive and select documents for a seven-volume compilation, *Documents Illustrative of the Origin, Development and Activities of the Chinese Maritime Customs Service* (1936–40). These initiatives were not just intended to preserve the historical legacy of the Customs; they also actively constructed an institutional folklore. A copy of *Documents Illustrative* was sent to every custom house, and a brief history of the Service penned by Wright in 1938 was circulated privately within the Customs.[75]

There were three recurring motifs in the Maze project to edit and preserve Customs history: its modernising legacy, the veneration of Robert Hart as the founding father of the institution and Maze's role in restoring service 'integrity'. Wright's privately circulated history emphasised its indispensable contribution to modernising China, as did T. R. Banister's survey of the aids to navigation system established by the Customs, *The Coastwise Lights of China* (1932). The foundations of Customs infrastructure were built by Robert Hart, who worked ceaselessly to promote China's advancement. Moreover, Hart's modernising impetus was global in scale. 'Long before internationalism had become a recognised ideal in world politics,' Wright explained, 'Hart had already built up, with men from every civilized nation in the world, the first great international civil service', a 'precursor to the League of Nations' no less.[76] Wright's magnum opus, a thousand-page biography of Hart, provided a laudatory corrective to the flood of lukewarm appraisals of Hart's career that emerged after his death in 1911, many of which pronounced him too sympathetic to Chinese interests and sensibilities. Hart 'espoused the Service,' Wright argued, 'putting leisure, domestic happiness, and the getting of gain behind him' in order to dedicate himself fully to China.[77]

The corollary to this posthumous reverence for Hart was that Maze, his nephew, was the natural heir of the great IG. Wright's histories and compilations of documents brushed over the Aglen inspectorate (1911–27), criticised for creating an *imperium in imperio*, as a temporary blip in a largely uninterrupted policy continuum from Hart to Maze. In Customs correspondence Maze emphasised how, like Hart, he intended to preserve foreign influence while also collaborating with the Chinese government.[78] Maze also prided himself on preserving what he saw as the integrity of the Service. 'Whatever Party emerges successfully out of the present struggle will, if this policy is pursued, inherit the enormous asset of an intact – not a dismembered – Customs Service,' he wrote to the Tianjin Commissioner Hayley-Bell in the midst of the Lenox Simpson debacle in 1930.[79] Even after the Manchurian custom houses were annexed by Japan in 1932 'integrity' remained the Service's watchword. It could also be used to justify politically suspect actions, such as making concessions to Japanese demands and deciding to keep the Inspectorate in Shanghai after the city was taken by the Japanese in 1937. At times Maze attempted to conserve a sanitised version of his own legacy as IG by underhand means, including doctoring the official record he would leave behind, tightly controlling the use of the Inspectorate archive and even taking certain Customs documents into his own possession against regulations.[80] Maze's manipulation of the Customs' historical record proved remarkably successful in retrospect. It certainly shaped the judgements and subjects of an entire generation of historians working in Europe and North America, most notably in the preoccupation with Hart's impressive legacy. Maze, too, has generally been treated favourably by historians since 1949, largely because of the carefully selected documents he placed in UK archives.[81]

Knowledge production and diffusion had always been a weighty matter for the Customs, but in the 1930s it became intensely political.

Conclusion

This chapter has outlined the ways in which the Customs' perception of its purpose in China and the foreign staff's views of their adopted country shifted in response to evolving external environments. As a Sino-foreign organisation, Customs attitudes were particularly finely attuned to changes in China's relations with the West. Knowledge produced about China by the institution and its personnel provides an insight into both the Inspectorate's perception of its role and responsibilities in China and the ideologies and attitudes of its foreign staff. Although there were many voices within the Customs, Hart's founding principle of disinterestedness was reinvoked by successive IGs between 1863 and 1949. Maze's talk of 'integrity' was just another permutation of Hart's original exhortation that the staff should remain aloof from political squabbles. More than anything the Service, with perhaps the exception of the Aglen Inspectorate, wanted to distance itself ideologically from imperialism. Certainly many members of treaty port foreign communities thought that the Customs did not do enough to support European and American interests and that Hart, in particular, was 'too Chinese' in his outlook. But rather than standing outside of imperialist ideologies and practices, the Customs actively contributed to them. Although certain Customs Sinologists distanced themselves from belligerent imperialist rhetoric, others reconfirmed the increasingly popular perception that China was weak, corrupt and deserving of punishment. Furthermore, Customs information-gathering projects themselves constituted a colonial project. As James Hevia has persuasively argued, various agents and organisations, including the Royal Asiatic Society, missionaries and the British Foreign Office, built an 'information empire' in China after 1842. As a result, by the end of the nineteenth century 'Euroamericans could now hold China in the palm of their hand, scan it, claim to understand it, and act on it – an alien empire had been decoded, classified, summarized, and, as a result, was known as it had never been known before'. These epistemological projects created a new China, not just in the Western imagination but also, more tangibly, by preparing the groundwork for colonial projects to 'reterritorialize' China. Imperialism rested upon detailed knowledge of the country's political and economic systems, culture and geography.[82] The Chinese Customs Service was at the forefront of this drive to produce knowledge about China and circulate it in the Western world.

Customs' knowledge production served to legitimise the Foreign

Inspectorate's position and thus informal empire in China more broadly. It demonstrated that the Customs was useful and that the foreign staff were experts who *knew* China. It also enabled the Inspectorate to construct and disseminate its own interpretation of its role, principles and achievements. Individual Customs officers, however, did not necessarily stick to the script provided by the Inspectorate. In Customs correspondence and in publications not sponsored by the Service they could be outspoken in their support for the foreign establishment. This eclectic range of voices broadened significantly in the twentieth century as the Customs began recruiting men and women from a more diverse range of backgrounds. This is not to say that the Inspectorate failed to cultivate a distinct Service ethos. Rather, the position of the Customs at a crossing point between the Chinese and foreign worlds meant that its employees could move freely between different ideological positions. Customs principles could be invoked opportunistically to lend legitimacy and authority when necessary, as could settler ideologies. Customs identities and allegiances, then, always involved negotiation and compromise between the institutional culture and the external context of imperialism.

Notes

1 Paul French, *Through the Looking Glass: China's foreign journalists from the Opium Wars to Mao* (Hong Kong: Hong Kong University Press, 2009), 82–3.
2 See, for example, *The Coming Struggle in Eastern Asia* (London, 1908) & *China's Crucifixion* (New York, 1928).
3 SHAC, 679(1) 31640, 'IG's Confidential correspondence with port commissioners, Jan–Aug 1930', confidential letter from Maze to Hayley-Bell, 16 May 1930.
4 For an account of the episode see Brunero, *Britain's Imperial Cornerstone*, 119–31.
5 *Documents Illustrative of the Origin, Development and Activities of the Chinese Customs Service*, vol. 1 (Shanghai: Statistical Department of the Inspectorate General of Customs, 1936–40), circular no. 8 of 1864, 36–47.
6 *Documents Illustrative*, vol. 1, circular no. 8 of 1864, 36.
7 *Documents Illustrative*, vol. 1, circular no. 24 of 1873, 313.
8 *Documents Illustrative*, vol. 1, circular no. 28 of 1870, 241–50.
9 For a summary of the decentralisation of power after 1860 see William T. Rowe, *China's Last Empire: The great Qing* (Cambridge, MA: Belknap Press, 2009), 204–7.
10 *Documents Illustrative*, vol. 1, circular no. 11 of 1870 (first series), 10 Dec 1870, 180.
11 *Documents Illustrative*, vol. 1, circular no. 20 (second series), 3 Mar 1877, 366–8.
12 *Documents Illustrative*, vol. 1, circular no. 51 of 1875 (first series), 360. Also see successive staff handbooks, such as *Provisional Instructions for the Guidance of the In-Door Staff* (Shanghai: Statistical Department of the Inspectorate General, 1877), 1.
13 *Documents Illustrative*, vol. 1, circular no. 8 of 1864 (first series), 21 June 1864, 43.
14 Hans Van de Ven, 'Robert Hart and Gustav Detring During the Boxer Rebellion', *Modern Asian Studies*, 40:3 (2006), 631–62.
15 Hippisley papers, MS. Eng. c. 7285, diary 1898–1905, diary entries 7 Sept 1898.
16 Horowitz, 'Politics, Power and the Chinese Maritime Customs Service'.
17 *Documents Illustrative*, vol. 1, circular no. 8 of 1864 (first series), 21 June 1864, vol. 1, 38.

18 Colin Mackerras, *Western Images of China* (Oxford: Oxford University Press, 1991), 44.

19 *Documents Illustrative*, vol. 1, circular no. 8 of 1864 (first series), 21 June 1864, 37.

20 *Documents Illustrative*, vol. 1, circular no. 24 of 1873 (first series), 18 Dec 1873, 313.

21 See, for example, Fairbank, 'Synarchy under the Treaties'.

22 Anne Veronica Witchard, *Thomas Burke's Dark Chinoiserie: Limehouse Nights and the queer spell of Chinatown* (Farnham: Ashgate, 2009), 11–12, 23–35 and 31–40.

23 See Charles Dickens's derisive account of the Chinese exhibits at the 1851 Crystal Palace Exhibition, 'The Great Exhibition and the Little One', *Household Words: A weekly journal*, 3:5 (July 1851), 356–60; Thomas De Quincey, *China: A revised reprint of articles from 'Titan'* (Edinburgh: J. Hogg, 1857).

24 Wichard, *Thomas Burke's Dark Chinoiserie*, 53–64

25 P. J. Marshall, 'Britain in China in the Late Eighteenth Century', in *Ritual & Diplomacy: The Macartney Mission to China, 1792–1794*, edited by Robert Bickers (London: Wellsweep, 1993), 11–29.

26 Robert K. Douglas, *Society in China*, 2nd ed. (London: A. D. Innes and Co., 1894), 1 and 331.

27 Horowitz, 'Politics, Power and the Chinese Maritime Customs Service'.

28 Hippisley papers, unpublished memoir, 52–3.

29 Hans J. van de Ven, 'Wade, Sir Thomas Francis (1818–95)', *Oxford Dictionary of National Biography*, edited by H. C. G. Matthew and Brian Harrison (Oxford: Oxford University Press, 2004).

30 See, for example, Friedrich Hirth, *The Ancient History of China, to the End of the Ch'ou Dynasty* (Freeport: Books for Libraries Press, 1969; first pub. 1908).

31 On van Aaslt see Han Kuo-huang, 'J. A. Van Aalst and His Chinese Music', *Asian Music*, 19:2 (1988), 127–30. For his book see *Chinese Music* (Shanghai: IMCS Statistical Department, 1884).

32 Isadore Cyril Cannon, *Public Success, Private Sorrow: The life and times of Charles Henry Brewitt-Taylor (1857–1938), China customs commissioner and pioneer translator* (Hong Kong: Hong Kong University Press, 2009).

33 For an overview of the Statistical Department's work see Andrea Eberhard-Bréard, 'Robert Hart and China's Statistical Revolution', *Modern Asian Studies*, 40:3 (2006), 605–29.

34 Thomas P. Lyons, *China Maritime Customs and China's Trade Statistics, 1859–1948* (Trumansburg: Willow Creek, 2003).

35 C. A. Gordon, ed., *An Epitome of the Reports of the Medical Officers to the Chinese Imperial Maritime Customs Service, from 1871 to 1882* (London: Baillière, Tindall & Cox, 1884).

36 See 'Documents relating to, 1º the Establishment of Meteorological Stations in China; and 2º Proposals for co-operation in the publication of meteorological observations and exchange of weather news by telegraph along the Pacific coast of Asia', *Chinese Maritime Customs Project Occasional Papers*, 3, 2008: <www.bristol. ac.uk/history/customs/papers/occasionalpaper3.pdf>.

37 Alfred E. Hippisley, *Proposal to Develop Trade and Improve Commercial Relations by Securing an Increase in Treaty Tariff in Return for Abolition of Internal Taxation* (Shanghai: Shanghai Mercury, 1902); Henry Kopsch, *Brevities on Eastern Bimetallism* (Shanghai: North China Herald Office, 1902).

38 For an overview of the rise of statistics in Europe see Stuart Woolf, 'Statistics and the Modern State', *Comparative Studies in History and Society*, 31:3 (1989), 588–604.

39 Woolf, 'Statistics and the Modern State', 595–7.

40 C. A. Bayly, *Empire and Information: Intelligence gathering and social communication in India, 1780–1870* (Cambridge: Cambridge University Press, 1996), especially chapters 6 and 7, 212–83.

41 *Documents Illustrative*, vol. 1, circular no. 28 of 1869 (first series), 12 Nov 1869.

42 Eberhard-Bréard, 'Robert Hart and China's Statistical Revolution', 619–20.

43 See Hevia, *English Lessons*, chapter 5, 123–5, for the ways in which the systematic

collection of information about China in the aftermath of the Arrow War made China known to the West in new ways, thus enabling colonial domination.

44 Eliza Scidmore, *China, the Long-Lived Empire* (New York: The Century Co., 1900), 5.

45 Gilbert Reid, 'The Ethics of Loot', *The Forum*, 31 (1901), 581–6.

46 See, for example, Mark Twain, 'To the Person Sitting in Darkness', *North American Review*, 172 (Feb 1901); E. J. Dillon, 'The Chinese Wolf and the European Lamb', *The Contemporary Review*, 79 (Jan 1901), 1–31; G. Lowes Dickinson, *Letters from a Chinese Official: Being an Eastern view of Western Civilization* (Garden City, NY: Doubleday, 1915; 1st edition 1901).

47 Robert Hart, 'The Boxers: 1900', *These from the Land of Sinim: Essays on the Chinese question*, 2nd ed. (London: Chapman & Hall, 1903), 166.

48 Bland papers, memoirs, chapter 8, 12.

49 Bickers, 'Bland, John Otway Percy (1863–1945)'.

50 Alexander Michie, *The Englishman in China during the Victorian Era as Illustrated by the Career of Sir Rutherford Alcock* (Taipei: Ch'eng-Wen Publishing Co., 1966), vol. I, 84–5 and 400.

51 See John King Fairbank, Martha Henderson Coolidge and Richard J. Smith, *H. B. Morse, Customs commissioner and historian of China* (Lexington: University Press of Kentucky, 1995).

52 Hosea Ballou Morse, *The International Relations of the Chinese Empire* (Taipei: Ch'eng wen Pub. Co., 1971; first published 1910–17), vol. 1, 617, and vol. 3, 446.

53 Hevia, *English Lessons*.

54 For a summary of popular fiction about China see Bickers, *Britain in China*, 43–54.

55 Louise Jordan Miln, *By Soochow Waters* (New York: Frederick A. Stokes Co., 1929).

56 L. C. Arlington, *Through the Dragon's Eyes* (London: Constable & Co., 1931); King, *In the Chinese Customs Service*; Rasmussen, *China Trader*; William Ferdinand Tyler, *Pulling Strings in China* (London: Constable & Co., 1929); G. R. G. Worcester, *The Junkman Smiles* (London: Chatto and Windus, 1959).

57 See Robert A. Bickers, 'History, Legend and Treaty Port Ideology, 1925–1931', in *Ritual and Diplomacy*, edited by Bickers, 81–92.

58 Hippisley papers, diary, especially entries in 1898.

59 School of Oriental and African Studies archives and special collections, MS 380683, Lancelot Lawford papers, letters to his wife 1913–17.

60 Bland papers, memoirs, chapter 1, 6.

61 Nicholas B. Dirks, *Castes of Mind: Colonialism and the making of modern India* (Princeton: Princeton University Press, 2001), especially chapter 3, 43–60.

62 George R. Trumbull, *An Empire of Facts: Colonial power, cultural knowledge, and Islam in Algeria, 1870–1914* (Cambridge: Cambridge University Press, 2009), 2.

63 Bayly, *Information and Empire*, especially chapters 2, 56–96, and 5, 180–211.

64 See, for example, his diary entry on 26 Jan 1899 discussing information provided by a former Chinese employee, now an 'expectant Taotai', about the political manoeu-vrings surrounding foreign railway concessions near Tianjin. Hippisley papers, diary 1895–1902.

65 SHAC, 679(1) 31961, 'Tientsin semi-official, 1910–13', S/O no. 37, Tianjin Commissioner J. F. Oiesen to IG Aglen, 26 Oct 1911.

66 SHAC, 679(1) 32365, 'Swatow semi-official, 1911–14', S/O no. 23, Shantou Commissioner Gilchrist to IG Aglen, 27 Oct 1911.

67 Lancelot Lawton took a positive view of the revolution in *Empires of the Far East*, vol. 1 (Boston: Small, Maynard & Co., 1932, first published 1912), 8.

68 SHAC, 691(1) 32365, 'Swatow semi-official, 1911–14', S/O nos 25 and 26, from Commissioner Oiesen to Aglen, 21 and 22 Nov 1911.

69 Tianjin Municipal Archives (hereafter TMA), W1–1–72, 'Outward semi-officials to postmaster general re. local situation during the revolution', S/O no. 99 from Tianjin to postmaster general Piry, 3 Mar 1912.

70 SHAC, 679(1) 32366, 'Swatow semi-official, 1915–17', S/O letter no. 195, Commissioner Lay to IG Aglen, 12 Apr 1916.

71 See, for instance, SHAC, 679(1) 22162, 'Disturbances at Swatow', despatch no. 6113, Commissioner Carey to IG Aglen, 2 July 1925 and S/O no. 436, 26 Sept 1925. Paul Cohen has discussed how various commentators invoked the spectre of the Boxer Rising in order to discredit anti-imperialist demonstrators; *History in Three Keys: The Boxers as event, experience, and myth* (New York: Columbia University Press, 1997), 238–60.
72 For the 1927–29 Customs succession crisis see Atkins, *Informal Empire in Crisis*; Brunero, *Britain's Imperial Cornerstone in China*, 79–98.
73 For a full account of Maze's attempts to influence the historical record see Robert Bickers, 'Purloined Letters: History and the Chinese Maritime Customs Service', *Modern Asian Studies*, 40:3 (2006), 691–723.
74 Stanley Fowler Wright, *China's Struggle for Tariff Autonomy, 1843–1938* (Shanghai: Kelly & Walsh, 1938); G. R. G. Worcester, *The Junks and Sampans of the Yangtze: A study in Chinese nautical research*, 2 vols (Shanghai: Statistical Department Inspectorate General of Customs, 1947–48).
75 Stanley Fowler Wright, *The Origin and Development of the Chinese Customs Service, 1843–1911* (Shanghai: privately circulated, 1936).
76 Wright, *Origin and Development*, 92 and 4.
77 Stanley Fowler Wright, *Hart and the Chinese Customs* (Belfast: W. Mullan, 1950), 855.
78 See Bickers, 'Purloined Letters', 699–700.
79 TMA, W1-1-4321, 'S/O letters from IG, 1930-1', confidential letter from Maze to Hayley-Bell, 14 May 1930.
80 Bickers, 'Purloined Letters', 691–723.
81 Brunero, *Britain's Imperial Cornerstone*; Clifford, 'Sir Frederick Maze'.
82 Hevia, *English Lessons*, 123–55. Quotation from 142.

CHAPTER THREE

'We want men and not encyclopaedias': joining the Customs Service[1]

Alfred E. Hippisley sailed in 1867 at the tender age of nineteen to China, where he joined over two hundred other Customs Britons. His path to China is telling of the ad hoc recruitment procedures practised in the formative years of the Inspectorate, when appointments were generally procured through personal connections, or even chance encounters, with Customs personnel. Hippisley was introduced to the Service by William Cartwright, his closest friend at the Bristol Grammar School, where Hippisley was head boy. Despite having no seafaring experience, in 1862 Cartwright unexpectedly left school to become a midshipman with the ill-fated Chinese flotilla organised by then-IG Horatio Nelson Lay and captained by Sherard Osborn. After the flotilla was disbanded the following year, Cartwright joined the Customs. His letters to his boyhood friend Hippisley 'described his life in such pleasant colours and the salaries issued as so liberal that I was fired by a desire to follow his example and obtain an appointment'.[2] In his brief and rather gauche letter of application to Robert Hart, written in 1864, Hippisley confessed that 'I am still pursuing my studies' and had thus 'not yet held any appointment'. His references, written by the headmaster and second master of Bristol Grammar School, were more effusive. Hippisley, they enthused, was possessed of a 'steady, industrious, persevering, & conscientious' character and 'actuated in his conduct by the principles of a Christian Gentleman'. What is more, the headmaster was convinced that 'he would assist in maintaining the influence of England abroad, by shewing an excellent example of a well-bred, well-educated & honourable English gentleman'.[3] Hart replied that there were unfortunately no available appointments at present. Besides, at the age of sixteen Hippisley was too young for the Service.

He was, however, impressed enough with Hippisley's credentials to promise him an Indoor Staff appointment should one become available in the future. In the meantime, Hart instructed, he should improve his conversational French and German, assets in Beijing's diplomatic community, also advising that 'for what little social pleasure life in China affords scope, you wd. find no cause to regret being a good performer on any one musical instrument'.[4] In 1866 Hippisley was able to reinforce his Customs connections in person when the IG, who was accompanying a Chinese official on a diplomatic trip, summoned him to London to take breakfast at the Berkeley Hotel. His future Customs career seemed well on course. Later that year, though, another much more attractive opportunity briefly presented itself when he received a partial scholarship to attend St John's College, Oxford. Heretofore he had never entertained the possibility of a university education, realising that, with eight children to support, it was impossible for his father to pay for such an extravagance. This dream was, however, dashed by his father's financial troubles, which meant that he could not subsidise the scholarship. The Customs it was, then. Hippisley stayed in the Service for forty-two years.[5]

The recruitment story of twenty-four-year-old Outdoor Staff man Albert Henry Rasmussen, colourfully told in his memoirs, is on the surface very different. Rasmussen was a wanderer, on the constant lookout for opportunity and adventure, a lifestyle inspired by romantic childhood visions of a seafaring life. At home in his native Norway he 'would sit for hours watching the ships going out, sick with longing. I never paid any attention to the inward bound ships; it was those outward bound I watched until they disappeared in the narrows by Dröbak.' Despite his father's opposition, Rasmussen ran away to sea at the age of fourteen and never looked back.[6] The experience was exhilarating. For the next ten years Rasmussen lived on the high seas, working on long-distance voyages to Brazil, Mexico and Ceylon before being deposited in Hong Kong in 1905. China was initially just another exotic experience. 'The strange new life I had entered, the fascination of the Orient, the colour and glamour of the teeming street and harbour life, satisfied me completely. All was new and fresh and wonderful,' he reminisced. There was, however, the problem of employment, as Rasmussen was now jobless in an unfamiliar land. According to the old China hands he met in Hong Kong, Shanghai, the city which featured most vividly in the international imagination as the gateway to wealth and opportunity for a white man in China, was the place to be in order to make his mark. Consequently, after being paid off by his ship Rasmussen travelled up the China coast and managed to procure a letter of introduction to the Chief Tidesurveyor, head of the Customs Outdoor Staff in Shanghai, from a Swedish missionary. After a perfunctory interview he was employed as a watcher, the lowest-ranking Outdoor position, thereby joining the small but steadily growing cohort of sixty-four Norwegians in the Service. The Customs, however, was not strictly what Rasmussen had in mind when he spoke of his intention to 'to stay and make a future for myself' in China. In fact he professed to have 'joined from dire necessity' and had no desire to remain a low-status Outdoor man for longer than was expedient. After five years of service he resigned to take up a more lucrative opportunity working for a China coast firm.[7] For Rasmussen the Customs was merely a convenient stopgap on the road to more promising ventures.

Hippisley and Rasmussen are just two individuals plucked from among thousands of Customs employees, yet their brief biographies provide an appropriate lens through which to study the archetypal foreign Indoor or Outdoor man, if he indeed existed. Furthermore, their recruitment stories significantly complicate our understanding of European migrations across and around the empire world, particularly when considering the factors that propelled and enabled these relocations and the types of people who sought employment overseas. Such a reassessment is important for several reasons, not least because the image of the colonist as invariably English, upper-class and singularly committed to the cause of imperialism continues to loom large. This chapter reconsiders such rough and ready assumptions about the men and women who staffed the empire world. I argue that most European Customs recruits were not motivated primarily by a desire to further imperialist interests in China. Rather, their concerns were rather more complex and opportunistic; they were shaped by colonial ideologies, concepts of nationality and citizenship, socio-economic class and personal ambition, particularly the promise of a reliable career.

David Lambert and Alan Lester's edited volume of essays *Colonial Lives Across the British Empire* presents an innovative theoretical approach to colonial migrations by reconceptualising the movements of people between different sites of empire as 'imperial careering', yet most of the lives collected in the book are those of elite or famous individuals.[8] This is, of course, partly a matter of sources, for working-class and marginal expatriates did not usually publish memoirs or travelogues or have their papers preserved for posterity. The archives of the CCS, then, with its vast personnel and recruitment records, present a rare opportunity to compare the socio-economic profiles, the career trajectories and the migratory impulses of the privileged and marginal alike. This chapter first discusses the political considerations taken into account when making appointments, particularly efforts to maintain the national balance in the staff. I will then explore the recruitment processes employed by the Inspectorate; this is followed by an analysis of the socio-economic profile of the foreign staff.

In this analysis, *Empire Careers* builds upon recent literature on imperial networks and 'careering' by considering the migrations of

Britons and non-Britons, elite and non-elite, within the same analytical framework. Works such as Zoë Laidlaw's *Colonial Connections* and Alan Lester's *Imperial Networks* have spatially reimagined the British empire as a network-like collection of multiple intersecting pathways, which in addition to connecting the colonies to the metropole also formed bridges *between* different colonial nodes. Capital, people, communications, goods and ideas flowed around the empire world through these networks.[9] Mobile individuals created, altered and exploited them in their movements around and *between* sites of empire, shaping colonial projects and discourses in the process.[10] Hippisley and Rasmussen drew upon these networks as a path into the Customs, in the sense of making use of trans-empire channels of travel and communication as well as exploiting personal connections to individuals in positions of influence. Hippisley's interest in the Customs was sparked by the cross-empire communications of his friend Cartwright. Indeed, it is unlikely that Hart would have taken an unsolicited application seriously were it not for Hippisley's link to his former school friend. His connections to the IG were cemented when Hart travelled to London. Rasmussen, as a Norwegian, was not an imperial subject, yet his career was also enabled by the global networks forged by colonial expansion. Even before joining the Customs he had traversed the globe as a sailor, stopping at present and former sites of multiple empires. On arriving in China he resourcefully made use of the local knowledge of sailors and traders whose trajectories converged in Hong Kong to gather information about his potential career options in China. As a Scandinavian he was also able to exploit regional connections to the Swedish missionary who wrote him a letter of introduction to the Shanghai Tidesurveyor. Histories of colonial networks have largely focused on the political influence and access to the patronage of powerful individuals enabled by imperial connections, yet Rasmussen's biography, and those of others like him, tell a different story. I contend that low-status and marginal Europeans also engaged in a type of 'imperial careering', which was often itinerant and unstable, by utilising a different but overlapping set of connections and networks to those exploited by their middle- and upper-class counterparts. This chapter aims to understand better the personal and family histories of individuals who sought work overseas, how their backgrounds determined their access to different colonial networks and how this influenced their decisions to join the Chinese Customs Service.

The internationalisation of the Customs staff

With few exceptions, trans-imperial careers have been explored within the boundaries of a single empire, usually the British Empire.[11]

However, on the fringes of formal empire and in sites where two or more empires converged, national and imperial allegiances and career trajectories often took on different shapes. In China multiple empires intersected and the foreign staff was a stage on which these imperial rivalries and collaborations were played out. The Inspectorate couched its multinational staff profile in terms of 'cosmopolitanism', but this benign rhetoric masked the political nature of Customs appointments. Each foreign power realised that increased national representation in the Customs staff meant a greater number of their subjects or citizens in positions of influence across China, something that could only further their ambitions.

Maintaining a system where national representation in the staff was proportional to each country's share of trade in China was a delicate balance to strike, and came into direct conflict with the Anglophone character of the Service. Out of a total of 11,000 foreign employees between 1854 and 1950 5,408 were British and, as Table 3.1 shows, Britons usually constituted fifty per cent or more of the total foreign staff, with the exception of the period of the Japanese occupation of China, 1937–45. As early as 1869 Hart acknowledged the tension between the vision of the Customs as, on the one hand, an institution modelled on the British civil service that competed with British colonial services for personnel and, on the other hand, a cosmopolitan league in the business of promoting multiple national interests:

> The Service is a Chinese Service: but it has cosmopolitan work to do, and existing conditions make it expedient that the composition of the Service should be cosmopolitan too. The circumstances under which it grew up tended naturally to fill its ranks with Englishmen; their present number – while still even below what it ought to be, were the proportion which Britain bears to other trade in China, alone considered, – continues to render it excessively difficult to be at once just to old employees and satisfy the requirements of other nationalities.[12]

Such seemingly contradictory concerns underscore the way in which collaboration and competition coexisted in interactions between different foreign powers with imperialist ambitions in China. For the Customs Inspectorate, this made recruitment a particularly thorny matter.

In the early decades of the Service, Hart made considerable efforts to appease foreign ministers in China who were chagrined by the British preponderance in the staff. As Table 3.2 shows, in Hart's recruitment drive of the 1860s a sizeable number of appointments were set aside for Americans, French and Germans. Hart had a predilection for men of certain nationalities: the Irish, because of his family roots, and the

Table 3.1 Key nationalities recorded as working in the Customs staff on 1 January at five-yearly intervals (percentage of the entire foreign staff in parentheses).

	American	British	Danish	French	German	Italian	Japanese	Norwegian	Russian	Total foreign staff	Chinese staff
1855	1 (25.0)	3 (75.0)	0	0	0	0	0	0	0	4	1
1860	9 (10.8)	49 (59.0)	0	1 (1.2)	2 (2.4)	0	0	0	0	83	12
1865	50 (15.7)	203 (64.0)	6 (1.9)	9 (2.8)	19 (6.0)	1 (0.3)	0	1 (0.3)	1 (0.3)	317	69
1870	53 (13.2)	235 (58.3)	9 (2.2)	28 (6.9)	40 (9.9)	1 (0.2)	0	4 (1.0)	4 (1.0)	403	98
1875	50 (11.1)	284 (63.3)	8 (1.8)	28 (6.2)	35 (7.8)	2 (0.4)	0	2 (0.4)	1 (0.2)	449	181
1880	50 (9.9)	307 (61.0)	12 (2.4)	29 (5.8)	47 (9.3)	3 (0.6)	0	3 (0.6)	2 (0.4)	503	251
1885	46 (8.3)	354 (60.0)	17 (2.9)	31 (5.2)	76 (12.9)	8 (1.4)	0	4 (0.7)	3 (0.5)	591	284
1890	56 (7.4)	446 (59.5)	23 (3.1)	29 (3.9)	96 (12.7)	12 (1.6)	0	16 (2.1)	4 (0.5)	753	394
1895	53 (6.8)	460 (58.6)	28 (3.6)	34 (4.3)	95 (12.1)	10 (1.3)	0	18 (2.3)	6 (0.8)	785	437
1900	86 (8.1)	574 (54.3)	31 (2.9)	57 (5.4)	133 (12.6)	13 (1.2)	4 (0.4)	36 (3.4)	10 (0.9)	1,057	675
1905	96 (7.6)	664 (52.3)	46 (3.6)	62 (4.9)	156 (12.3)	23 (1.8)	15 (1.2)	50 (3.9)	15 (1.2)	1,269	1,285
1910	68 (4.9)	691 (49.5)	46 (3.3)	72 (5.2)	171 (12.2)	32 (1.3)	77 (5.5)	64 (4.6)	48 (3.4)	1,396	1,244
1915	72 (4.9)	736 (50.2)	59 (4.0)	39 (2.7)	142 (9.7)	33 (2.3)	102 (7.0)	57 (3.9)	78 (5.3)	1,466	1,303
1920	81 (6.1)	681 (51.0)	50 (3.7)	27 (2.4)	0	29 (2.2)	199 (14.9)	47 (3.5)	68 (5.1)	1,336	1,443
1925	86 (5.9)	772 (53.1)	46 (3.2)	22 (1.5)	0	28 (1.9)	216 (14.9)	30 (2.1)	83 (5.7)	1,454	1,952
1930	76 (5.9)	662 (51.8)	32 (2.5)	21 (1.6)	0	29 (2.3)	212 (16.6)	26 (2.0)	76 (5.9)	1,278	2,393
1935	74 (6.8)	688 (62.8)	29 (2.0)	10 (0.9)	0	24 (2.2)	75 (6.8)	28 (2.6)	60 (5.5)	1,096	3,062
1940	70 (5.1)	559 (40.5)	22 (1.6)	7 (0.5)	0	17 (1.2)	538 (40.0)	25 (1.1)	46 (3.3)	1,380	3,766
1945	14 (1.0)	206 (15.3)	15 (1.1)	2 (0.1)	0	1	1,001 (74.5)	9 (0.7)	32 (2.4)	1,344	4,035
1949	7 (2.3)	208 (69.1)	12 (4.0)	0	0	3 (1.0)	0	12 (4)	10 (3.3)	301	4,646

Total number employed by the Customs 1854–1950

	American	British	Danish	French	German	Italian	Japanese	Norwegian	Russian	Total foreign staff	Chinese staff
	984	5,408	268	251	775	125	1,495	293	361	11,000	11,272

Source: Data extrapolated from service lists database of employees withdrawn from service

Table 3.2 Number of appointments of key nationalities to the Customs Service (figures calculated for five-year periods)

	American	British	Chinese	Danish	French	German	Italian	Japanese	Norwegian	Russian	Total staff appointed
1855–1859	9	56	10	0	3	2	0	0	0	0	128
1860–1864	105	406	58	10	12	32	0	0	2	1	716
1865–1869	42	163	29	4	29	36	2	0	4	5	338
1870–1874	21	173	77	5	7	22	1	0	0	1	336
1875–1879	32	234	99	14	14	34	4	0	3	5	494
1880–1884	31	208	106	13	9	64	7	0	9	6	490
1885–1889	41	270	235	14	8	61	6	0	17	2	704
1890–1894	43	280	184	13	16	42	2	0	15	6	653
1895–1899	127	536	428	25	43	131	6	4	42	16	1,484
1900–1904	143	563	1,059	43	32	118	20	11	54	19	2,284
1905–1909	80	592	1,191	24	29	104	20	74	49	51	2,296
1910–1914	65	545	472	36	24	116	7	41	28	82	1,498
1915–1919	80	312	378	20	2	11	12	138	21	43	1,105
1920–1924	81	494	857	22	15	0	15	72	9	78	1,722
1925–1929	32	161	899	6	6	0	9	35	10	22	1,196
1930–1934	25	193	1,294	7	0	0	4	19	12	12	1,589
1935–1939	8	28	1,183	3	1	1	2	498	7	3	1,739
1940–1944	4	3	1,193	1	0	0	1	602	1	6	1,818
1945–1949	5	82	1,511	8	1	0	7	0	10	3	1,649

Source: Data extrapolated from service lists database of employees withdrawn from service

Americans, whom he pronounced 'the most serious' in the entire service.[13] Channelling most Indoor Staff recruitment through the London Office after 1874 enabled Hart to evade pressures from ministers in Beijing to appoint their own nominees. In response to pressure from the Russian government in 1880 Hart instructed James Campbell, head of the London branch, to appoint three Russian assistants. 'Russia begins to notice that there are many Russian merchants and no Russian Customs' employés, and I must get out of the difficulty this is preparing for me *before the trap snaps: so, look alive*', Hart urged.[14] Without this offshore recruitment base the Customs would be forced, in Hart's words, to 'take the Legation candidates when the "balance of power" demands attention', men who could become political pawns of their ministers.[15]

The Sino-Japanese War (1894–95) and the ensuing Scramble for Concessions (1897–98) saw China carved up into 'spheres of influence' and a corresponding clamour for increased representation in the foreign staff. Japan's victory and subsequent political and economic influence in Northeast Asia prompted the first wave of Japanese recruitment to the Service in the late 1890s.[16] Russia, previously a minor player in the Customs, steadily increased its representation after extracting the leasehold of Port Arthur on the Liaodong Peninsula. Germany's rise was especially dramatic in the late nineteenth century. Germans overtook the Americans as the second-largest national contingent in the Customs, a trend that was commensurate with Germany's broader political and economic encroachments, which culminated in the seizure of Jiaozhou Bay in 1897.[17] In 1899 Hart wearily complained that 'the Japs have not followed up their attack yet, but the Americans have asked for more men and the Russians reminded me that I am expected to go on adding. The result is we are over-manned.'[18] Hart was not exaggerating; in the period 1895–99 the number of foreign Customs appointments shot up to 1,050, as compared with 469 in the preceding five years (see Table 3.2). It was in the late 1890s that the Customs finally lived up to its talk of cosmopolitanism. By the first decade of the twentieth century the staff had been fully internationalised; over twenty-two different nationalities were represented, compared with only seven in the 1850s.

While the staff profile did become truly multinational in this period, this very internationalisation sparked a counter-impulse to preserve the British character of the Service. In a time of intense imperial competition, both in China and in other sites of empire, jingoistic feeling was running high. In the context of Great Game rivalries, Hart's reluctance to appoint Russians to the Service had as much to do with curbing Russian influence in Northeast Asia as with maintaining a fair representation of all nationalities. This desire was shared by other high-ranking Britons. Hippisley, for example, devoted lengthy sections of his diary to dissecting supposed 'Russian intrigues' in China and was particularly incensed about a proposed custom house controlled by Russian authorities at Dalian in the leased territory of the Liaodong Peninsula. A rumour that the Russian authorities were poaching Russian staff from the CCS in order to run the establishment only strengthened the British conviction that Russian employees were not to be trusted.[19]

Imperialist competition intensified further in the first two decades of the twentieth century, a time when the Foreign Inspectorate itself took on a more unambiguously imperialistic role. For instance, under the terms of the Boxer Protocol in 1901 the CCS assumed control of all Native Customs stations, which administered the domestic transit tariff and had previously been independent from the Foreign Inspectorate, within a 50 *li* (17.9 miles) radius of the treaty ports. A portion of the revenue from these Native Customs stations was then earmarked for repayment of the Boxer Indemnity. Furthermore, after Aglen succeeded Hart as IG in 1911 the CCS assumed direct responsibility for collecting and banking customs duties for the first time, placing the revenues in foreign banks. Foreign loans and indemnities were henceforth serviced directly from these banks. Against the backdrop of these broader trends, Aglen's response to a petition for increased French representation in 1913 makes perfect sense. In a blustering appeal to the British minister in Peking, Aglen surmised that France 'wants to reduce the British interest in the Service to the same dimension as that of the other big powers and above all to eliminate all that is distinctively British or that gives a distinctively British tone to the administration'.[20] The Foreign Office brushed him off, yet the IG's readiness to make recourse to British authority to protect British interests speaks volumes about the Inspectorate's empty talk of disinterested service of China.

The suspension of foreign recruitment in 1927 and its official termination in 1929, with the exception of technical experts, meant that when Maze's turn as IG came around in 1929 the issue of maintaining the national balance had become redundant. As Table 3.2 shows, foreign appointments did not altogether cease after 1927, although they did drop significantly to make way for a steep rise in Chinese recruitment and promotion. In the anti-imperialist climate of the late 1920s and early 1930s the most important staffing issue for the Customs was the respective positions of the foreign and Chinese staffs. Japanese aggression in China from 1931 onwards changed the game again. From the late nineteenth century Japan had pressed for increased representation and for the appointment of Japanese Commissioners at key ports of Japanese influence such as Qingdao, held by Japan 1915–22, and

Dalian, held by Japan 1905–45. After 1932 the Manchurian Customs stations were lost to the Japanese puppet state of Manchukuo and the Japanese takeover of the Customs accelerated after the outbreak of full-scale war in 1937. A massive intake of Japanese recruits followed in 1938 and, thereafter, the Inspectorate was subjected to a constant stream of demands to appoint Japanese to influential posts and commissionerships.[21] The dismissal of all British and American employees in December 1941 following the attack on Pearl Harbor increased the Japanese preponderance in the foreign staff further. In January 1945 the Japanese quota stood at 1,001 – almost seventy-five per cent of the entire foreign staff (see Table 3.1). When all Japanese employees were dismissed at the end of the war in August 1945, then-IG Little found himself in charge of a small but long-serving cohort of 339 foreigners and 4,105 Chinese employees.[22] The Inspectorate had almost achieved full Sinification of the staff and the days of 'tutelage' by foreign employees were quite clearly numbered.

Understanding concerns about national prestige and imperial rivalries is essential to explaining recruitment trends 1854–1949. Although certain IGs, notably Hart, appeared to be genuinely proud of the Customs' multinational staff profile, it is equally true that the Inspectorate used the concept of cosmopolitanism as a legitimising tool. Calling attention to the Service's cosmopolitan credentials placed it in a different category from colonial institutions bent on advancing the ambitions of a single European power. Yet it is clear that while the foreign staff could be a site of multinational co-operation it was also a platform for national rivalries. Furthermore, the politics of nationality shed light on how multiple and sometimes contradictory projects were at work within colonial institutions. In the case of the Customs, the aim of creating a broad-based, unified staff that could 'modernise' China along Western lines conflicted with pressures to further the influence of individual countries, particularly Britain.

Joining the foreign staff: connections and credentials

Recruitment to the Indoor, Outdoor and Marine Staffs proceeded along very different lines and, therefore, partly explains the distinct career trajectories found in each branch. There were three main distinguishing features of the Indoor Staff recruitment methods developed in the nineteenth century: patronage, a desire to promote China as a site of imperial careering and a conviction that 'character' was the best determinant of a candidate's suitability. In the very early decades, however, there was no coherent recruitment system. From 1854 until at least 1870 employees were largely plucked from among the nascent foreign communities coalescing along the China coast. This meant that the Indoor Staff was a motley crew of former student interpreters at the foreign legations, cousins and brothers-in-law of high-ranking employees, down-at-the-heels members of the European nobility and adventurers. An early employee, Prosper Giquel, was a naval officer who first came to China in 1857 to join the Anglo-French assault on China during the Arrow War. After the conclusion of the war he joined the Customs and later, while on special leave, found fame as commander of the Sino-French force operating out of Ningbo against the Taiping rebels.[23] News of vacancies spread by word of mouth, either through the professional and social networks within and between China's new foreign communities or, as was the case with Hippisley, through personal connections between Customs men in China and friends and family at home. The foreign legations, with their steady inflow and outflow of young student interpreters, proved a fertile source of personnel throughout the nineteenth century. C. Kleczkowski was plucked from the French Legation in 1860 and served as a Commissioner until 1867, when he committed suicide by throwing himself down a well in Xiamen.[24] W. T. Lay had been in China as a student interpreter only for a year before he left to join the Customs in Guangzhou in 1862, and Hart himself started out his China career as a student interpreter before resigning in favour of the Customs in 1859. After the Inspectorate moved from Shanghai to Beijing in 1865 this recruitment source became even more fruitful as Hart made personal acquaintances among the staff of the legations. H. M. A. Bismarck, son of a former interpreter at the German Legation, used to play with Hart's children as a boy and was appointed to the Customs as a result of this personal connection in 1898.[25] Edwin Denby, son of the American minister in Beijing, obtained a post in 1887 largely on the strength of Hart's connections to his father, despite being two years short of the official minimum age.[26] The intermittent warfare between China and the West in the nineteenth century also presented recruitment opportunities; the navy, in particular, proved a fruitful source of men. More often than not, however, Hart entrusted senior staff with the task of handpicking new employees while on leave in Europe or America on special commissions.

The establishment of a permanent London Office in 1874, headed by Hart's deputy, James Duncan Campbell, as Non-Resident Secretary (NRS) 1874–1907, standardised recruitment to a degree, yet appointments were still tightly controlled by Hart. The first step to obtaining an Indoor appointment was to secure a *personal* nomination from the IG, a policy that led to grumblings about nepotism in some quarters. By relying upon personal connections the Customs was explicitly modelling itself on the recruitment procedures of British imperial administrative services. Zoë Laidlaw has demonstrated how personal connections to powerful holders of patronage at the Colonial Office, either directly through ties of family and friendship or indirectly through intermediaries, were essential to obtaining senior colonial posts in the early nineteenth century. The financial insecurity of a career overseas, the desire for promotion, and attempts to outmanoeuvre rivals meant that colonial officials continuously cultivated their connections to patrons, or would-be patrons, in the metropole. This system was also designed to enhance of the power of London over the colonies.[27] Although the Colonial Office's reliance on personal networks diminished after 1835, it is clear that patronage, nepotism and non-advertisement of posts remained common features of the recruitment procedures of overseas services as late as the twentieth century. A similar system existed in the consular service, and even the most junior appointments to the Colonial Administrative Service were procured through patronage until 1931.[28] The Customs operated slightly differently. Metropolitan connections were nowhere near as important as a personal tie to Robert Hart, who had the power to approve or veto any candidate. Neither was this system entirely inflexible. Nominations could, for example, be solicited by sending an application to the IG supported by sufficient recommendations 'as regards antecedents and character'.[29] In any case a more systematic recruitment channel was unnecessary considering that only ten to fifteen Indoor vacancies arose annually.

Even after the formation of the London Office and failed attempts to recruit through more regular channels, such as the Cambridge Appointments Board, access to personal trans-imperial networks was the most dependable way to attain an appointment.[30] Access to such networks could be obtained through the briefest of encounters. B. E. Foster Hall, for example, who worked in the Indoor Staff 1913–43, obtained his position through a chance meeting with a schoolboy whose father worked in the London Office, which 'resulted in a visit to Westminster the next day, an interview, a written application to the Inspector General in Beijing, a qualifying examination three weeks later, and appointment to the Service within a month of having first heard of it!'[31] Educational ties between existing employees and potential candidates often provided a route into the Customs, as Hippisley's case suggests, and also enabled the Customs to attract a higher calibre of men by integrating the Service into old boy networks. The American Commissioner Edward Drew, for instance, managed to lure four recent graduates from his alma mater, Harvard University, into the Customs while on home leave in 1874, including the future high-flyers H. F. Merrill (employed 1874–1916) and H. B. Morse (employed 1874–1909).[32]

Family connections to the Service, which I will return to later in the chapter, were also advantageous.

As much as it may have pained Hart to recognise it, the Customs was considered a second-rate career by many likely candidates looking for an overseas career. Commenting glumly on a potential recruit, B. Currie, who had defected to the Indian Civil Service (ICS) in 1896, Hart conceded that 'Indian opportunities cannot be surpassed'.[33] The IG was acutely aware that the Customs competed for personnel with high-status colonial and diplomatic institutions. What is more, the Foreign Inspectorate's subordination to the Chinese government could also be off-putting, especially at times when patriotic fervour was running high. Therefore Hart was especially preoccupied with making a name for his service on a global stage. Well-connected Commissioners on leave in Europe or America, such as Drew, were expected to raise the Customs' international profile. Employees of all levels advertised the Customs as a viable career option through trans-empire webs of communication, knowledge and personal connections, whether by promoting China and the Customs at international exhibitions or by spreading awareness by word of mouth among former schoolmates. Attracting members of the European nobility, such as Baron Eugène de Meritens, in the Customs 1862–71, and Count Kleczkowski, in the Customs 1860–67, served the same purpose of enhancing its international prestige. By the latter decades of the century Hart could report that men of stature were encouraging their sons to join the Customs. Sir Harry Parkes, former China consul and British minister to Japan, asked in 1883 for a nomination for his son, which Hart believed showed that the Customs 'is taking a high stand as a public Service'.[34] When the Spanish minister to China, Cologan, also requested an appointment for his son in 1901 Hart surmised that his 'desire to put his son in the Customs (rather than the diplomatic service) shows the estimation in which the Service is held, and also the confidence there is in its duration'.[35]

The introduction of an interview and examination held at the London Office after 1874 was also intended to enhance the reputation of the Service, and was a nod towards a more meritocratic system of recruitment. This process assessed four main criteria: academic ability, 'character', medical fitness and social qualities. The exam was clearly an attempt to place the Customs on a par with other intellectually elite overseas services such as the ICS and Eastern Cadetships, which introduced competitive qualifying examinations in 1858 and 1869 respectively and, in the case of the ICS, an additional year of university study.[36] Yet, despite the Inspectorate's insecurities about the esteem in which it was held, the main aim of the exam, which usually tested mathematics, composition and foreign languages, was to assess basic competence rather than set up a 'factitious or extravagant standard of scholarship'.[37] In 1880 Campbell, who examined potential recruits, complained that most of the candidates he had seen were of such a low standard that they would have failed the qualifying exam for the consular service, a damning assessment given its low entry requirements.[38] Still, the Inspectorate was not looking for a show of academic brilliance. It sought nothing more than 'youthful, likely men, who can read, write and count'.[39] 'Don't send me duffers: don't send me geniuses', Hart tellingly instructed Commissioner Edward Drew, charged with recruiting new blood in 1874.[40] Besides, the examination was never applied uniformly to all recruits. Sometimes it was competitive, and sometimes it was merely a qualifying test. Non-Britons were usually exempted from taking it, as they could hardly be requested to travel all the way to London for this purpose. Edwin Denby was appointed in 1887 after a token exam in Beijing consisting of only '15 questions in common arithmetic – not at all the regular Customs exam, which comprises numerous branches'.[41]

Of far more importance to the Inspectorate than academic achievement was 'character', a nebulous concept that was nonetheless ubiquitously employed by the recruitment boards of overseas administrative services as a marker of promise and suitability.[42] As Hart advised Campbell in 1875, 'a man of average attainments, healthy constitution, cheerful temperament, and possessing the appearance of being gifted with good common sense and a prepossessing exterior, would suit us much more than a short-sighted, weak-chested, lugubrious, impracticable "double-first"'.[43] 'Character' encapsulated an assortment of physical and mental qualities considered to be held by men of a certain class, including a striking bearing, a well-developed sense of duty, social ease and level-headedness. Accordingly, special attention was paid to the appearance of potential recruits. Hart had an eye for a 'specially prepossessing looking youth' and the photographs of prospective assistants were forwarded to Beijing for his inspection.[44] In placing such importance upon appearance and demeanour the Inspectorate was drawing upon clear imperial reference points. By the late nineteenth century physical traits such as a strong jaw, muscular build and firm handshake were viewed as embodying the defining attributes of the elite. These features also ostensibly distinguished colonisers from colonised. In the context of colonialism, a system that hinged upon the discursive maintenance of racial difference, the physical appearance and mannerisms of imperial administrators were all-important. A commanding presence and physical vigour were deemed essential to preserving authority over colonised peoples.[45] Social confidence was a key component of 'character'. Poise in social situations demonstrated that a man was of the correct stock to be placed in a position of authority. It both denoted potential to command the public and suggested that a newcomer would be a good 'fit' with expatriate society. The Indoor Staff, according to Hart, needed men who were 'likely to learn how to live in China, how to get on with messmates, how to talk to the public'.[46] Self-assurance and good manners would, practically speaking, enable 'griffins' to adapt to their new environment and be accepted into insular expatriate society, while at the same time enhancing the public image of the Service.

The premium placed upon character also barred Indoor Staff candidates of the wrong race or class. Hart's comments about the Belgian postal clerk J. A. van Aalst expose the Inspectorate's class prejudices. 'Like all men who make their way up from nothing he is of course without that foundation of character which heredity really gives: the responsibilities of position through three or four generations and the amenities of respectable life give form and solidity to the *nebulae* with which "the first of his name" cannot help starting', he surmised. 'It *is a mistake to help them up too high.*'[47] Similarly, although the Customs always employed a sizeable Chinese staff, people of mixed Chinese and European ancestry – Eurasians in treaty port parlance – were viewed with intense suspicion. Fear of racial mixing in China's foreign communities is discussed in detail in Chapter 5, so it suffices to say here that Eurasians were troubling because their very presence was clear evidence of the transgression of racial boundaries. In the eyes of senior-ranking Customs men, Eurasians lacked the good character necessary to succeed in the Service. In 1910, for example, the current NRS Bruce Hart explained that he had rejected the candidate Jack Brinkley because he 'is Eurasian both in features and demeanour, and he has the elliptical mode of expression (*vide* his papers) typical of the half-caste'.[48] In 1908 the Lappa Commissioner expressed similar reservations about employing an Australian, Henry Leung, whose father had emigrated from the Guangzhou region to New South Wales in 1856. He explained that Leung was not seeking the position of clerk (reserved for Chinese applicants), but rather aspired to join the Indoor Staff, which at that time was implicitly understood to be a European-only branch. The Commissioner's comments reveal the racialised understanding of 'character':

This would mean the introduction of a new element into the ranks of the Assistants, i.e. that of an Australian Chinese registered as a British subject, with preponderating foreign appearance in dress and manners, and I doubt whether the prestige of the Service, foreign and native, would be benefited by the acquisition of such a man who, a blending of both, does not sail under his true colours.[49]

No matter how 'foreign' his appearance and mannerisms, Leung's race was a permanent impediment to developing a true European character. His European traits were viewed as mere affectations, marking him as an imposter. Given that candour and sincerity were defining features of 'character', this automatically barred him from the Service. Yes, the Customs was a hybrid institution, but until the late 1920s its justification for existing – the notion that China needed a period of tutelage from an elite cohort of foreign experts – rested on a strict division of the foreign and Chinese staffs. Applications from individuals such as Brinkley and Leung risked exposing the dubious logic behind this rationale.

In marked contrast to Hart and Campbell's volley of letters discussing the minutiae of Indoor Staff recruitment practices, later IGs were notably less voluble on the subject. In large part this is a testimony to Hart's success at publicising the Service as a feasible career option, which meant that by the turn of the century there was no shortage of willing candidates. Furthermore, by the time that Aglen succeeded Hart as IG in 1911 recruitment procedures had become routine and the personal qualities desired in Indoor men had been squarely decided upon. By Maze's time as IG regular recruitment of foreigners had ceased; the last non-Japanese foreign assistant was appointed in February 1927. Maze's task, which was also that of his successor in 1943, L. K. Little, was to preserve the integrity of the Customs and ensure that the jobs of the remaining foreign staff were safe for the time being.

The main distinguishing feature of recruitment to the Outdoor and Marine branches was the use of itinerant seafaring populations, which congregated in large treaty ports such as Shanghai and Guangzhou, as labour pools. Rasmussen's almost accidental route into the Customs was by no means unique; the foreign Outdoor ranks were filled with similarly transient characters looking for temporary employment in China between seafaring jobs. The Customs could prove a more amenable billet than life on a merchant ship, and also provided a means by which such men could stay in China for an extended sojourn. This meant that tidewaiters, lightkeepers and marine officers were usually employed on the spot as vacancies arose, either by the port Commissioner or Tidesurveyor, without any Inspectorate oversight, although technical experts, such as mechanics, were sometimes recruited through the London Office. The Inspectorate's apparent indifference to Outdoor and Marine recruitment in contrast to the voluminous correspondence regarding Indoor candidates is telling of the disparity in status afforded to the different branches.

The casual nature of Outdoor and Marine recruitment helped to shape the often peripatetic nature of the imperial careers embarked upon by working-class men and women. The effort expended in recruiting Indoor Staff in Europe and America and the expense of paying their passages to China was evidence of a long-term investment in these employees. For the Inspectorate the pay-off was a higher degree of loyalty and the expectation on the part of many Indoor recruits that the Customs offered a career for life. By contrast, the more off-hand attitude towards the Outdoor and Marine staff spoke of the lack of esteem afforded to these branches and contributed to the perception that Customs work was merely a convenient temporary employment solution in between more promising enterprises. The Inspectorate was little interested in ensuring a more reliable and skilled pool of Outdoor men by creating a more rigorous recruitment system and offering improved conditions of employment. In part this grew out of empire-wide fears of a possible inversion of class hierarchies as the colonies presented working-class settlers with greater opportunities for social mobility. These anxieties sometimes resulted in vigorous efforts to defend the status quo, a trend that fed into the Customs' determination to preserve the elite status of the Indoor Staff.[50]

By the twentieth century, however, the drawbacks of this system, which attracted uncommitted candidates who were likely to decamp after a short period of service, were becoming clear. In the view of the Shanghai Tidesurveyor, C. P. Dawson, this system inevitably led to the employment of 'men of poor education, unsteady habits, and without the good character which is so necessary for men who almost immediately after being employed are put in positions of trust'.[51] Yet a European avenue of recruitment was not seriously pursued until a critical staff shortage during the First World War forced the Inspectorate to take action.[52] During the war years, from August 1914 to October 1918, 943 foreign employees withdrew from the Customs, mostly from the Outdoor ranks. These figures include 146 Germans and Austrians who were dismissed as enemy subjects in August 1917 after China entered the war. By way of contrast, in the year immediately prior to the outbreak of war, from August 1913 to August 1914, only 164 foreign employees withdrew from service. In response to depleting Outdoor numbers Aglen instructed the current NRS, Paul King, to appoint fifty former British Navy men through the London Office as tidewaiters to fill the void. A few years later in 1920, when Outdoor numbers were still below quota, King was again compelled to appoint forty-eight more men, forty of whom were recruited through the Admiralty.[53] Within a couple of years, however, this avenue of recruitment had proved a resounding failure. As early as 1918 disgruntled naval recruits began to jump ship, unhappy with Customs living conditions and terms of employment.[54] Even as late as 1925 these London recruits continued to gripe about their treatment at the hands of the Customs. The current NRS, Cecil Bowra, was nonplussed, indignantly protesting that each man had been 'plainly told that he is engaged for serious work and not for a life of play and amusement'.[55] Outdoor men engaged in London, it emerged, were singularly unsuited to the Customs; their expectations of life and work in China often bore little relation to its disappointing reality. Men appointed on the spot in Shanghai or Canton were much more aware of and resilient to the conditions of life in a Chinese port. After the suspension of foreign recruitment in 1927, a further 560 non-Japanese foreign 'technical experts' were employed on short-term contracts. This contract system of labour merely compounded the pattern of impermanence that had characterised employment in the Outdoor and Marine branches for the past seventy years. This pattern of temporary careers and Inspectorate indifference in the case of the Outdoor branches and, in contrast, a high degree of interest and investment in Indoor Staff careers, highlights the diverse career trajectories experienced by men and women of different social statuses across the empire world. As will become clear in the following part of this chapter, the social, educational and economic backgrounds of individuals constrained and enabled the paths of their imperial careers in significant ways.

The origins of a Customs man

Chapter 2 explored how multiple imperial ideologies were interpreted and adapted in the China context, and how new types of European and American knowledge about China were disseminated. This is essential to understanding why Europeans and Americans began to view China and the Customs as a feasible and attractive career option by the late nineteenth century. Although the average Customs recruit probably would not have consulted any of the new scholarly tracts about China, it is probable that they would have encountered popular histories, and it is even more likely that they would have been familiar with the salacious tales of Louise Jordan Miln, Sax Rohmer and of the former Customs man turned author Putnam Weale. The Customs itself had become more of a known quantity by the end of the century, thanks to Hart's self-publicising drive. Although Hart grumbled about the cost and bother caused by participation in international exhibitions – in Vienna (1873), Paris (1878 and 1900) and the London fisheries (1883) and health (1884) exhibitions – they undoubtedly raised the Customs' international profile. Press acclaim for Robert Hart's achievements only enhanced the Service's standing in Britain, and Juliet Bredon's biography of her uncle, *Sir Robert Hart: The romance of a great career*, published in 1910, ensured that Hart's memory lived on long after his retirement. All of this rendered China and the Customs familiar and knowable to people in Europe, North America and the settler colonies.[56] This knowledge may well have been sensationalised or inaccurate, yet it enabled potential Customs candidates to imagine China as one among many potential sites of imperial careering.

Exploring the pre-Customs lives of the foreign staff can shed much light on the reasons why people from certain socio-economic backgrounds chose to embark on a career overseas. In his study of the lives and careers of two prominent ICS officers, Clive Dewey argues that 'the members of one of the most powerful elites the world has ever known, the Indian Civil Service at the high noon of empire, were the prisoners of values they absorbed in their youth'.[57] In this book I argue that rather than being lifelong 'prisoners' of childhood 'indoctrination' the ideologies and personal identities of individuals were often reformulated over the course of an imperial career. However, Dewey's approach does highlight how the values, connections and expectations formed in the family and educational context influenced the decision to work overseas. In Britain, as Andrew Thompson has observed, people of different social backgrounds experienced a range of associations with empire, both positive and negative, which influenced their perceptions of the desirability of an imperial career.[58] This chapter now turns to consider how the pre-Customs experiences and identities of foreign employees can explain the reasons why China and empire stood for opportunity for a diverse range of individuals.

As discussed earlier in this chapter, the early Indoor Staff was a diverse assemblage of former consuls and interpreters, mercenaries, naval officers and even the occasional aristocrat. On becoming IG in 1863 Hart vowed to 'get rid of all our "bad hats"' by shaping the Indoor Staff into a proficient and professional administrative corps.[59] As a result, the staff profile gradually became more homogeneous, consisting largely of career administrators who were capable but not brilliant. This new wave of Indoor recruits from the 1870s onwards was plucked from the professional middle classes, in Britain, elsewhere in Europe and in North America. The fortunes and social status of men and women of this social class were closely entwined with empire, given that they staffed the administrative ranks of imperial institutions. Here I will sketch the socio-economic profile of the Indoor Staff, using a sample of ninety-three application forms filled in by candidates between 1899 and 1926, seventy-four of whom were eventually appointed.[60] In doing so I will highlight the various ways in which men of the professional middle class were connected to imperial networks.

In a British-dominated institution with an ancillary headquarters in London it was often more difficult for non-Britons to demonstrate the connections and qualifications required to obtain a position in this Anglophone service. This is reflected in the fact that sixty out of this sample of ninety-three applicants were British. The rest of the sample is comprised of eight Frenchmen, eight Germans, a handful of Russians, Belgians, Austrians, Italians and Swedes, and a lone Norwegian, Dutchman and Indian. Among the sixty British applicants, ten were born in Ireland (Irish were always listed as British in the service lists), a testimony to the integration of Ireland into imperial networks.[61] It is also a sign of the tenacity of Robert Hart's Ulster roots. Accusations of nepotism were habitually levelled at Hart, and it has to be said that these allegations *did* contain some truth: Hart appointed his brother, two brothers-in-law, his son, numerous cousins and three nephews.[62] Even more striking is the finding that nineteen men out of this sample of ninety-three were born outside of Europe. What is more, seventeen of these men were British, meaning that over one-quarter of the entire British contingent were born overseas, in India, Australia, Japan, Southeast Asia and China itself. This trend speaks to the prevalence of multigenerational imperial careers. The fathers of eleven candidates in this sample – out of a total of eighty-two for whom the father's occupation is recorded – worked as consuls, missionaries, engineers and merchants in China or Japan. Percy Bencraft Joly, appointed to the Customs in 1909, was born in Guangzhou where his father was the British consul, schooled at the China Inland Mission School at Yantai before finishing his education at King's College School, London, and listed his hometown as Seoul. Alexander Forbes, appointed to the Customs in 1906, was born in Tianjin in 1885 where his father was secretary of the Taku Tug and Lighter Company. A third example, the Austrian Dr Gustav Ritter von Kreitner, appointed 1911, was born in 1886 in Yokohama where his father was consul-general. The fathers of five more had empire careers as doctors, military officers or lawyers in Australia, India and Penang. Individuals who embarked on imperial careers are frequently imagined as intrepid adventurers or pioneering settlers. Yet this sample suggests that by the early twentieth century empire careers had become so commonplace that young expatriates were often simply building upon family traditions of shifting between different sites of empire. This not only normalised the idea that the empire world offered numerous sites of professional opportunity; it also connected individuals to multilayered personal networks developed over generations.

This is nowhere more apparent than in the Customs lineages encouraged by the Inspectorate. In her study of the relationship between family and empire in late-imperial India Elizabeth Buettner stresses 'the integral role of family practices in the reproduction of imperial rule and its personnel, accounting for the substantial degree of family continuity among the middle classes engaged with the raj'.[63] Within the family imperial ideologies and practices were passed down and perpetuated, as were ready-made professional connections to the empire world. In the specific context of the Customs, children could be imbued from an early age with Service philosophies and folklore, and fathers could use their connections to the Service to secure reliable employment for their sons. Four out the sample of ninety-three applicants mentioned fathers who worked for the Customs, but there are countless other examples in the archives. In many cases a family relationship to a former high-ranking Customs man was qualification enough for employment. Informing Campbell in 1877 of his nomination of W. Davies, the son of a former Commissioner, Hart advised that 'as he is an old Commissioner's son, I don't want him to compete: it will suffice to see that he is qualified'.[64] In addition to employing numerous members of his own family, Hart also granted appointments to the son and cousin of his right-hand-man in London, James Campbell.[65] *Three* generations of the Lowder family were in the Customs 1882–1940. The creation of Customs genealogies demonstrates the joint role of the family and imperial institutions in perpetuating systems of patronage. A lesser-known service such as the Customs, which frequently had trouble finding suitable staff of multiple nationalities, had a vested interest in doing so. The sons of 'Customs families' presumably experienced a degree of loyalty to the Service even before joining and began their new careers pre-primed in its work, principles and purpose.

The Customs did not seek Indoor men from elite backgrounds, who were liable to expect too much from the Service and China. It did, however, require that Indoor men at least had 'reputable' beginnings, with the accompanying social traits that this implied. With a few exceptions, the men in this sample belonged to professional, middle-class families, a rising and expanding sector of European society from the late nineteenth century onwards.[66] A wide variety of father's occupations are recorded – ranging from analytical biologist to musician, to commander of the Guardia Nobile (the Vatican City's police force) – yet the vast majority worked in solid and established professions, as, for example, army or naval officers, clergymen, doctors and surgeons, barristers, merchants, civil engineers, architects and teachers. The educational background of Indoor applicants also indicates their middle-class origins. Although a handful of the British candidates attended highly prestigious public schools, such as Marlborough, Westminster, Stonyhurst and Shrewsbury, the vast majority of men in my sample were educated in the minor public schools that proliferated in the nineteenth century in response to demand from the expanding middle classes for a cheap education that would provide social and intellectual training for professional careers.[67] Almost all of the non-British men had received a parallel education at classical gymnasiums and lycées; only two had received a more technical and scientific education at Realschulen.

Although much has been made of the intertwined nature of imperialism and the public school system in Britain, with the public schools feeding the machinery of empire with a stream of young men socialised into imperial ideologies, the motivations behind middle-class imperial careering were more complex. Public schools indisputably fostered a sharper awareness of and attachment to empire, while also cultivating the qualities of 'character' and connections to old boy networks necessary to obtain a post in the colonial bureaucracy.[68] It would, however, be a mistake to view a sense of imperial duty fostered at school as the driving force behind middle-class migrations around the empire world. A desire for adventure, for independence and, most importantly, a reliable career provided a strong impetus. As Andrew Thompson has convincingly demonstrated, the growth of the professional middle classes and the growth of empire were intertwined in Britain. As empire expanded, so did the state, creating a demand for career administrators and technical experts and thereby providing opportunities for middle-class men who lacked the financial means to establish themselves in a professional career at home. The professional identity of this class was, therefore, inextricably tied up with empire.[69] For men whose families could rarely afford to provide them with a private source of income, financial needs were a major consideration when choosing a career. The Customs compared favourably with many other available employment options, paying £400 annually for a fourth assistant B (the lowest rank in the foreign Indoor Staff) entering the Service in the late nineteenth century as compared with a £250 entry salary for the British civil service.[70] Practical concerns were fundamental to the appeal of the Customs for young men whose economic circumstances made it imperative to secure quickly a stable and profitable job with clear prospects for advancement.

The centrality of these concerns is borne out by the low university attendance rates among Customs men, something that is perhaps unsurprising given Hart's contempt for candidates with an 'impracticable "double first"'. For men of this social class, university was an expensive luxury. Edward Drew's success in recruiting fellow Harvard graduates in 1874 was a distinct anomaly. Only twenty-six of the applicants in the sample attended university, something which set the Customs further apart from more esteemed imperial administrative services that recruited a large proportion of their personnel through Oxbridge, such as the ICS and Sudan Political Service.[71] University 'attendance', moreover, did not necessarily mean that the candidate had been awarded a degree, as more often than not Customs men had failed to graduate or else fared badly in their exams. For many prospective candidates the Customs was a fortuitous career option followed up almost out of desperation after their university careers were stymied by financial difficulties or academic failure. As recounted at the beginning of this chapter, Hippisley's hopes of taking up a scholarship at Oxford were scuppered owing to his father's financial ruin. The university career of J. O. P. Bland at Trinity College Dublin was also cut short in 1883 owing to his family's financial problems. 'It was not a case of having heard the East a callin', but simply of *res angusta domi*,' wrote Bland about the circumstances of his appointment, as his father 'could ill afford to have me on his hands for four or five years'.[72] James Anderson, in the Indoor Staff 1914–41, found himself in dire financial straits after he failed his first-year exams at Cambridge, causing his father to cut off all support.[73] All three decided to join the Customs as an expedient alternative to university. The Inspectorate prized practicality over academic prowess in its employees, something which demonstrated an astute awareness of both the Service's position as a low-status imperial institution and the humdrum realities of Customs work, which did not require an intellectual bent.

The previous employment of candidates also shows that the Customs did not seek any particular expertise in its Indoor recruits. Because candidates were required to be between the ages of nineteen and twenty-three the vast majority had not seriously pursued an alternative career before applying to the Customs and, for those who *had* worked, their experience bore little relation to the work they would perform in the Customs. A handful had worked as secretaries and clerks and a fair number had served in the armed forces, but none had any particular knowledge of customs work. For four men in my sample the Customs was a fall-back career after studying for and being rejected by either the consular service or the ICS. This lack of useful skills was by no means prejudicial to a Customs career. Relatively blank slates such as these were, in fact, coveted by the Inspectorate; young men with limited working experience and no special expertise could easily be moulded into the institutional ethos. The Inspectorate envisaged that its Indoor Staff would set an example of duty, honesty and dependability to the Chinese bureaucracy. 'Character' rather than expertise was all that was needed to fulfil these expectations.

The lack of a formal recruitment procedure for the Outdoor and Marine staffs means that the application forms which are such a rich source of information about the pre-Customs lives of the Indoor Staff are often missing for these branches. A rough picture of the changing socio-economic profile of the nineteenth-century Outdoor and Marine Staffs can, however, be pieced together from various types of personnel documents collected over the century of the Foreign Inspectorate's existence. Firstly, a sample of 250 memos of service of European and American Outdoor men who were stationed at Shanghai at some point during their careers before 1887 provides basic details of place of birth and previous employment.[74] This sample also presents a representative national mix for the late nineteenth century, encompassing 138 British (including Irish) employees, thirty-five Americans, thirty-three Germans, nine Swedes, seven Frenchmen, and a sprinkling of other nationalities. Secondly, a smaller sample of thirty-three application forms filled out by British Outdoor and Marine candidates recruited 1883–1926 includes further information about pre-Customs lives, such as educational background and fathers' occupations.[75] Finally, the profile of the European and American staff can be contrasted with that of forty Japanese tidewaiters recruited between 1936 and 1940.[76]

European and American personnel in the uniformed branches occupied a social milieu very different from their Indoor counterparts in their pre-Customs lives. Fathers' occupations are not usually recorded for men in these branches, but this information is listed for twenty-nine of the sample of thirty-three British Outdoor and Marine applications. Working in a wide spectrum of occupations, including agricultural labourer, warehouseman, builder and shopkeeper, the majority of these recruits came from a distinctly working-class, or occasionally lower-middle-class, background. Similarly, all but one of the men in this sample attended state- or council-run board schools, and occasionally church-funded schools, and the vast majority left school at the age of fourteen or fifteen after obtaining a basic secondary education. One of the most arresting differences with the Indoor Staff is the scant evidence of multigenerational traditions of imperial careering. Combining the sample of 250 nineteenth-century Outdoor men with the thirty-three applicants to the Marine and Outdoor staffs, only eighteen – less than one per cent – were born outside Britain, as compared with over twenty per cent of Indoor candidates. A family history of living overseas was, moreover, a great deal more common among Britons – fifteen of the eighteen were British. Rather than taking this as evidence that working-class Europeans did not engage in trans-imperial careering, I would argue instead that they sustained patterns of global migrations different from their middle-class counterparts. As we have seen, middle-class expatriates tended to work as consuls, doctors, imperial administrators, high-ranking military officers and senior employees of foreign trading houses. All of these professions provided for a lengthy career overseas, either in a single location or through a series of protracted stays in multiple sites of empire, usually accompanied by one's family, with the expectation of eventual retirement at home. Working-class and lower-middle-class Europeans did not have access to the higher-status professions that enabled this type of empire career, but they could follow at least two different paths. Firstly, *permanent* emigration to British settler colonies or the Dominions, rather than circular professional migrations around the globe, was fervently promoted to these social classes from the late nineteenth century, a trend that is apparent in the handful of British Outdoor candidates in this sample born in Australia.[77] Secondly, and more relevant to the specific demographic that formed the Outdoor Staff, working-class overseas careers were often more itinerant, consisting of short-lived sojourns in numerous places, including frequent back and forth movements between 'home' and outposts of empire. The low-paid and peripatetic nature of these occupations, such as sailor or soldier, discouraged wives and families from accompanying them, meaning that fewer Outdoor candidates were born overseas. Of the twenty-nine British men in this sample for whom their father's occupations are recorded, eight (just over twenty per cent) worked in maritime occupations, including master mariner and maritime engineer, which suggests that multigenerational patterns of professional movements across the empire world also existed, to a lesser extent, among this demographic.

A huge proportion of Outdoor and Marine candidates had themselves previously worked in maritime occupations, a pattern that remained consistent from the 1880s to the 1920s. The previous occupations of 199 of the sample of 250 nineteenth-century Outdoor men and all of the thirty-three men recruited 1883–1926 are recorded. Of these combined samples, around half (117) had formerly worked as sailors, master mariners, mates or ships' stewards. The vast majority of these men did not travel to China with the specific aim of joining the Customs in mind, unlike many of their Indoor counterparts. Rather they arrived in China in the course of their professional journeys around the world, on ships carrying goods between China and Europe, America, Southeast Asia and India. Rasmussen, as mentioned at the beginning of this chapter, had travelled far and wide before ending up in China. So had, the Coast Inspector William F. Tyler, who before joining the Customs in 1899 travelled to Australia, New Zealand and the United States, and Christopher Briggs (in the Marine Department, 1932–39), whose pre-Customs career with the merchant marine took him to South Africa, Australia, South America, Japan and Canada.[78] Although they did not have access to the networks of power and patronage that enabled the imperial careers of middle-class young men, Outdoor and Marine recruits often had substantial experience of living and working overseas.

For these branches the Inspectorate evidently preferred seasoned men with a degree of technical expertise. All ten of the engineers and mechanics in the sample of applications from 1883 to 1926 had prior experience of engineering. In part this speaks to the technical nature of the work these branches often performed, which required some level of vocational training. More striking is the fact that thirty-nine out of the sample of 199 nineteenth-century Outdoor men for whom former occupations are recorded (almost twenty per cent) had previously worked for the Chinese Customs Service itself. In part this willingness to re-employ men who had either been proved incompetent or who had left for more lucrative ventures was evidence of desperation; the Outdoor branches, with their low pay and status, were not attractive career options and the Customs struggled to hold on to personnel.

The most dramatic transformation in the personnel profile of these branches came with the upsurge in Japanese recruitment in the late 1930s and early 1940s, a time when Japan's territorial encroachments in China were rapidly swallowing up Customs stations in north and east China. The sample of forty Japanese Outdoor applications collected 1936–40 describes a group of men who were heads above their European and American counterparts in terms of educational and professional achievement. Most had stayed in full-time education for between eleven and fifteen years, eleven of the forty had attended university or foreign language classes, and another eight had attended technical, commercial or mercantile marine schools. Most listed previous employment in higher-status occupations; eight had worked in the Japanese police force, six in the Shanghai Municipal Police and five had reached positions of responsibility in the Japanese customs. Several laid claim to prior professional careers in Japan, including teacher, editor of a magazine, interpreter and civil servant (four of the sample). Why the discrepancy between the profiles of the Japanese and European Outdoor staffs? The Foreign Inspectorate's racism is at least partly responsible; race, rather than nationality, primarily determined one's eligibility to join the foreign staff, meaning that Japanese candidates had to be of a higher calibre in order to compete with Europeans and Americans. The specific conditions of wartime China also came into play. For many lower-middle-class Japanese, China's colonisation represented a wealth of opportunities for professional, financial and social advancement. Unlike the European and American seamen, in China for a brief sojourn, Japanese candidates, like the administrators of the Indoor Staff, clearly foresaw making a career out of the Customs. Thus the Customs attracted a more educated and expert cohort of Japanese recruits.

Conclusion

In his memoirs Alfred Hippisley recalled how his passage to China to take up his Customs appointment in 1867 sharpened his understanding of the British empire and his place within it:

> The Union Jacks flying at each of our ports of call (Egypt alone excepted), evidence that each and all of them – Gibraltar, Malta, Aden, Pointe de Galle, Singapore, Penang, and Hongkong – formed part of the dominions of the Crown, and the White Ensigns on at least one man-of-war in each harbour gave me a far more vivid idea and a vastly greater pride in the extent and power of the British Empire than previous reading had ever given.

For Hippisley, China was just another node within a vast network of sites that constituted empire. Little distinction was made in the minds of expatriates between 'formal' and 'informal' colonies. A middle-class Briton could ostensibly move between many of these places during the course of an imperial career. While passing all of these outposts of empire en route to beginning what would be a lifelong career overseas, it struck Hippisley that most British cabinet ministers had never set foot in these distant lands that they ruled from afar, and thus 'had no adequate conception of the varying character and diverse needs of the Colonies overseas, and no adequate appreciation of the enormous responsibilities they assumed in lightly undertaking the government of them'.[79] The arduous task of putting the colonies in order, of promoting British interests abroad and of gathering knowledge about distant lands and peoples fell to imperial administrators like Hippisley, men who were willing to leave their home for a decades-long 'exile' overseas in service of the British empire.

Such was the romanticised self-perception of expatriates across the empire world. Yet the real intent and impetus behind these relocations was considerably more complex. As discussed in Chapter 2, the work of the foreign Customs staff was often given meaning and legitimacy by certain imperial ideologies, which were necessarily reformulated in the specific context of China and the Customs. However, while a sense of duty to one's country, to empire and to peoples and governments considered less advanced than one's own may have partly inspired imperial careers, other motivations and circumstances were more important and differed substantially according to social class. For example, the professional identity of many middle-class European families, particularly

Britons, and even the very growth of this social class were increasingly intertwined with imperial expansion, which provided new career opportunities for professional administrators and technical experts. By the late nineteenth century many young middle-class men were following well-trodden paths of imperial careers established by their forebears. In this context embarking on an overseas career in the Customs was a commonsensical choice.

In selecting young middle-class men who rarely possessed any technical or professional expertise for the Indoor Staff, the Customs was self-consciously contributing to and perpetuating empire-wide standards. 'Character', formed through hereditary class background, the public school socialisation process and a decent grounding in a classical education, was the most important attribute that administrators across the empire world brought to the institutions they served and was essential to sustaining the fiction of white prestige. 'Character' was a malleable concept, which in the colonial context could be easily remoulded to exclude various undesirables from the personal and professional networks necessary to reach positions of authority. By employing men of good character to staff the executive branch the Inspectorate hoped to style itself as a professionalised administrative service and a peer of other more elite imperial institutions.

Often pushed to the margins of colonial society and denied access to the networks of power and patronage that enabled the careers of middle-class imperial administrators, the connections and opportunities available to working-class men overseas were more unpredictable and uneven. This meant that family traditions of work overseas, while they existed, were often fragmented. These men did, however, make use of imperial networks of a different sort. In particular the ships that transported goods and people around the empire world enabled many working-class Europeans and Americans to embark on an overseas career. The fragile nature of their connections to systems and institutions of colonial power, however, meant that their imperial careers often followed more unstable and peripatetic courses than their middle class counterparts.

The case of the Customs foreign staff can significantly broaden our understanding of imperial career trajectories. As a site where the economic and political interests of several imperial powers converged, which was never formally and fully incorporated into the empire of any one foreign power, the imperial networks that intersected in China were particularly fluid and heterogeneous. China, and the Customs, therefore offered an unparalleled chance to embark on an imperial career, particularly for individuals who might otherwise have had limited access to such opportunities. Rasmussen, for example, despite his home country's lack of colonial possessions, was able to make use of imperial pathways and regional connections to forge a career in China. The appeal of empire, and of China, was far-reaching and, in the staff of a multinational service such as the Customs, the whole range of people for whom the empire world spoke of opportunity was represented.

Notes

1   An earlier version of this chapter was first published as: Catherine Ladds, '"Youthful, Likely Men, Able to Read, Write and Count": Joining the foreign staff of the Chinese Customs Service, 1854–1927', *Journal of Imperial and Commonwealth History*, 36:2 (2008), 227–42. Title quote taken from *I. G. in Peking*, vol. 1, letter A/39, 18 Dec 1881, 398.

2   Hippisley papers, MS Eng. c. 7286, 'Memoirs 1848–67', 16–17.

3   Hippisley papers, MS Eng. c. 7288, 'Correspondence, 1864–89', letter from Hippisley to Hart, 9 Dec 1864; letter from John W. Caldiert, headmaster of Bristol Grammar School, to Hart, 3 Apr 1865; letter from H. Seymour Roberts, second master of Bristol Grammar School, to Hart, Apr 1865.

4   Hippisley papers, MS Eng. c. 7288, 'Correspondence, 1864–89', letter from Hart to Hippisley, 1 Aug 1865.

5   Hippisley papers, MS Eng. c. 7286, 'Memoirs 1848–67', 21–2.

6   A. H. Rasmussen, *Sea Fever* (London: Constable, 1952), 14–16.

7   Rasmussen, *China Trader*, 3, 4, 17, 42.

8   Lambert and Lester, *Colonial Lives*.

9   Laidlaw, *Colonial Connections*, esp. chapter 2, 13–38; Lester, *Imperial Networks*, 5–8.

10 Lambert and Lester, *Colonial Lives*, 'Introduction', 1–31.

11 An exception is Brown, 'Gregor Macgregor: Clansman, conquistador and coloniser on the fringes of the British Empire'.

12 *Documents Illustrative*, vol. 1, circular no. 26 of 1869 (first series), 'Service Re-organization', 174.

13 *I. G. in Peking*, vol. 1, Z/341, 20 May 1888, 704.

14 *I. G. in Peking*, vol. 1, A/26, 14 Dec 1880, 351.

15 *I. G. in Peking*, vol. 2, Z/1346, 9 Oct 1904, 1431.

16 Peter Duus, Ramon Hawley Myers, and Mark R. Peattie, eds, *The Japanese Informal Empire in China, 1895–1937* (Princeton: Princeton University Press, 1989), 'Introduction', xix–xxiv.

17 John E. Schrecker, *Imperialism and Chinese Nationalism: Germany in Shantung* (Cambridge, MA: Harvard University Press, 1971), chapter 1, 1–42.

18 *I. G. in Peking*, vol. 2, Z/819, 26 Feb 1899, 1189.

19 Hippisley papers, MS Eng. c. 7285, 'Diary, 1898–1905', 30 Jan 1903.

20 The National Archives of the UK (hereafter TNA), FO371/1629, Aglen to Jordan, Oct 1913, 141–6.

21 For Japanese recruitment to the Customs see Bickers, 'Anglo-Japanese Relations and Treaty Port China', 35–56.

22 Figures calculated for 31 Aug 1945. Service lists database of employees withdrawn from service.

23 Fairbank et al., eds, *Robert Hart and China's Modernization*, 447, n. 120.

24 *I. G. in Peking*, vol. 1, Z/37, 3 Oct 1876, 225, n. 7; SHAC, 679(2) 84, 'Amoy Customs: Despatches to IG, 1862–1868', dispatch no. 52, 15 Aug 1876.

25 *I. G. in Peking*, vol. 1, 21 Nov 1872, 94, n. 4.

26 Library of Congress (LOC), MSS84834, Denby Family Papers, 1850–1911, letter from Edwin Denby (Beijing) to Graham Denby (Evansville IA), 9 Oct 1887.

27 Laidlaw, *Colonial Connections*, chapter 5, 94–126.
28 See Platt, *Cinderella Service*, 71–4; Anthony Kirk-Greene, '"Not quite a gentle-man": The desk diaries of the Assistant Private Secretary (Appointments) to the Secretary of State for the Colonies, 1899–1915', *English Historical Review*, 472 (2002), 622–33.
29 SHAC, 679(3) 1599, 'London Office: dispatches to I.G., 1910', Memo: Admission to the Chinese Customs Service Indoor Staff, 20 Dec 1899.
30 SHAC, 679(3) 1600, 'London Office: Dispatches to IG', dispatch no. 3,807, NRS Bruce Hart to acting IG Bredon, 11 Feb 1911.
31 B. E. Foster Hall papers (private collection), 'My Life and Work in China, 1913–1943'.
32 Fairbank et al., *H. B. Morse*, 19–22.
33 *I. G. in Peking*, vol. 1, Z/907, 20 Oct 1901, 1286.
34 *I. G. in Peking*, vol. 1, Z/117, 8 Apr 1883, 458.
35 *I. G. in Peking*, vol. 2, Z/907, 20 Oct 1901, 1286.
36 Kirk-Greene, *Imperial Administrators*, 72–3.
37 SHAC, 679(2) 1190, 'London Office: Dispatches from IG', dispatch no. 26. 24 Feb 1874.
38 *Archives of China's Imperial Maritime Customs*, vol. 1, A/201, Campbell to Hart, 11 June 1880, 523–4.
39 *I. G. in Peking*, vol. 2, A/26, 14 Dec 1880, 351.
40 Houghton Library, Harvard University, MS Chinese 4, Sir Robert Hart Papers, letter from Hart to Drew, 21 Mar 1874.
41 LOC, MSS84834, Denby Family Papers, 1850–1911, letter from Edwin Denby (Beijing) to Graham Denby (Evansville IA), 9 Oct 1887.
42 See Kirk-Greene, '"Not quite a gentleman"'; P. J. Cain, 'Character and Imperialism: The British financial administration of Egypt, 1878–1914', *Journal of Imperial and Commonwealth History*, 34: 2 (2006), 177–200.
43 SHAC, 679(3) 1190, 'London Office: Dispatches from IG,' dispatch no. 94, 17 July 1875.
44 *I. G. in Peking*, vol. 2, Z/788, 27 Mar 1898, 1157.
45 J. A. Mangan, *The Games Ethic and Imperialism: Aspects of the diffusion of an ideal* (London: F. Cass, 1998), esp. chapter 3, 'Manly Chaps in Control: Blues and Blacks in the Sudan', 71–100.
46 *I. G. in Peking*, vol. 1, A/26, 14 Dec 1880, 351.
47 *I. G. in Peking*, vol. 1, Z/182, Hart to Campbell, 21 June 1884.
48 SHAC, 679(3) 1597, 'London Office: Dispatches to IG, 1909', dispatch no. 3,710, NRS Bruce Hart to Acting IG Bredon, 5 Oct 1910.
49 SHAC, 679(3) 1347, 'Lappa Dispatches 4491–4580', dispatch no. 4492, 5 June 1908.
50 See Lester, *Imperial Networks*, 46–53.
51 SHAC, 679(1) 26898, 'Inspector general's circulars, vol. 9, second series, nos. 1,202–1,400, 1905–6', Shanghai Chief Tidesurveyor, C. P. Dawson's, memo, enclosed in IG circular no. 1,357, 2 July 1906.
52 SHAC, 679(3) 1602, 'London Office: Dispatches to IG, 1913', dispatch no. 3,967, NRS Hart to IG Aglen, 12 Aug 1913.
53 SHAC, 679(1) 15073, 'Withdrawal of Out-door Staff London recruits', letter from NRS King to IG Aglen, 9 Oct 1917; SHAC, 679(3) 1609, 'London Office: dispatches to IG, 1920', dispatch no. 4,416, King to Aglen, 16 June 1920.
54 SHAC, 679(1) 15073, 'Withdrawal of Out-door Staff London recruits, 1920'.
55 SHAC, 679(3) 1623, 'London Office: dispatches to IG, 1925', dispatch no. 4,793, NRS Bowra to IG Aglen, 13 Mar 1925.
56 See Lachlan Strahan, *Australia's China: Changing perceptions from the 1930s to the 1990s* (Cambridge: Cambridge University Press, 1996), 1–14, for a discussion of Australian views of China and how these stereotypes helped to render an unfamiliar place and culture familiar.
57 Dewey, *Anglo-Indian Attitudes*, vii.
58 Andrew S. Thompson, *The Empire Strikes Back?: The impact of imperialism on*

Britain from the mid-nineteenth century (Harlow: Pearson Longman, 2005), esp. chapters 1 and 2, 9–82.

59 Fairbank et al., eds, *Robert Hart and China's Modernization*, journal entry on 18 Mar 1864, 73.

60 This sample is collected from files in SHAC, nos 679(3) 1579–1582, 679(3) 1590– 1591, 679(3) 1597–1603, 679(3) 1608–1612, 679(3) 1621–1625, 679(2) 1209, 'London Office: dispatches to IG'.

61 See Zoë Laidlaw, 'Richard Bourke: Irish liberalism tempered by empire', in *Colonial Lives*, edited by Lambert and Lester, 113–44.

62 Richard O'Leary, 'Robert Hart in China: The significance of his Irish roots', *Modern Asian Studies*, 40:3 (2006), 538–604.

63 Buettner, *Empire Families*, 2.

64 *I. G. in Peking*, vol. 1, Hart to Campbell, 25 Jan 1877, 235.

65 *Archives of China's Imperial Maritime Customs*, vol. 1, A/4, Hart to Campbell, 8 Sept 1879, 457.

66 For the growth of the middle class in Britain see Harold Perkin, *The Rise of Professional Society: England since 1880* (London: Routledge, 2002).

67 T. W. Bamford, *Rise of the Public Schools: A study of boys' public boarding schools in England and Wales from 1837 to the Present Day* (London: Nelson, 1967), 17–38; Colin Shrosbree, *Public Schools and Private Education: The Clarendon Commission, 1861–64, and the Public Schools Acts* (Manchester: Manchester University Press, 1988).

68 J. A. Mangan, *'Benefits Bestowed'?: Education and British imperialism* (Manchester: Manchester University Press, 1988).

69 Thompson, *The Empire Strikes Back?*, 17–28.

70 Campbell, *James Duncan Campbell*, 30.

71 Kirk-Greene, *Imperial Administrators*, 17 and 170.

72 Bland papers, memoirs, chapter 1, 1.

73 Perry Anderson, 'A Belated Encounter: Perry Anderson retraces his father's career in the Chinese Customs Service', *London Review of Books*, 20:15 (1998), 6.

74 Sample taken from SHAC, 679(9) 3019, 'Memo of service collected to 31 December 1887, members of foreign Outdoor Staff, Shanghai'.

75 Sample taken from SHAC, file nos 679(2) 1593; 679(2) 1599–1612; 679(3) 1621–1624, 'London Office; dispatches to IG'.

76 Sample taken from SHAC files 679(1) 15038; 679(1) 15039; 679(1) 15040; 679(1) 15044, 'Recruitment of Japanese Officers'.

77 See Constantine, 'British Emigration to the Empire-Commonwealth since 1880'.

78 Tyler, *Pulling Strings in China*, 1–29; Christopher Briggs, *Hai Kuan: The Sea Gate* (Stockport: Lane Publishers, 1997), 12–70.

79 Hippisley papers, MS Eng. c. 7286, 'Memoirs 1848–67', 25.

CHAPTER FOUR

'That chaotic and Gilbertian Service': working life in the Customs

On 28 February 1932 Breaker Point lighthouse near Shantou was overrun by communist rebels, an event that had cataclysmic consequences for two foreign lightkeepers and their families. In the attack foreign employees, and those Chinese with a close association to them, were deliberately targeted. Although all of the Chinese lights staff were left behind unscathed, the British lightkeeper Charles H. Edwards, his Chinese wife and four of his children, and a Russian colleague, A. N. Andreyanow, and his wife (also Chinese) were kidnapped and held to ransom. 'The Reds says that the ransom money must be paid inside of a month otherwise they will kill us,' pleaded Edwards in a note to the Shantou Commissioner.[1] The women and children were released by the end of March, but over the ensuing months the Customs, the Chinese government and the British consular and military authorities in China all equivocated over taking action to free the remaining prisoners. Although the British consul at Shantou and the commander-in-chief of the British China Station initially seemed gung-ho about the possibility of using HMS *Whitehall* to transport Chinese troops to the site of the kidnapping, nothing came of this proposal.[2] Also, by 1932 the age of gunboat diplomacy had long since waned, meaning that a direct British military intervention was out of the question. The Customs proposed paying a reduced ransom of $10,000 per lightkeeper, but government authorities in Nanjing vetoed this decision, claiming that it would encourage more kidnappings. Exasperated by the prevarications of both the British and Chinese authorities, Edwards's elderly father, who lived in Xiamen, decided to attempt to negotiate his son's release himself. However, on travelling to Shantou to solicit help from the various authorities involved in the case, Edwards Senior was coolly received by the British consul, Customs Commissioner, Chinese Superintendent and the central government's Pacification Commissioner. He returned to Xiamen defeated.[3]

Unable and somewhat unwilling to take any official action, the Shantou Commissioner, H. G. Fletcher, enlisted the help of Christian missionaries and their converts in the hinterland to scout for information about the whereabouts and condition of the captives. Although rumours that the bodies of the lightkeepers had been found 'riddled with bullets' began to circulate in the Hong Kong press in May – and were corroborated by the Guangzhou authorities – on the basis of reports from informants Fletcher insisted 'it is practically certain that our men are alive and well'.[4] By January of 1933, however, these hopes were dashed by news, reportedly from an 'ex-communist of some standing', that both men had died some time ago. The exact date of their deaths remained unclear; Andreyanow reportedly died from natural causes and Edwards was shot dead by his captors as they were being pursued by Chiang Kai-shek's troops.[5] The Inspectorate's botched handling of the affair had very real and long-term consequences for Edwards's family. Not only were his wife, Chian Kim Edwards, and seven children deprived of a husband and father; they also lost a rent-free home at the lighthouse and Edwards's salary, leaving the family practically destitute. They were able to survive only with the help of Edwards's brother-in-law, Mr Dudley, an examiner in the Customs.

The kidnapping at Breaker Point and the inadequate response to Edwards's and Andreyanow's plight introduces several pertinent issues to do with the experience of working for the Customs. Above all it is suggestive of the complex personal and professional consequences of working within a different state's administration. The Customs' status as a foreign-run organisation that operated under the auspices of the Chinese state made its staff particularly susceptible to the political vicissitudes of twentieth-century China. The decision to target an isolated outpost of foreign power and to kidnap only the foreigners and their families was a calculated one. Not only did the communists assume that foreigners would fetch a higher ransom (although they miscalculated on that score); their actions also made a political point about the injustice of foreign control over China's primary revenue-generating organ. The events at Breaker Point were especially dramatic, but across China the Customs became unavoidably embroiled in local and national revolutions, endemic civil war, the growth of popular anti-imperialist sentiment and Japan's encroachments.

The lacklustre response to the events at Breaker Point also hints at the way in which race, class and nationality intersected to determine an employee's professional status and their ability to negotiate difficult local conditions. Lightkeeper was the lowest-ranking position in the Customs for a foreigner, which partly accounts for the Inspectorate's tepid reaction to the kidnapping. Furthermore, Edwards was of mixed

British and Chinese ancestry – a 'Eurasian' to use the treaty port terminology – and was therefore not regarded as a true Briton, regardless of what his birth certificate may have said. Andreyanow was in an even sorrier position. As a stateless Russian refugee, who appears to have fled his homeland in the course of the Russian Civil War (1917–23), Andreyanow lacked consular representation and extraterritorial protection in China. Indeed, the voluminous correspondence surrounding the case focuses almost entirely on Edwards, and barely mentions his equally unfortunate colleague. The aftermath of the attack on Breaker Point also sheds light upon the knotty issue of which authority ultimately had jurisdiction over foreigners in the Chinese government's employ. The British consular and military establishment, various Chinese government departments and the supposedly impartial Foreign Inspectorate were all involved in the protracted official conversation about the incident, yet no authority was ultimately willing to shoulder the responsibility of rescuing Edwards and Andreyanow. In the early 1930s Britain was beginning to retreat from China, Chiang Kai-shek's government was in power and openly championed an anti-imperialist agenda, and the Foreign Inspectorate was more fully subordinated to the central government in Nanjing than ever before. In this context, no one wanted to take responsibility for the fate of employees of an increasingly contentious and, in the eyes of many, outmoded institution.

In disentangling these issues, this chapter contends that employees of imperial institutions were required to steer creatively through a range of often-contradictory political currents in their professional lives. In the case of the Customs these forces included official directives from the Inspectorate, changes in central government, specific local political conditions and international trends that manifested themselves in China, such as the waxing and waning of various imperial powers. The description of the Foreign Inspectorate as a 'chaotic and Gilbertian service', quoted from the Indoor Staff employee Paul King and his wife Veronica King's novel based on their Customs experiences, captures the unpredictable nature of Service working environments, which varied tremendously from port to port.[6] Rather than its being an impregnable bastion of imperial power, versatility and compromise were vital to the day-to-day running of the Customs. In order to situate these issues within their proper context it is important to begin by outlining the diverse working conditions of the Service's many branches. This chapter then examines how the Inspectorate's policies were interpreted, implemented and challenged at a local and national level. Exploring the foreign staff's relations with local Chinese power-brokers, representatives of foreign power and local communities and considering how the position of the Foreign Inspectorate changed in response to external influences demonstrates that, despite its protestations to the contrary, the Customs was intensely political.

Working life in the Customs

Whereas much scholarly energy has been devoted to studying the intricacies of colonial policy and the ideologies of empire, the question of *how* these policies and principles were implemented by imperial administrators has often been ignored. Because the lower-level staff of imperial institutions carried out the groundwork of colonial policies, and formed a frontline of contact between local communities and foreign power, it is important to understand their everyday working lives. The structure and conditions of the typical work day shed light on how foreign power was exercised, and the bureaucratic structures that influenced its deployment. In many overseas services new recruits were first introduced to institutional principles and practices during a training period. In the foreign Customs staff, however, there was no explicit and organised attempt to mould new recruits into a committed and elite corps of professional administrators, despite the creation of a Customs College in Beijing in 1908 to train Chinese candidates. This marked the Customs as a mediocre cousin of the more well-regarded imperial administrative services that the Inspectorate wished to emulate, such as the Tropical African Services and the Indian Civil Service (ICS), both of which had inaugurated thoroughgoing preparatory training courses by the early twentieth century.[7] By comparison the most new appointees to the foreign Indoor Staff could hope for by way of training was a few months of language study before taking up their posts. J. O. P. Bland reminisced nostalgically about the summer of 1883 that he and other new arrivals spent learning Mandarin with 'patient and courteous Chinese teachers' in Beijing's Western Hills, an interlude that he described as 'a picnic of the rarest kind'.[8] Similarly, many Customs language students were sent to Nanjing in the late nineteenth century. Intensive language tutoring was, however, always offered on an ad hoc basis, and by the second decade of the twentieth century appears to have been abandoned altogether. Instead, the Inspectorate provided new recruits with an allowance to pay for private language tuition from local teachers. Most employees, however, clearly did not put much effort into language study, much to the Inspectorate's chagrin. In 1910, after soliciting reports from Commissioners on the language abilities of the foreign staff, the Inspectorate concluded that 'study of Chinese is not taken seriously'. In an attempt to force foreign assistants into more diligent study, the Inspectorate announced the commencement of regular language examinations in 1911, after which

Chinese language abilities across the Indoor Staff rose considerably. There were three levels of examination and only those who passed the highest level were eligible for promotion to Deputy Commissioner.[9] By contrast, foreign members of the Outdoor Staff and Marine Department received no language training whatsoever, although they were rewarded with salary bonuses and sometimes promotions if they made the effort to learn.

This paucity of training was largely due to the basic nature of the work at the junior levels of the Service. Unlike ICS probationary officers and Colonial Administrative Service (CAS) cadets, who were expected to shoulder a great deal of responsibility early on in their careers, new Customs men were not required to make important or independent decisions.[10] Instead they gradually accumulated knowledge and responsibility through experience. This was the result of a specific service structure and mindset that emphasised a clear system of ranks and thus discouraged exhibitions of individual flair on the part of junior employees. Staff Secretary Hugh Prettejohn's assertion that 'several years' service as a "Tidewaiter" is essential for the moulding and disciplining of the junior officer', made in response to a proposed reorganisation of the Outdoor Staff in 1930, perfectly illustrates this entrenched attitude.[11] More than an obsession with hierarchy, though, the lack of training for foreign staff points to a particular perception of their role in China and the qualities they were expected to bring to the Customs. With the exception of technical experts and experienced seamen in the Marine Department, the majority of newcomers to the foreign staff did not possess any proven talent for Customs work. Rather, they were a visible emblem of foreign tutelage of China. Their domination of the most prestigious ranks and branches of the Customs staff loudly declared that only foreigners possessed the skills and character necessary to modernise China. Likewise, the creation of a Customs College exclusively for Chinese recruits implied that, while these qualities were intrinsic to the foreign staff, they needed to be painstakingly taught to Chinese employees.

As Table 4.1 demonstrates, the Inspectorate General presided over two departments, the Revenue Department and the Marine Department, each of which consisted of multiple subsidiary branches. In addition a separate Works Department, not shown in the diagram, was created in 1912 to plan and survey building works, but this was subsumed into the Marine Department and Inspectorate General in 1930. In the ports the Commissioner had supreme authority over all custom house employees, including the Marine Department staff and the Tidesurveyor (head of the Outdoor Staff). In all branches the hybrid character of the Service and foreign monopoly on positions of power

Table 4.1 Staff structure of the Chinese Maritime Customs Service c. 1920

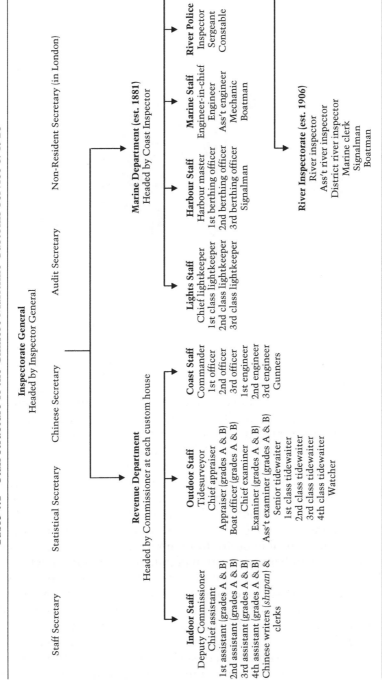

Inspectorate General
Headed by Inspector General

Staff Secretary   Statistical Secretary   Chinese Secretary   Audit Secretary   Non-Resident Secretary (in London)

Revenue Department
Headed by Commissioner at each custom house

Marine Department (est. 1881)
Headed by Coast Inspector

Indoor Staff
Deputy Commissioner
Chief assistant
1st assistant (grades A & B)
2nd assistant (grades A & B)
3rd assistant (grades A & B)
4th assistant (grades A & B)
Chinese writers (*shupan*) &
   clerks

Outdoor Staff
Tidesurveyor
Chief appraiser
Appraiser (grades A & B)
Boat officer (grades A & B)
Chief examiner
Examiner (grades A & B)
Ass't examiner (grades A & B)
Senior tidewaiter
1st class tidewaiter
2nd class tidewaiter
3rd class tidewaiter
4th class tidewaiter
Watcher

Coast Staff
Commander
1st officer
2nd officer
3rd officer
1st engineer
2nd engineer
3rd engineer
Gunners

Lights Staff
Chief lightkeeper
1st class lightkeeper
2nd class lightkeeper
3rd class lightkeeper

Harbour Staff
Harbour master
1st berthing officer
2nd berthing officer
3rd berthing officer
Signalman

Marine Staff
Engineer-in-chief
Engineer
Ass't engineer
Mechanic
Boatman

River Police
Inspector
Sergeant
Constable

River Inspectorate (est. 1906)
River inspector
Ass't river inspector
District river inspector
Marine clerk
Signalman
Boatman

1   Chinese employees at the Tianjin Custom house, 1905

and prestige until the 1930s created a multitude of structural inefficiencies. For example, despite the fact that the majority of people who had dealings with the Customs were Chinese, most official business was conducted in English until the 1930s, which necessitated the employment of an army of Chinese clerks and *shupan* (writers) to translate and copy documents prepared by higher-ranking foreign staff with rudimentary Chinese language skills. Similarly, in order to preserve the privileged position of the foreign staff, Europeans and Americans, often newly arrived in China with little understanding of Customs work, were placed above Chinese clerks with occupation-specific knowledge and understanding of local conditions. Moreover, the Chinese government's understandable desire to retain as much influence as possible resulted in a cumbersome system of joint administration, whereby the Foreign Inspectorate's Commissioner and his staff in each port worked alongside a Chinese Superintendent. Ostensibly Customs work was efficiently apportioned between the two authorities; the Commissioner oversaw administrative affairs and the superintendent was in charge of political business and supervising the banking of the revenues, until the Inspectorate assumed responsibility for this after 1911. For John K. Fairbank this system of joint administration of the Customs perfectly illustrated his thesis of 'synarchy', whereby the Commissioners 'maintained a careful parallel relationship' to the Superintendents and 'the foreign inspectorate of customs thus functioned in a partnership'.[12] In reality this arrangement necessitated the expensive maintenance of two separate establishments when one could have got the job done.

The Indoor and Outdoor Staffs were the two original branches of the Foreign Inspectorate and remained at the core of its work. Although several extra ranks were added to these staffs over the years, their basic structure remained more or less intact until 1949. The Indoor Staff, so called because most of its work was conducted inside the custom house, was styled as the elite, executive arm.

Although the Indoor Staff was an overwhelmingly male environment, it also employed a small number of women. Eighty-one female typists and secretaries are recorded in the service lists. All but five were recruited in the 1930s and 1940s. Although this number included a handful of Britons, Americans and Japanese, the vast majority of these female employees were Chinese and earned salaries less than half those of male Chinese clerks. A 1931 memo circulated to all custom houses instructed Commissioners to investigate the feasibility of employing 'lady-typists' capable of carrying out the routine clerical work usually performed by clerks or foreign assistants. This was explicitly framed as a cost-saving measure. 'The proposed arrangement, moreover, is an economical one in that the pay of 2 lady-typists of 10 years' service each (totalling Hk. Tls. 120 *per mensem*) is less than the pay of 1 Clerk of the same period of service (Hk. Tls. 150 *per mensem*), and so on, more or less, up and down the scale', reported the Shantou Commissioner in his response to the memo.[13]

The clerical work performed by this branch was by no means challenging. Indeed it was the undemanding nature of the work combined with short working hours and relatively high salaries that attracted many young men to the Indoor Staff. Edwin Denby, writing to his brother about the terms of his employment in 1887, described how 'office hours are from 9 to 3, with the usual hour for tiffin. My duties are clerical, and neither very complex nor hard . . . Chief among many dangers that assail me and my plans is this, that I may not have sufficient strength of character to give up the comparatively easy life in China for the monotonous and loathsome existence of a struggling lawyer at home.'[14] Others baulked at the humdrum nature of the work. Willard Straight, an American who joined the Indoor Staff in 1901, ruminated on his work in his diary. 'As a career plus the satisfaction of working for the work's sake I doubt its usefulness,' he wrote. 'The work is done in a routine way and requires only clerical ability until one becomes a Commissioner or an Assistant-in-Charge and is

Table 4.2 Annual salaries of foreign Customs employees in *haikuan taels*, c. 1898

Indoor Staff		Outdoor Staff		Marine Department	
4th assistant B	1,800	Watcher	600	4th cl. lightkeeper	360
3rd assistant A	3,600	1st cl. tidewaiter	1,320	3rd cl. berthing officer	1,200
1st assistant A	5,000	Examiner	1,800	Engineer	7,200
Commissioner	9,500–18,000	Tidesurveyor	4,800	Coast Inspector	9,500

Source: SHAC, 679(1) 26896, 'Inspector General's circulars, vol. 7, second series, nos. 801-1,000, 1897–1901', circulars no. 848 (second series) 3 Oct 1898, no. 849 (second series) 4 Oct 1898 & no. 860 (second series) 18 Nov 1898; SHAC, 679(1) 16826, 'Commissioners' reports on Out-Door Staff petitions for increase in pay in reply to circular no. 2,545', enclosure in Swatow dispatch no. 5,022, 27 July 1916. The haikuan tael was a measurement of silver devised by the CCS in which Customs tariffs and employee salaries were paid.

given the responsibility for the port. With luck it might be attractive; without luck or a pull it is a damned drudge.'[15] Yet despite the routine and often undemanding nature of their work, foreign Indoor employees were given conspicuously preferential treatment. As Table 4.2 shows, c. 1898 the lowest-ranking foreign Indoor employee was paid an annual salary treble that paid to the lowest foreign position in the Outdoor Staff. Similarly, Indoor employees were entitled to their first home leave of up to two years on half-pay after only seven years of service, and then every five subsequent years. Outdoor Staff leave allowance was much less generous; employees were entitled to their first leave of six months on full pay, with the option of extending it for a further six months unpaid, after nine years of continuous service, and then every seven following years.[16] The fact of the matter was that foreign Indoor employees were prized neither because they performed irreplaceable work nor because they offered unique expertise. Rather their presence helped to establish the Customs' international reputation as a top-notch administrative service on a par with more elite colonial bureaucracies. What is more, only well-educated European and American young men of the 'right sort' were deemed to possess the qualities necessary to set an example of good character, sense of duty and initiative for Chinese bureaucrats to emulate.

The Outdoor Staff, by comparison, worked longer and harder days performing the labour that lay at the core of the Customs' responsibilities, principally examining and valuing cargoes and some preventive (anti-smuggling) work. Notwithstanding the indispensable nature of their work, Outdoor men, much like the staff of the other uniformed branches, were considered as socially and professionally inferior by the Inspectorate. Resentment of the preferential treatment of the Indoor Staff was always latent, but became much more palpable after 1918, particularly among the British Outdoor Staff. The growing strength of labour unions in Britain prior to and during the First World War was the international context and inspiration for the more vocal demands for more equal treatment emanating from the uniformed branches in the interwar period. More often than not these complaints were made by disgruntled individuals acting alone. In 1919, for example, the Nanning Commissioner R. F. C. Hedgeland, in a memo scathingly entitled 'Bolshevik Mutterings of a 3rd Class Tidewaiter', reported that W. T. Johnson, a British war veteran who had joined the Outdoor Staff in 1917, was discontented with the favoured position of the Indoor Staff in the port. Enclosed in Hedgeland's communication was a letter he had received from Johnson, apparently prompted by the Commissioner's decision to exclude him from a leaving party held in honour of two foreign residents of Nanning, seemingly because of his social status. 'I am quite well aware of the fact that I'm a person of but very little importance, but really I don't like to be insulted on account of that, nor do I like to be treated as a leper,' wrote Johnson, evidently stung by this slight. Hedgeland's analysis of the affair was largely derisive, yet also betrayed fears that such murmurs of discontent had the potential to spark a more serious upheaval.

> At a small port Mr. Johnson would not be likely to find much indorsement [sic] of his views – at Nanning he has not found any – but if he goes to a large port it would be well if he were watched, as a man of his stamp, endowed with the faculty of ready speech which burns to express itself in action, might succeed in gaining ascendancy over the more sober and steady-going men with the result that a staff which might be healthy to-day would not unlikely become a centre of infection tomorrow.[17]

The perception that malcontents such as Johnson threatened to transform the Outdoor Staff into a hotbed of communist agitation redoubled later that year when a Customs Outdoor Staff union, routinely referred to in official correspondence as the 'Shanghai Soviet', was formed in Shanghai by the chief examiner H. Wyatt, calling for increased pay, a retirement scheme, higher benefits and improved working conditions. Wyatt refused to dismantle the union and was forced to resign as a result.[18] Against the global backdrop of rising fears of communism and the UK police strikes in 1918–19 – which perhaps provided some inspiration to the Customs union leaders – evidence of dissidence made senior employees nervous. Anti-communism was, of course, becoming part of mainstream Western politics at this time. The Shanghai Municipal Police's investigations into suspected Soviet spies and its fears of Bolshevik infiltration in the early 1930s illuminate this growing paranoia in the China coast context.[19] High-ranking Customs staff viewed unionisation with trepidation not just because of fears of the class system overturning but also because granting Outdoor men a higher professional status would, they believed, erode foreign prestige in the Customs more generally. If the position of working-class foreigners was elevated, Chinese agitation for pay and benefits commensurate with those of the foreign staff was sure to follow, something which would only lead to the eventual dissolution of foreign power in the Service.

Men joining the Marine Department and Coast Staff entered a very different world. The often-technical nature of their jobs, which encompassed anti-smuggling work, maintaining aids to navigation, meteorological work and coastal and riverine surveying, combined with the fact that these employees usually lived and worked aboard ship or in lighthouses, meant that they worked on the peripheries of institutional structures and hierarchies. Although the head of the Marine Department, the Coast Inspector, was in theory answerable to the Shanghai Commissioner, he was in reality granted a large degree of autonomy, as was the River Inspectorate, created in 1906 to improve navigation on the Yangzi.[20] An independent work life was central to the appeal of these branches. Jack Blackburn, for example, a former lieutenant commander in the Royal Navy who worked in the River Inspectorate 1934–37, wrote home: 'I often think that the life which I have longed to live has come, able to dress as I like, and do as I like within reason etc.'[21] The lightkeepers who staffed and maintained the system of coastal aids to navigation also enjoyed a great deal of autonomy and were visited only infrequently by their higher-ups. Work in these branches veered between monotony and danger. Lightkeepers went for days or even weeks at a stretch with minimal work to perform and very little human contact, yet lighthouses were also easy pickings for marauding pirates or rebels, as the Breaker Point episode illustrates. Anti-smuggling work, too, was hazardous – there are numerous reports in the archives of Customs employees being killed by smugglers – yet the danger could also be exhilarating. In his published memoir W. F. Tyler, who joined the Marine Department as an officer assigned to preventive work in 1889, reminisced about the 'narrow bays overshadowed by high hills and sooty darkness, where I lay in wait like a spider for its fly'.[22] In sum, life and work in the Marine Department and Coast Staff was infinitely more varied, independent and at times

2   The Nanjing Customs boatmen in uniform, 1900

more exciting than either the stuffy monotony of the Indoor Staff or the tightly regulated Outdoor Staff.

The bureaucratic structure and authority of the Foreign Inspectorate rested on the maintenance of a strict hierarchy. In the ports the Commissioner held sway, rendering him the closest Customs equivalent to the indefatigable district officer (DO) of colonial administrative services. As Anthony Kirk-Greene has observed, the typical DO was expected to perform a 'tutti-frutti of assignments' and was therefore required to display a virtuoso talent for leadership and versatility. As thorough training in such a bewildering array of duties would have been impossible, and the DO's 'success, his effectiveness, his very ability to do and to be, were basically rooted in the assumption of his authority: I am the DO, *ergo quidque est*. His word was law; he was the law.'[23] Customs Commissioners were not all-powerful and, as will become clear later in this chapter, they competed for authority with other Chinese and foreign officials. They *were*, however, expected to run their custom houses in a paternalistic manner and maintain an unswerving influence over their staff. Commissioners were charged with fostering esprit de corps among their subordinates and with tutoring juniors in Service principles and responsibilities. They also acted as a buffer between the custom house and the Inspectorate through which all communications between lower-level staff and the IG had to pass.[24] This meant that it was all but impossible for junior employees to air grievances against the Commissioner to a higher authority without fear of repercussions.

Furthermore, the Commissioner's role as a conduit for information passing between his staff and the Inspectorate meant that employees were effectively at their chief's mercy when it came to annual perform-ance reports, which often determined career trajectories. By the twenti-eth century standard practice was to promote junior employees on the basis of seniority as vacancies arose until they reached the mid-level ranks, after which advancement was based on merit. Given the numer-ous ranks in the Service, routine promotions could be expected approxi-mately every two years, although employees would be passed over if they proved incompetent or failed to make sufficient progress in their Chinese studies.[25] Commissioners were instructed to submit an annual confidential report on each employee's conduct and progress, used to determine who should be promoted and who should be held back. This system was open to a host of abuses and many embittered employees believed that their advancement was being unfairly obstructed by mali-cious confidential reports. In 1938, for example, the chief assistant at Mengzi, H. J. de Garcia, travelled to Shanghai to clear his name with the Inspectorate after a slew of negative confidential reports submitted by his Commissioner, H. Y. J. Cloarec, which Garcia complained were made 'out of spite and personal feelings disregarding the interest of the service'.[26] As punishment for his impudence de Garcia was passed over for promotion until his departure from the Service seven years later. In these and similar cases the Inspectorate was less concerned about the alleged malice of the Commissioners than about the complainants' audacious circumvention of Service protocols, which jeopardised the carefully maintained hierarchy on which Customs authority rested.

The Customs establishment in four ports: Shanghai, Shantou, Yichang and Harbin

The Inspectorate insisted that the foreign staff were ideally placed to act as impartial mediators between Chinese and foreign economic interests. In reality their very position at a crossroads between the Chinese and foreign worlds rendered Customs work political. The essential ambiguity of the Inspectorate's status – not quite foreign, yet not quite Chinese – left it open to a host of pressures from agents of foreign and Chinese power alike, not to mention from the public. Maintaining disinterestedness was, then, a difficult task at best, and was often compromised by the foreign staff's need to negotiate with foreign and Chinese powerbrokers at a local, national and international level. Furthermore, because Customs work was fundamentally intertwined with the deployment of political power, both foreign and Chinese, changing geo-political contexts at a local level had a profound effect on the experience of working in any given custom house.

A brief investigation of the impact of political environments at four ports, Shanghai, Shantou, Yichang and Harbin, serves to illustrate the diverse situations in which Customs employees worked. The staff of various custom houses navigated specific regional challenges which necessitated developing local solutions to local problems. Shanghai, one of the original five treaty ports 'opened up' by the Treaty of Nanjing in 1842, swiftly developed into a centre of international commerce, making its custom house the most important in China. The custom house, with its granite columns and 90 metres-tall clock tower, stylistically modelled on Big Ben, dominated the neo-classical pomposity of the world-famous Bund. Personnel in the Shanghai custom house, which in the twentieth century employed hundreds at any given time, had a greater sense of working for a large, carefully graded bureaucracy than those stationed at other ports, some of which required a staff of only seven or eight.

The international influences on Shanghai's development lent the city a cultural, intellectual and commercial dynamism, creating a distinct urban character.[27] Marie-Claire Bergère has therefore described Shanghai as 'the other China', a place that was 'the China of the minority; marginal China, but just as authentic as the rural China'.[28] Shanghai's cosmopolitanism and cultural eclecticism made it a coveted posting. There were, however, also distinct drawbacks. Shanghai's position as the central node of foreign power in China coupled with its well-earned reputation as a site of political ferment meant that it bore the brunt of anti-foreign demonstrations in the 1920s. Most notoriously, the foreign-administered International Settlement district was the site of the May Thirtieth protests in 1925, during which eleven unarmed demonstrators were killed by the British-controlled Shanghai Municipal Police.[29] The sheer visibility and importance of the Shanghai Customs establishment meant that it inevitably got caught up in these tumultuous political events. The rise to power of Chiang Kai-shek's Nationalist Party in 1927, for example, caused unprecedented difficulties for the Shanghai Customs, most notably when the local party organisation orchestrated a boycott of British and Japanese goods in June 1927.[30] Although relations between the Customs and the Nationalist Party improved after Maze's appointment to the IG-ship in 1929 and his subsequent conciliatory gestures towards the National Government, the Customs was now operating on a different footing. This was especially keenly felt in Shanghai. Reviled for its foreignness yet also valued as an arena of modernity, Shanghai 'became a pole, even a vital nerve center, for the new regime, which strove to establish its grip over the city', a policy that extended to foreign-controlled institutions such as the Customs.[31] Nationalist-sponsored efforts to limit foreign domination of the Customs and bolster Chinese influence emerged in the shape of a Shanghai Customs Association for Chinese staff in 1929, which thrived despite the Inspectorate's prior suppression of earlier staff associations and unions. The Shanghai Commissioner resignedly explained that because of the Nationalist government's endorsement of the associa-tion 'it does not come within the Commissioner's competence to dis-establish it'.[32] After Shanghai's occupation by Japanese forces in 1937 the custom house found itself in an increasingly untenable situation, exacerbated by the dismissal of approximately one hundred British and American employees from Shanghai in mid-December 1941. Also, the city's wartime position as a thriving hub of smuggling and profiteering rendered the Customs establishment all but impotent.[33]

The southern fishing village of Shantou in Guangdong province became a treaty port in 1861 under the terms of the Sino-French Convention of 1860, and quickly emerged as a thriving trading centre in south China. Shantou was considered an amenable posting in Customs circles, with plenty of work, a moderately sized foreign com-munity, good bathing beaches and hunting in the hinterland. It was, however, prone to natural disasters; the majority of the town's popula-tion perished in a typhoon in 1922. What is more, Beijing's influence over this remote southern region had always been less than watertight and the area's inhabitants had thus developed a fiercely independent mentality. The region spawned several rebellions, most infamously the Taiping Rebellion of 1850–64, and was a prime location for regional military and political coups before 1927. Sun Yat-sen launched several quixotic attempts at republican revolution in the provincial capital, Guangzhou, in 1895, 1900 and again in 1911, and was even invited by the southern warlord Chen Jiongming to become 'president' of a newly formed Chinese People's Government in the city in 1921–22. Warlord power shifts were particularly dramatic in this region and the Customs was often caught in the crossfire. Commissioners endeav-oured to remain aloof by reiterating the Customs dictum of neutrality, but they inevitably faced pressure from warlords who had designs on the revenue.

The inhabitants of Guangdong province also had a long history of opposition to foreign encroachments, most famously in the anti-British resistance in the aftermath of the First Opium War.[34] When com-bined with a determination to retain as much autonomy as possible this meant that the Customs, a foreign-run organisation that represented the power of the central government in Beijing, was resented as an impostor in Shantou. The Customs was perpetually engaged in stand-offs and negotiations with local power-holders and merchant groups who resented the imposition of new policies by outsiders. In 1881, for example, it was caught up in an ongoing dispute with the Shantou Merchants' Guild, which resisted the levying of fines for evading Customs regulations. Commissioner A. Huber found the guild 'a proud and powerful body accustomed to dictate to the other merchants foreign and native and sometimes to the local authorities also'. The Guild proved to be a formidable enemy, especially as it had the support of the local *daotai* and an army general who held sway in the district. The disagreement was resolved only when a magistrate was brought in to adjudicate.[35] Property disputes were a recurrent source of friction between the Customs and the Shantou public. According to Commissioner Currie writing in 1909, so frequent were attempts to dispossess the Customs of its land that Commissioners had to maintain the 'utmost vigilance' in order to 'detect and stop any encroachment or establishment of fancied rights'.[36] The effects of the growth of anti-imperialism, both popular and official, from the mid-1920s onwards is discussed in more detail later in this chapter, but it is important to note that they were especially keenly felt in Shantou. The nationwide wave of anti-British boycotts that followed the bloody suppression of the May Thirtieth demonstrations in 1925 hit the Shantou Customs hard and, what is more, local officials seemed to collude in the protests. The frustrated Commissioner reported that 'the political machinery of the local government seemed to have been devised for the express purpose of inviting incidents and inculcating severe lessons of patience and self-restraint'.[37] Attempts to undermine the Customs' authority only intensified in the 1930s. Local mindsets and long-standing attitudes towards central authority and foreign interference, then, often tested the limits of Customs power.

Yichang, situated on the Yangzi, was a small river port opened to foreign trade in 1877 by the Chefoo Convention (1876), and was the most important commercial conduit into western China until the stretch of the Yangzi between Yichang and Chongqing became navigable by large steamships in the 1890s. A small town which offered little in the way of entertainment or foreign society, Yichang was never a particularly desirable billet. Furthermore, by the 1920s Yichang was a port in decline, its trading importance having been eclipsed by Chongqing, although it did retain strategic importance as a base for the River Inspectorate. In 1930 the Yichang Commissioner pointed out that 'this port is living on its past glories', and that it

[95]

employed an absurdly large staff considering its unimportance.[38] Yichang became an even more undesirable posting in the early 1930s. This was an unstable frontier region for Chiang Kai-shek's National Government and it consequently saw a great deal of military activity, embroiling the Yichang Customs in an ongoing struggle with local military leaders who insisted on housing troops in Customs-owned buildings free of charge.[39] This in itself was disruptive, yet worse was to come when Yichang became a target of Japanese bombing raids from 1938 onwards owing to the town's strategic importance as a gateway for shipping to the wartime capital of Chongqing. In March 1939 the Commissioner reported that Yichang had suffered thirty bombing raids since January 1938; during the most recent approximately a thousand buildings had been razed and inestimable numbers of lives lost.[40] During the war years Customs personnel were always on guard and ready to evacuate at a moment's notice. The example of Yichang, then, illustrates that the Customs, as a government agency, was inevitably pulled into regional and international conflicts. Its semi-foreign status only gave its staff minimal protection in times of hardship and danger.

Harbin was situated on the Sungari River in the far northeast, a region that had a long history as a crossroads between China, Russia and the various nomadic tribes from which the Manchu people, founders of the Qing dynasty, were descended. In 1898 engineers working for the Russian-controlled China Eastern Railway (CER) chose the small settlement at Harbin as the base for a project to connect the Trans-Siberian railway to Vladivostok. After the completion of the railway in 1905 international trade in Harbin boomed, as did the town's population, leading the Customs administration to put down roots there in 1907. Yet multiple and contested claims to jurisdiction over the city created a bureaucratic nightmare for the Customs. Initially the city was divided into two distinct zones, one administered by the CER and the other controlled by Chinese authorities. The Chinese Customs administration was thus forced to work alongside a Russian-controlled custom house, a situation which led to endless disputes about the boundaries of each establishment's authority.[41] In 1917, after the October Revolution undermined Russian authority in China, which was based on treaty agreements and leaseholds extracted by *imperial* Russia, the Chinese authorities nominally seized control of the entire city. Subsequent attempts to eliminate the CER's influence and an aggressive policy of promoting Harbin's Chinese identity in the 1920s engendered an even more fractious relationship between Russian authorities and the Customs.[42] In 1924 the current Commissioner warned his successor that 'Harbin is a hot-bed of political intrigues at all times, the Railway being the storm centre'.[43] In the context of the city's byzantine power struggles, maintaining a neutral stance was essential, albeit difficult.

Harbin's frontier status also meant that the Customs became entangled in the tense international political situation after 1917; both the Beiyang government and, after 1927, Chiang Kai-shek's National Government were hostile to the Soviet regime. What is more, the political divisions of the Russian Civil War spilled over into China. The remnants of the anti-Bolshevik White Army and its supporters, known as 'White Russians', arrived in Harbin in droves, and many of them joined the Customs, leading to ideological feuds with representatives and supporters of the Soviet Union. At times this created a dangerous situation for the Russian Customs staff, especially those who worked at Harbin's satellite stations along the China–Russia border, such as Sanxing, Suifenhe, Tongjiang and Manzhouli. During a Sino-Soviet border clash in 1929 Russian members of staff stationed at Customs outposts close to the fighting were evacuated owing to fears of a potential bloodbath perpetrated by advancing Soviet troops on their anti-Bolshevik compatriots. Should the Soviet Union triumph, the Harbin Commissioner predicted, 'there will be a dreadful stampede of Russians and, undoubtedly, a carnage of those who are left behind'.[44] In 1932 the Japanese added an extra layer of complexity to an already fraught political situation when the Harbin Customs was subsumed into the puppet state of Manchukuo.[45]

As these four examples demonstrate, local and regional power structures, domestic and international conflicts, entrenched attitudes towards outsiders and changing political sentiments shaped the Customs working environment in significant ways. Although at times Commissioners could plead disinterestedness in order to escape entanglement in local disputes, its special position in China often placed it at the centre of political issues. Although the power of imperial institutions is often imagined as absolute, in the case of the Customs local civil and military power-holders and the public worked to constrain its authority. This chapter now goes on to explore several themes raised by these regional case studies in more depth. Firstly, as the case of the Russian-dominated Customs staff in Harbin shows, the nationality of employees could influence the experience of working for the Customs in important ways. Secondly, I will consider the relations between Customs staff and Chinese and foreign officials, and the contests for authority that resulted from their overlapping jurisdictions. Lastly, the profound changes wrought on the Customs working environment by the growth of anti-imperialism and rise to power of the Nationalist Party will be examined further.

Nationality and the problem of Customs cosmopolitanism

The Inspectorate styled the hotchpotch national composition of its staff as cosmopolitanism, a label that implied a sophisticated international camaraderie. For the most part, men of different nationalities *did* seem to get along. For many, working side by side with foreign colleagues was an amusing novelty and some appear to have revelled in the aura of urbanity it conferred upon them. 'At the beginning of the summer there were six in the mess, two Englishmen, aforesaid Irishman, one Frenchman, one half German & half American,' wrote the American Edwin Denby about his first messmates in 1887. 'How is that for a cosmopolitan array!'[46] Yet, as discussed in Chapter 3 with regard to Customs appointments, multinational co-operation coexisted uneasily with competition. National allegiances were not extinguished on joining the Customs, and when disagreements arose within the staff the parties involved were apt to reach first for xenophobic slurs. Hart's attempts to build a truly cosmopolitan service were continually thwarted by nationalist sentiment. In an 1875 letter to the American Commissioner Edward Drew, who had informed him about discontent over promotions in the Indoor Staff, Hart thundered:

> The unhappy ones say: 'Confound the I.G.! He made that bacon-and-beans eating Yankee Drew a Commissioner before he had three year's service; he made that frog-eating Frenchman Dechamps Commissioner when he only had 3½ years service; he made that sour-crout-assimilating German Kleinwachter a Commissioner when he had only 4 years service; and after these enormities, he has had the audacity to make his own potato-peeling-Paddy-of-a-brother Commissioner before he had 6 years service. Confound him and again confound him!'[47]

Much of this resentment came from Britons. When men of other nationalities were promoted above them they were apt to take it as a national slight, or as evidence that Hart did not promote British interests sufficiently.

After the annexation of leaseholds and spheres of influence in the 1890s, the strategic distribution of nationalities in custom houses across China became a highly politicised matter. In 1899, one year after China conceded Jiaozhou Bay to Germany, the German minister to China extracted an agreement to staff the newly formed Qingdao custom house exclusively with Germans.[48] Russia followed suit with negotiations for a similar agreement at Dalian and Port Arthur (Lüshunkou) after leasing the Liaodong Peninsula in 1898. Other countries extracted similar agreements, official and unofficial. For example the colonial authorities in Hong Kong resented Customs interference to begin with, but the employment of non-British officers in the Kowloon custom house, positioned on the edge of the colony, only aggravated the situation. According to the Kowloon Commissioner writing in 1939, 'officers of British nationality are almost essential in this district, for in all our frontier work we come into contact with Hong Kong Government officers and nationality plays a large part in promoting harmonious relations'.[49] The career trajectories and employment conditions of various national cohorts often mirrored the rise and fall of their home countries' imperialist ambitions in China. Although this was true of all nationalities to some extent, I will focus here on the abrupt change in fortunes experienced by Customs Russians after 1917.

Until 1917 Russian influence in the Customs was, much to the chagrin of the British establishment, in the ascendant, especially in the northeast. In addition to Port Arthur and Dalian, a Russian preponderance was considered strategically desirable in Harbin. In this international city a polyglot personnel, able to speak Russian, French and Japanese in addition to English and Chinese, was needed. Also, Russian employees helped to smooth the often-testy relations between the Customs and the China Eastern Railway authorities. After 1917 thousands of 'White' Russian refugees fled to China; in Shanghai alone the Russian population increased twelvefold in the period 1918–30, numbering over 13,000 by the end of the decade.[50] Yet Russian political influence did not increase commensurately. Furthermore the proportion of Russians in the Customs remained more or less constant, at just over five per cent of the foreign staff, until the late 1930s. The Customs' reluctance to exploit this new labour source had much to do with the plummeting status of Russians. The October Revolution transformed Russians in China from representatives of a threatening colonial power to stateless refugees and humble guests of the Chinese government. Moreover, stripped of extraterritorial protection, the mainstay of foreign power and prestige, Russians became less and less useful for the Foreign Inspectorate. Its organisational structure assumed freedom of movement on the part of its foreign employees, but the Chinese government's new requirement that all Russians obtain permission from the Waiqiaobu (Immigration Bureau) before moving to a different residence, something that was extremely difficult to obtain, severely limited Russian mobility.[51] Without the protective armour of extraterritoriality Russian employees were not able to perform unpopular Customs operations with the same degree of impunity and, what is more, they could imperil both the safety and the much-lauded impartiality of the Foreign Inspectorate. In 1931, for example, the assistant-in-charge at the Tongjiang customs post under the Harbin jurisdiction, D. N. Smirnoff, was approached by the local Customs Superintendent to assist in an opium-smuggling scheme. When Smirnoff refused, the Superintendent threatened that 'he was a Russian émigré and was likely to find himself in trouble and later arrested by a military court and shot as he had no protection'.[52] While it would have been unthinkable for a Superintendent to make similar threats to foreigners with extraterritorial protection, Russians were now considered fair game.

The Russians who remained in the Customs after 1917 were by and large anti-Bolshevik, leading to strained relations between 'White' Russian employees and Soviet officials. This conflict threatened to mire the Customs in political feuds and derail its efforts to establish its authority in the former Russian sphere of influence in Manchuria, especially in Harbin. Whereas Russian employees had previously been valued as intermediaries who could sweeten the Customs' relations with the CER, after the Chinese government officially recognised Soviet control of the railway zone in 1925 they became an encumbrance. In 1930 the Danish Commissioner, P. Barentzen, complained that Russian employees were now all but useless in the port and suggested that several '"near-Russians" – i.e. natives of Poland or the Baltic states who would presumably not offend the Soviet Consular, Customs and Railway officials' be sent to Harbin to replace them.[53]

The character of Russians was also impugned by officials and the public, foreign and Chinese alike, after 1917. At a time when international anti-communist feeling was reaching fever pitch, all Russians seemed suspect. Anti-Russian feeling was most pronounced in the northeast border region where Chinese and Russian interests clashed on a regular basic. Hostility towards Russians in Aigun (present-day Heihe), opposite the Siberian city of Blagoveshchensk on the Amur River, was especially vituperative. Commissioner Hedgeland reported in 1923 that a Political and Economic Union formed by Chinese merchants had issued a manifesto denouncing several Customs Russians in the port as Bolsheviks, accusing them of misconduct and demanding their immediate dismissal. 'The Chinese here profess to view all Russians with considerable mistrust and at present a customs officer of Russian nationality acts as a sort of "Bogey" to which public apprehension is directed,' Hedgeland surmised. Such was the extent of this ill-feeling that Hedgeland even proposed transferring all Russian employees out of the port, although nothing came of this suggestion. A breakdown in trading relations leading to the temporary closure of the border at Aigun the following year only exacerbated the situation.[54]

At the conclusion of the Northern Expedition to unify China in

1927, achieved through an alliance between the Chinese Communist Party and the Guomindang with Comintern support, Chiang Kai-shek purged the party of communists and ousted Soviet advisers from China. The National Government subsequently eyed Russians with mistrust as potential communist agents. In 1936, for example, the Guanwushu (Customs Administration), which supervised the CCS, instructed the the Shanghai Commissioner to investigate the Russian examiner D. A. Morozoff along with the British boat officer J. A. Crossland and Latvian tidewaiter J. D. Grundel on charges of passing knowledge of exports and imports to the Soviet Union. They were also, rather improbably, accused of disseminating Bolshevik propaganda and transporting Soviet spies under the guise of working as Chinese Customs officials. The case against them was shaky and seemed to be largely based on tenuous rumours that Morozoff's wife was a 'notorious Soviet spy' and vague claims that Grundel was somehow 'connected with the USSR'.[55] The Shanghai Commissioner gave each man a warning and the matter was not pursued further, yet this incident nonetheless demonstrates how easily Russian employees, and those who associated with them, could fall under suspicion in the unsettled political environment of the 1920s and 1930s. Every Russian was regarded as a possible spy who could insidiously plant the seed of Bolshevism in the Customs staff.

Social snobbery had much to do with the scorn with which Russians were regarded after 1917. The destitution of the refugee community coupled with their lack of extraterritorial protection meant that in status terms Russians now occupied a grey area somewhere in between the Chinese and foreign communities. Stella Benson, novelist, waspish commentator on expatriate life in small-port China and wife of a Customs Commissioner, summed up the thoughts of many British expatriates when she declared in 1926 that the Russian refugees 'are the debris of the White Army, mostly scamps and prostitutes'.[56] Many newcomers were forced to survive on charitable handouts, and those lucky enough to find employment were generally confined to low-status jobs that were previously the preserve of Chinese workers.[57] Social prejudices as much as fears of communism fed into common assumptions that Russians in China were slippery characters, politically suspect and easy to manipulate for dubious ends. The fate of Customs Russians shows that the experiences of men and women who worked in the empire world were dictated by their home countries' imperial fortunes as much as by personal ambition and ability. Extraterritoriality was not just an abstract concept; it had tangible meaning for those who benefited from its protection or else suffered from the loss of it.

The Customs in relation to foreign and Chinese authority

The case of the Customs Russians demonstrates how the shifting character of the foreign staff was intimately entwined with external political events. Similarly the often-tense relations between the Customs and other representatives of foreign and Chinese power demonstrate that the Foreign Inspectorate was an intensely political institution. In particular the foreign staff could become a battleground on which foreign and Chinese authorities attempted to assert their jurisdiction over foreigners resident in China, especially in the nineteenth century when the exact parameters of foreign authority were constantly in flux. This situation is thrown into stark relief by the dramatic events of 1891, when a British junior employee in the Indoor Staff, Charles Mason, was accused of conspiring with a Chinese secret society, the Gelaohui (Elder Brothers Society), to overthrow the regional government in Jiangsu. During his leave, Mason travelled to Hong Kong where he attempted to recruit various foreign beachcombers and out-of-work sailors as mercenaries. He also arranged for an illegal shipment of arms, which was intercepted in Shanghai. On the night of 13 September Mason disembarked in his current port of Zhenjiang on the Yangzi and was promptly searched by his colleagues in the Customs, who had received word from Shanghai about his possible involvement in arms smuggling. Five pounds of dynamite and a pair of derringer pistols were found in his luggage, thus sparking a fraught diplomatic incident.

Both the Foreign Inspectorate and the British consular establishment surmised that Mason's involvement in the plot was probably minimal and that he was either out for notoriety or suffering from delusions of grandeur.[58] Nonetheless, the episode, which was breathlessly reported in the treaty port press, was a distinct embarrassment for the Customs; the implication of a foreign officer in a seditious anti-Qing uprising severely undermined the Inspectorate's claims that the European and American staff – unlike Chinese bureaucrats – were loyal servants of China unaffected by regional political machinations.[59] More importantly the episode gave rise to a tussle between the Qing and the British diplomatic establishment over which authority foreign Customs employees were ultimately answerable to. From the beginning local Qing officials and the Zongli Yamen (Bureau of Foreign Affairs) argued that Mason, as an employee of the Chinese government engaged in a plot against the Qing state, should be tried in a Chinese court. When it became clear that the British authorities would not co-operate with this proposal, the Zongli Yamen insisted that Mason be punished immediately and severely under British law. Moreover Chinese officials should be given leave to interrogate him about the details of the plot and his co-conspirators. The British minister, Sir John Walsham, failed even to reply to most of the Zongli Yamen's dispatches. What is more, much to the Qing's chagrin, the British authorities were reluctant to take any action whatsoever, beginning proceedings against Mason only over two weeks after the discovery of the plot and only after considerable pressure from the Chinese government. Walsham dismissed the Zongli Yamen's appeal for a joint investigation into the case, claiming that, his employment notwithstanding, Mason was still a British subject and therefore enjoyed extraterritorial protection. When the case eventually went to trial in the British consular court in Shanghai, Mason was charged not with inciting rebellion but rather with the considerably lesser offence of illegally possessing explosives. He was sentenced to nine months in prison and, to add insult to injury, the British refused to guarantee that Mason would never again be permitted to return to China. The Zongli Yamen was outraged at the light sentence, which seemed to confirm its suspicions about the injustice and abuses inherent in the system of extraterritoriality.[60] As for Mason, after leaving the Customs he turned his hand to writing several reasonably popular tales of Chinese political intrigues and smuggling on the China coast under the penname Julian Croskey, including a purported memoir about his dabbling in China's murky underworld of secret societies and gun running.[61]

The Mason affair highlights how the ambiguous status of the foreign staff, who were caught between two spheres of jurisdiction, periodically led to struggles for control that sometimes reached the highest levels of the Chinese government and the foreign diplomatic establishment. Throughout the entire span of its existence, the Inspectorate's insistence that its foreign employees were first and foremost servants of China and should therefore be regarded as having a 'Chinese character' for legal purposes caused intermittent conflict with foreign consuls. Foreign powers were reluctant to relinquish their authority over their citizens in China, especially those strategically placed in the Chinese government's employ. As Eileen Scully has shown, extraterritoriality not only worked to protect foreign nationals from Chinese law; it also created a means by which foreign powers could retain control over their own nationals overseas who might otherwise subvert their home government's interests.[62] The Foreign Inspectorate and foreign consuls, particularly the British establishment, were engaged in a perpetual war of attrition throughout the latter half of the nineteenth century in which both sides attempted to assert their authority over Customs employees. 'If England would allow us to take our chance and lead in War as we teach in peace, and if English Consuls were warned to keep their hands off (and give support to) Englishmen in Chinese employ, we could make England and China the best of friends,' complained Hart wearily in 1881.[63]

This quandary came to a head when Customs men became embroiled in legal disputes. One such high-profile incident occurred in 1880 when a British watcher at Guangzhou, E. Page, who had shot and killed a Chinese smuggler while on duty, was summoned by the British consul to stand trial for manslaughter. Hart seized this opportunity to make a point about the legal accountability of foreign Customs employees. As the Chinese authorities believed that Page had acted in the line of duty, Hart argued, the arrest was unlawful. Hart promised to defend Page 'to the nth' and to prosecute the consul for unlawful arrest, but was eventually forced to back down in the face of diplomatic ire.[64] A similar case emerged in 1883, involving a British examiner in the Outdoor Staff, Mr Roberts, who was imprisoned for withholding evidence when acting as a witness in an opium theft case tried at the British consular court. In his defence Roberts cited a rule that forbade Customs employees from giving evidence that had come to their knowledge purely through Customs work without permission from the Chinese government. The case led to a showdown between the Shanghai Commissioner (Glover) and the British consul (Hughes) about their respective jurisdictions over British Customs employees, which ultimately reached a stalemate.[65]

Hart's insistence that foreign employees should be regarded as having a 'Chinese character' for legal purposes was somewhat disingenuous, often running counter to realities on the ground. The fact was that the Foreign Inspectorate existed to protect both Chinese *and* foreign interests. In fact, from the 1850s until the 1880s, when the consular presence in China's rapidly opening treaty ports was patchy, Customs Commissioners were bound by treaty agreements to perform consular functions when the need arose.[66] By the turn of the century, by which time Qing power had weakened significantly and the extent of foreign authority had been more squarely decided upon, legal battles between the Customs and the diplomatic establishment petered out. Mutual antipathy, however, remained in several ports, especially in small, isolated towns, far away from the restraining control of central authority. In small backwaters, where the consul and the Customs Commissioner were often the pre-eminent foreign authorities in the port, battles of egos frequently erupted. In the isolated port of Tengyue in the southwest in the early 1930s, for example, this competition grew into seething antipathy between the Commissioner (Macdonald) and the British consul (Wyatt-Smith). Wyatt-Smith seemed intent upon defaming the Customs, circulating rumours that Macdonald knowingly employed opium smugglers as his servants and that almost all Customs staff were embezzling the revenue. In any case, Macdonald explained, Wyatt-Smith's slanderous tales were not taken seriously;

his alcoholism, 'megalomania' and propensity for 'conducting himself with local Shan prostitutes' were well known to the port's foreign community.[67] These confrontations were both personal and political. Consuls and Commissioners represented two different but overlapping colonial projects in China; thus, their ideas about how foreign power should be deployed and how foreign nationals should act sometimes clashed.

The Commissioner's relationship with Chinese officials was equally tricky and varied tremendously from port to port. The question of the Commissioner's position vis-à-vis his Chinese counterpart, the Superintendent, was especially vexatious throughout the century of the Foreign Inspectorate's existence. John K. Fairbank saw joint administration of the Customs as a perfect example of a harmonious partnership between China and the West. But, although the system of dual control does demonstrate a degree of co-operation, it is clear that both parties often resented having to share their power. In an 1864 circular Hart urged his staff to remember that the dominance of foreigners in the Customs was an understandably sensitive issue for Superintendents and recommended that 'the more the Commissioners keep in the background, the better will it be for the duties they have to perform, and less will be the chances of their becoming the objects of ill-feeling'. In an oblique explanation that reveals the wooliness of this issue, Hart added that, although in reality the Commissioner and Superintendent were of equal rank, the Commissioner must give the *appearance* of exercising less power than the Superintendent; 'A judicious sinking of self will not in any way derogate from one's respectability or real influence,' he advised.[68] This circular set the tone for the Inspectorate's vacillation on the issue, made even more complex by several obfuscating directives over the decades. Commissioners could not abnegate too much power to the Superintendent if they wanted to maintain foreign prestige. Yet they also could not afford to alienate Chinese power-holders, who were useful allies when enforcing unpopular Customs policies.

In any case few Superintendents took these foreign interlopers particularly seriously, especially in the nineteenth century when the Customs was not well-established in most ports. 'I am "gradually creating for myself a position of influence with the Chinese officials",' wrote H. B. Morse to fellow Commissioner A. E. Hippisley in 1898, 'but deep down I feel that the advice I give is rather a "counsel of perfection," and that my friends here do not wish to know how best (for China) they should act. In the essentials they do not act on my advice.'[69] Customs men were often perplexed that their beneficent advice was rejected and tended to chalk it up to obduracy or short-sightedness rather than, for example, their lack of understanding of local conditions or resentment

3 A ceremony to burn seized opium attended by Customs employees and
Chinese officials, Nanning, 1920

of foreign interference. Furthermore Commissioners frequently struggled to assert their control over trade; the public much preferred to
deal with a *Chinese* establishment and the Customs was conspicuously foreign in the eyes of many communities. This problem persisted
well into the twentieth century. In 1914, for example, Francis Unwin
warned his successor as Shanghai Commissioner that he had 'ceased
since 1912 to be the recognised head of the local Customs establishment' because 'native officials, high and low, have a natural tendency
to address the Superintendent on all occasions and to treat him generally as the *de facto* as well as the *de jure* head of the Customs'.[70] The
dual system of control, then, often did not lead to partnership so much
as to the perception that there were two different Customs establishments, one Chinese and one foreign, working side by side. This attitude
intensified in the 1930s, when foreign control of the Customs was more
forcefully contested by both the government and the public. The same
Superintendent in Harbin who attempted to draw D. N. Smirnoff into
an opium smuggling scheme in 1931 also tried to intimidate a Chinese
member of the Indoor Staff, Mr Pooth, who had intercepted a parcel
of opium addressed to the Superintendent. 'Being a Chinese he had
no business to disclose their opium activities to the Commissioner,

a foreigner,' the Superintendent warned Pooth.[71] Foreign Customs Commissioners were never truly viewed as *Chinese* officials by the Superintendent and most found it difficult to maintain the delicate power equilibrium that the Inspectorate strove for. The system of dual control never really existed in perfect form; its main function was to provide a semblance of Chinese control over the organisation and the façade of a Sino-foreign partnership.

Backlash: Customs authority on the wane, 1925–49

Customs authority, then, always rested upon constant negotiation, political manoeuvring and compromise with other power-holders, but the most severe threats to its influence emerged concurrent with the intensification of anti-imperialist sentiment from the mid-1920s onwards. The period 1925–49 saw fundamental changes to the Foreign Inspectorate's position in China. Popular anti-foreignism, the restrictions placed on the Inspectorate's autonomy by Chiang Kai-shek's government and Japanese encroachments all destabilised the foreign staff's dominance. The Customs was the most obvious and far-reaching example of foreign power in China; there were custom houses in ports the length and breadth of the country, the public interacted with Customs officials on a regular basis and the European and American staff themselves were conspicuously foreign, in appearance, dress and mannerisms, when placed against the backdrop of a small town. The sheer visibility of the Customs, then, meant that anti-imperialist protestors were inevitably drawn to it.

The Customs and Chinese nationalism

Some of the earliest protests came from *within* the Service. In Tianjin in 1912, to give one example, five Chinese members of staff distributed a circular letter among students at the College of Communications calling for an end to foreign control of the Customs.[72] As anti-imperialism became a mainstream political position in the treaty ports from the mid-1920s onwards, Chinese staff began to feel more and more uneasy about working for a bastion of foreign power. In 1927 the Commissioner R. F. C. Hedgeland recommended that Mr Huang Shan Chienghsi in the Guangzhou office, a Guomindang supporter given to vocally advocating an end to foreign domination of the Customs, should be fired. 'There is a clear conspiracy of a group of the young and more extreme men to force on others views which are not to the liking of the latter,' Hedgeland deduced, adding that anti-imperialist agitation threatened to destroy the authority of the foreign staff.[73] Seven years later it emerged that a Chinese Assistant in the Sandu Dao custom house, Ngu Iong Hieng, had been zealously disseminating anti-foreign propaganda and urging local residents to boycott foreign goods – obviously objectionable behaviour for an employee of an organisation charged with administering foreign trade.[74] To the senior foreign staff, dissent from within the Customs ranks seemed to indicate a worrying rejection of decades of foreign-led tutelage from those who were supposed to have benefited from it the most. Despite the tendency of senior foreign Commissioners to downplay anti-imperialism within the staff as the malcontent rumblings of an obstreperous minority, nationalism was clearly a majority position in many ports. Staff unions, often vocally opposed to foreign control, were widespread. The Chinese staff union in Shantou, which reached the peak of its activities in 1927, specifically aimed to oust the current Commissioner, a Dane named J. Klubien, from the port. More worrying still were suspicions that his deputy, the Portuguese A. J. Basto, had encouraged the union. Klubien claimed that Basto 'deliberately misinformed' him about the union's actions, refused to follow his orders and 'fanned the fire instead of putting it out' in an attempt to ingratiate himself with the dissenting staff.[75] This episode demonstrated how the Commissioner's authority, the linchpin around which the Customs establishment revolved at a local level, was severely shaken in the late 1920s. The collusion of senior *foreign* employees in anti-foreign movements turned the carefully constructed hierarchy of Customs authority on its head.

These anti-imperialist actions on the part of the Customs' very own staff also point to the deep uncertainty with which many Chinese viewed their positions as employees of a foreign-run organisation in the 1920s and early 1930s. Ambivalence about foreign influence was characteristic of the broader May Fourth era, a time of exhilarating yet confusing change. Politically, both the Communist Party and the Guomindang advocated alternative visions of China's future. In the cities women and youth were gaining confidence and Confucian ethics and hierarchies were being rejected by some. Foreign ideas were an essential component of this new culture, particularly the oft-reiterated Enlightenment-derived rhetoric of 'science and democracy' and an emphasis on individual autonomy. At the same time foreign power was at its height in the early 1920s. Politically minded urban youth embraced aspects of Western and Japanese culture, yet were increasingly convinced that foreign encroachments were preventing China from becoming a strong, modern nation-state.[76] The Chinese Customs staff found themselves in a predicament. By the twentieth century they had usually been educated in modern schools, knew at least some English and saw in the Customs a chance to get ahead in life by working for a prestigious foreign-run organisation. But in the politically charged context of the late 1920s their work branded them as co-conspirators of the imperialists. Some chose to make the best of both worlds, retaining their professional positions while also demonstrating their nationalist credentials by protesting against foreign domination of the institution.

Chinese Customs employees and the servants of the foreign staff, considered traitors by many of their nationalist compatriots, usually bore the brunt of anti-imperialist movements.[77] Headlines in the Chinese press defaming 'Customs Officers who are running dogs of the imperialist, disgraceful to China's sovereignty and who deceive their brethren' were commonplace.[78] In small ports hostile press could turn the entire community against the Customs, making life dangerous for the Chinese staff. The wave of anti-British sentiment in the aftermath of the May Thirtieth episode lasted for several years after 1925 and was acutely felt in Shantou, where, the Commissioner admitted in 1931, the custom house had long been 'in a state of active defence against the Municipality'.[79] The city's strike committee attempted to drive out the foreigners by obstructing their efforts to buy food and fuel. It was, however, the Chinese who worked for foreign organisations and households who were subjected to special attack. 'The strike was not many days old before letters from a so-called "Blood and Iron Society" began to reach the Chinese members of my Staff, warning them to cease work for foreigners, under penalty of death,' reported the Commissioner, Frederick Carey. Most continued in their positions, but were clearly uneasy. Despite Carey's being given a police guard by the local authorities, the servants' union managed to break into Carey's house and kidnap six of his servants. Unnerved by this incident, all servants working for the foreign Indoor Staff absconded from work the next day and some joined the strike union. 'From the point of view of the older foreign residents of Swatow, the unhappiest feature of this strike is the intense bitterness displayed by the domestics towards their quondam employers, under whom they have been working for years on apparently amicable terms, but whose houses they are now the most active in picketing,' Carey lamented.[80] A similar situation existed in other ports, particularly in the south. More so than any other foreign-run organisation the Customs became a potent symbol of both the foreign stranglehold on China's economic and political institutions and the country's perceived lack of patriotism. In the eyes of anti-imperialist campaigners, those who worked for the Customs or for its foreign staff seemed to represent what was fundamentally wrong with China: a lack of nationalist backbone and a willingness to collude with foreign oppressors.

It is no coincidence that some of the most vociferous anti-Customs agitation took place in the south, the traditional cradle of rebellion and anti-foreign action. Intermittently in the 1920s, this region, particularly Guangdong province, was the stronghold of the Nationalist Party, first led by Sun Yat-sen and after 1925 by Chiang Kai-shek. The Nationalists came to power on the back of an explicitly anti-imperialist agenda in 1927. Chiang Kai-shek's government may have struck judicious deals with foreign powers and taken a gradual approach to reclaiming China's sovereignty, but its long-term plan was unmistakable. Popular anti-imperialist agitation in the late 1920s and early 1930s was encouraged and sustained by the government's stance. Furthermore, although the ultimate success or failure of Nationalist attempts at state-building and centralisation is up for debate, it is clear that the position of the Foreign Inspectorate was transformed by both the new ruling party's ideology and its reorganisation of the government.[81] The Customs, like the Sino-foreign Salt Inspectorate, was incorporated into the Ministry of Finance in 1928 and its supervisory board was downgraded in status from that of a *ju* (the Shuiwuju or Revenue Board) to that of a lower status *shu* (the Guanwushu or Customs Administration).[82] A shrewd recognition that the Customs could provide the new government with its most stable revenue stream partly motivated these efforts to bring the Foreign Inspectorate more closely under Nanjing's supervision. The authority of the Guomindang's party-state was never absolute. Regional warlords remained in power in many areas and the government's control over the countryside was flimsy, meaning that the land tax revenues continued to flow to local power-holders rather than the central government. By contrast, even custom houses on the peripheries of Nanjing's control were obliged to submit their revenues to the central government. The Guomindang's recovery of tariff autonomy in 1928, a major vindication of Chiang Kai-shek's anti-imperialist agenda, made the Maritime Customs even more valuable. Throughout the Nanjing decade (1927–37) Customs revenues covered over half of the government's expenditures.[83]

Nanjing's anti-imperialist agenda, centralising impetus and the importance of the Customs revenues to funding the government's state-building, foreign debt repayment and military 'pacification' efforts all resulted in a loss of autonomy for the Foreign Inspectorate. Frederick Maze, who became IG in 1929, was well aware of the need to capitulate to central authority and secured his appointment to the post of IG on the strength of his willingness to do just that.[84] There were clear ramifications for the foreign staff, who up until this point were answerable only to the IG. Suddenly in 1928 the foreign staff found that they were politically accountable to Nanjing. As a result the Inspectorate now needed to be much more careful about its allocation of senior positions. The British Commissioner Joseph Stephenson discovered this to his cost after he returned to China from a stint as Non-Resident Secretary in the London Office in 1931 expecting to take up the position of Shanghai Commissioner, only to find that the government had vetoed his appointment. 'It is inconceivable to me why you should have continued to consider the possibility of my appointment to Shanghai when you knew that my appointment to the post was not acceptable to the Chinese Authorities,' he remonstrated to Maze.[85] The Inspectorate had always insisted that the Customs was an impartial organisation and that, therefore, the political credentials of the foreign staff were irrelevant. In the late 1920s, however, the political hue of appointments was clear for all to see. As the Staff Secretary observed in 1937, 'it should be considered that with keen competition from the Chinese in the Service, coupled with the watchful eye of the Kuan-wu Shu [Guanwushu] nowadays, the utmost care must be exercised in allotting billets, especially to foreigners, in order not to cause adverse criticism and bring discredit to the foreign staff as a whole'.[86] Just a few years earlier the opinion of Chinese officials about foreign Commissioners would have been a minor concern. The Customs was finally becoming a truly Chinese organisation.

In this broader political context the issue of race, specifically the relative positions of the foreign and Chinese staff, became highly charged by the late 1920s. This had, of course, always been a cause of latent unrest. The Customs could not afford to draw racial boundaries as overtly as other colonial administrative services such as the Eastern Cadetships, the service that administered Ceylon, Hong Kong, the Straits Settlements and the Federated Malay States, which after 1904 required candidates to document European descent on both sides of the family.[87] Nonetheless, inequality between Chinese and foreigners was entrenched in the staff structure. Chinese were paid less than their foreign counterparts, received fewer benefits and until the late 1920s were largely prevented from occupying positions of authority. The first Chinese assistant was not appointed until 1912. Yet Chinese employees had never meekly accepted foreign seniority. Especially in the early years, with the memory of the First Opium War and Second Anglo-Chinese War still fresh, Chinese staff frequently challenged foreign dominance. 'If any Chinese writer refuses to act under a foreign one, *dismiss him on the spot*,' Hart instructed Charles Hannen, Commissioner at Jiujiang, in 1867 after several incidents of *shupan* (writers) refusing to recognise the latter's authority.[88] It was also common for Chinese staff to circumvent the Commissioner and appeal directly to the Superintendent in the 1860s. As foreign control of the Customs became more established, incidents of this type occurred less and less frequently, but the growth of popular nationalism in the 1920s placed them at centre stage once again. Emboldened by the National Government's apparent support of anti-imperialist action and the suspension of foreign recruitment in 1927, Chinese staff became more vocal about this unfair treatment. In 1936 the clerks at the Shanghai custom house submitted a petition to the IG demanding equal status with assistants and pointing out that they essentially performed the same work as their foreign counterparts.[89] This sparked a flurry of similar petitions from various ports, forcing the Staff Secretary to launch a Customs-wide investigation into the similarities and differences between the duties executed by assistants and clerks.[90] Knowing that they had the government's backing, individual Chinese employees also complained about foreign privilege with greater confidence in the 1930s. A 1937 letter from Tsao Yu Chien, a former officer in the Marine Department who had recently been discharged after only two months of service for not showing enough respect for his foreign colleagues, encapsulated the sentiments of many Chinese staff. Foreigners would do well to remember that the Customs is a Chinese organisation, Tsao argued, meaning that 'although they are given suitable posts by Chinese, it was only meant as kindness of Chinese people [sic], and does not entitle them to any power . . . Chinese people are not half civilized and their knowledge at the present time is not under standard, so they cannot be considered as slaves and kept under control'.[91] Such explicit defiance of foreign authority would have been unimaginable two decades earlier. Fired up by the language of nationalism employed by both the Guomindang and the Communist Party and the perception that China's position in the world was rapidly changing, individuals such as Tsao gained a new-found confidence.

By contrast foreign employees experienced deep unease about their future prospects in China. Foreign recruitment ended in 1927, with the exception of so-called 'technical experts', and Maze promised to accelerate promotions of Chinese to positions of authority. Senior staff had long insisted that the Foreign Inspectorate's eventual goal was to gradually replace foreigners with Chinese. Hart had been outspoken on this point. 'The Customs edict will, sooner or later, push Chinese more to the front in the Inspectorate ranks,' Hart predicted in a 1906 letter soliciting H. B. Morse's opinion on promoting clerk Ting I-hsien to the post of Assistant Statistical Secretary. Ting's appointment 'will show the Chinese generally that ability is appreciated, and that there is no objection whatever on account of nationality to Chinese in the higher ranks provided they are fit,' Hart calculated.[92] Most foreign employees, however, certainly objected. Sinification of the staff – the gradual replacement of foreign with Chinese employees – raised the spectre of delayed promotions and even dismissals of foreigners, leading to a pervasive malaise. In 1929 Commissioner Howell in Tianjin reported a 'widespread feeling of unrest among junior foreign Assistants' who were anxious about 'how far promotion will be retarded by the advancement of Chinese over their heads'.[93] Maze replied that the positions of foreign employees were 'reasonably protected' but acknowledged that he could give no concrete guarantee that the services of foreigners would not be dispensed with in the near future.[94] In reality there was little cause to worry that a flood of Chinese into senior positions would erode foreign promotion prospects. Although a couple of Chinese were appointed to high-profile positions as a symbolic gesture calculated to demonstrate that the IG was taking Sinification seriously, such as Hu Fu-sen who became Staff Secretary in the early 1930s, very few Chinese had reached positions of authority by 1936. As Table 4.3 shows, only five Chinese Commissioners and one Tidesurveyor had been appointed by this date. Large numbers of Chinese entered the lower ranks while the number of junior foreigners declined steeply, yet this is more an indication of the phasing out of foreign recruitment rather than evidence of foreigners being held back to make way for Chinese promotion.

Given that the promotion prospects of *existing* employees were not threatened, it is clear that, in the words of the Tianjin Commissioner Edward Howell, 'a dislike of the prospect of serving under the orders of a Chinese' was at the root of the foreign staff's noisy opposition to Sinification.[95] As Chinese moved further up the ranks, senior foreign staff resented these encroachments on their authority, as they saw it. The Shantou Commissioner H. D. Hilliard requested in 1934 that his Chinese deputy, T. Manuel Wong, be replaced by a foreigner, claiming that Chinese were unsuitable for such a position of responsibility. 'I regard your reference to the respective merits or advantages of Chinese and foreign staff as illogical,' the IG's secretary, Lancelot Lawford, admonished. 'It is the man, not the nationality, that is of importance'.[96] Despite his misgivings, however, Lawford granted Hilliard's request, an indication that the process of Sinification still had a long way to go. The Swedish Tidesurveyor at Tianjin, J. W. Ryden, who had worked for the Customs since 1903, also vocally opposed accelerated promotion of Chinese. Responding to a letter about the situation from Commissioner Luigi de Luca in 1932, Maze agreed that 'touchy old servants' such as Ryden were bound to 'resent the dwindling of their authority which these changes have brought about'. Since the changes were inevitable, Ryden must 'sink his personal prejudice for the general welfare'.[97] Many more accounts of outrage and anxiety reached the IG from ports across China. Foreigners bridled at the prospect of Chinese control of the Service because it seemed antithetical to the Customs mission, as they saw it. Their very presence in the staff had long been

Table 4.3 Numbers of Chinese and foreign nationals in senior positions 1928–36

| | Indoor Staff | | | | | | | | Outdoor Staff | | | | | |
| | Commissioner | | Deputy Commissioner | | Assistant | | Tidesurveyor | | Appraiser | | Examiner | |
	Ch.	Fo.	Ch.	Fo.	Ch.	Fo.	Ch.	Fo.	Ch.	Fo.	Ch.	Fo.
1928	–	41	5	24	165	162	–	44	–	30	–	301
1929	–	45	8	22	182	142	–	48	–	28	11	311
1930	4	37	2	28	213	119	1	50	–	42	30	280
1931	3	36	3	28	232	111	1	44	–	42	31	270
1932	4	39	3	25	244	97	1	51	–	45	61	255
1933	4	39	2	24	237	77	1	47	–	41	97	215
1934	4	32	3	24	240	71	1	48	1	44	120	195
1935	4	31	7	22	235	66	1	46	2	50	180	180
1936	5	33	6	16	236	62	1	52	3	60	294	157

Source: SHAC, 679(1) 14237, 'Staff Secretary's office: semi-official and confidential correspondence during 1937: Kiungchow-Santuao', confidential letter from Staff Secretary Hu Fu-sen to Non-resident Secretary John Macoun, 13 Nov 1937

justified by the argument that China needed a period of guidance from foreigners, who occupied privileged positions because they supposedly possessed bureaucratic expertise and a superior character. Recognition of the equality of foreigners and Chinese was a fundamental reversal of this rationalisation. Furthermore, if, as the Nationalist government contended, foreign tutelage in the Customs was no longer necessary, foreign privilege in the Service was untenable. Thus, many feared being pushed to the margins. The conflict between the rank and file foreign staff and the Inspectorate on the issue of Sinification in many ways mirrors the deep divisions between settlers and the foreign diplomatic presence in China that emerged after 1927. In the case of Britain, as Robert Bickers has demonstrated, the efforts of diplomats to dismantle the props of the British presence in China in response to fierce clashes with Chinese nationalists in the 1920s exacerbated the rift between the British imperial state and China coast settlers.[98] The foreign Customs staff, too, became disillusioned with their leaders, who were intent upon renegotiating the Foreign Inspectorate's relationship with the central government.

The foreign staff and the wartime state

The National Government did not push for the total and immediate dissolution of the Foreign Inspectorate in the 1930s because the Customs provided a vital source of revenue and because, as war with Japan loomed, Chiang Kai-shek could not afford to alienate potential diplomatic allies. Japanese expansionism wrought dramatic changes on the Customs working environment, while also testing the Inspectorate's dictum of political neutrality to the limits. The annexation of Manchuria by Japan in 1931 and the subsequent establishment of the puppet state Manchukuo the following year created a vast fissure in the Customs establishment as the Manchurian Customs stations one by one broke away from the Inspectorate.[99] As tensions between Japan and China grew, Customs employees near the border with Manchukuo were thrust into the centre of a looming international conflict. Custom houses in this region fielded ongoing attempts by the Japanese authorities to seize control of their revenues. After years of pressure, for instance, the Japanese consul-general succeeded in forcing Nanjing to deposit the Tianjin and Qinhuangdao revenues in the Yokohama Specie Bank in 1937.[100] Moreover Japanese encroachments created overlapping and contested spheres of jurisdiction, which had the effect of encouraging lawlessness. Policing smuggling in this frontier region near to Korea and Russia had long been difficult, but the Japanese occupation made it virtually impossible to carry out this most basic Customs function. Smuggling was most virulent at Shanhaiguan, a pass at the eastern end of the Great Wall just outside the coastal city of Qinhuangdao on the border of Manchukuo where, as the Tianjin postmaster described it, an illegal drug trade was carried out in the 1930s by 'low class Japanese and Koreans' collaborating with 'a crowd of Chinese whom the authorities are powerless to touch'.[101] According to the beleaguered Qinhuangdao Commissioner, H. C. Morgan, the smuggling was carried out with the connivance of both the Japanese and Chinese military authorities, who rubbed salt in the wound by taunting Customs officials about their inability to make seizures. 'It was not pleasant to be Commissioner here at that time and to be in a position of such ignominious powerlessness, and to know that newspapers all over China were referring to this state of affairs,' admitted Morgan in a 1936 letter to the Staff Secretary requesting a transfer.[102] More than anything, the inability to enforce Customs regulations was humiliating for Morgan and other Commissioners in similar positions. Wartime conditions stripped many foreign Commissioners of their remaining power in China. Japanese military personnel and civilians alike, buoyed up by ultra-nationalism and Japan's military muscle in the region, routinely refused to comply with Customs regulations. The situation was worst at Shanhaiguan where Customs officers attempting to detain and assess cargoes arriving on Japanese vessels or military trucks were regularly assaulted by defiant Japanese importers. On one occasion, reported the Tianjin postmaster, a Customs patrol attempting to seize a ship intent on evading import duties was fired upon by the Japanese crew, armed with 'clubs, sabres and pistols', seriously injuring one officer.[103] The Japanese Young Men's League of North China, a nationalist organisation thought to be connected with the Japanese military, also inflamed tensions with the Customs. In objection to the supposedly partial treatment of Europeans, the League obstructed searches of Japanese passengers at Tianjin. The Commissioner, Carlos Bos, strenuously denied the accusation and deduced that 'the charge of discrimination is a pretext invented by these young Japanese to make themselves conspicuous'.[104] In the 1930s the Customs found itself beleaguered from all side, by Japanese, by nationalist Chinese and even from discontented elements within its own staff. This made Customs work singularly unappealing. The enhanced power and prestige, both imagined and real, endowed upon Europeans and Americans in the colonies by virtue of their race was one of the main reasons why imperial careering was so attractive. Without it there was little incentive to stay.

The Customs had always been a vehicle for foreign powers to further their influence in China, but the Japanese presence in the staff, bolstered as it was by aggressive political and military power, was especially controversial after 1932. After all, no other foreign power had ever exhibited such clear intentions to annex extensive swathes of Chinese territory, not even at the height of the Scramble for Concessions in the 1890s. As popular movements calling for Nanjing to resist Japan gathered pace across the country, the presence of Japanese in the government's employ was especially galling. Long-serving Japanese staff such as Commissioner Kurematsu Yuuji, stationed at Yichang in the early 1930s, saw themselves as impartial intermediaries working to unite Chinese and Japanese interests. In 1931 Kurematsu boasted that his special position as a Japanese national working for the Chinese government had enabled him to arbitrate a settlement between the Chinese magistrate and the Japanese consul over the presence of a Japanese gunboat at Yichang.[105] Kurematsu also raised the hackles of his staff by trying to suppress Chinese nationalism in the port. In contravention of Inspectorate rules he refused to forward to the IG a 1933 petition from Chinese staff who desired to form a patriotic association. In his defence Kurematsu claimed that rather than encouraging further antagonism through nationalist organisations his main aim was 'to foster the feeling of friendship between the two nations with the slogan *pro-Japan* and *pro-China* [original emphasis]'. Maze, however, was livid and reminded Kurematsu of the political repercussions of his actions.[106] As Japanese gained increasing influence in the Service in the late 1930s, as shown in Table 4.4, such tensions became all the more common.

With the outbreak of full-scale war in 1937 the most important custom houses were swallowed up into Japanese-occupied China. Maze had worked hard to preserve what he saw as the integrity of the Customs in the 1930s, but this unfortunately meant that he had made no provision for the likely event of a Japanese takeover. Pushing the Customs dictum of political neutrality to the extreme, the Inspectorate continued to operate more or less as usual out of Shanghai 1937–41. Most of the staff stayed at their posts while the revenues from custom houses in occupied China were deposited in the Yokohama Specie Bank. Commensurate with the expansion of the occupied zone, the Japanese contingent increased precipitously after 1938. Maze may have dressed up these concessions to Japanese pressure as faithfulness to the Customs tradition of disinterestedness, but to most Chinese they were highly political acts.[107] While the Customs' attempts to avoid involvement in local political disputes could be understood, working for the invader and its puppets was something else entirely. The obligation to work alongside Japanese enemies – no matter how long they had served in the Customs – was an infinite source of resentment for the Chinese staff, who feared being tarred as collaborators. In November 1938, for example, one month after the fall of Guangzhou to Japan, the Commissioner requested immediate transfer for one of his Chinese

Table 4.4 Numbers of Japanese, Chinese and non-Japanese foreigners in the Customs 1931–49 (1 July each year)

	Non-Japanese foreign employees	Japanese employees	Chinese employees
1931	1,009	205	2,726
1932	979	198	2,765
1933	1,003	86	2,749
1934	1,043	77	2,990
1935	1,010	71	3,242
1936	994	69	3,498
1937	956	83	3,743
1938	914	269	3,713
1939	862	541	3,778
1940	824	553	3,883
1941	780	612	3,893
1942	515	765	4,324
1943	481	873	4,261
1944	345	1,001	4,088
1945	340	1,001	4,112
1946	311	0	4,166
1947	323	0	4,510
1948	303	0	4,656
1949	289	0	4,627

Source: Service lists database of employees withdrawn from service. These figures include staff working for both the Chongqing and the Kishimoto Inspectorates after 1942 with the following exceptions. The Chongqing Inspectorate service list for July 1942–July 1943 and the Kishimoto Inspectorate service list for July 1944–July 1945 are missing and therefore not included in the table. Similarly, the 1949 service list is missing, meaning that all employees still in the Customs in 1949 – including those who left at some point during that year – are recorded as having withdrawn from service in February 1950

clerks, Mei Huan-tsao, because he 'has developed anti-Japanism to such a degree that he feels he might not be able to control himself in such an office as this, where he would be brought into contact with the Japanese'.[108] During the war the Inspectorate was inundated with similar requests for transfers from those unable to tolerate working alongside or under Japanese.

Worse was to come. The loss of the Manchurian customs houses in 1932 and the occupation of much of eastern and northern China in 1937–38 tore vast rents in the Customs establishment, but it was in the 1940s that the Inspectorate's position, and that of the foreign staff, irreversibly deteriorated. As an international organisation, until December 1941 the Inspectorate in Shanghai was able to remain more or less obedient to Chiang Kai-shek's government in Chongqing, although it had been forced to hand over the revenues to a Japanese bank. All this changed on 8 December 1941, the day after the attack on Pearl Harbor, when the Inspectorate was brought under the jurisdiction of Wang Jingwei's collaborationist government. Maze was dismissed and replaced as IG by Customs Chief Secretary Kishimoto Hirokichi on 11 December. Two days later all British and American employees in occupied China were dismissed as enemy subjects, but the Kishimoto Inspectorate retained the services of most Chinese, approximately one thousand Japanese and one hundred foreigners of neutral nationalities. All those of Allied nationalities who stayed in occupied China after 1941 faced internment after 31 January 1943. On 12 January 1942 a second Inspectorate was established from scratch at Chongqing, headed first by officiating IG C. H. B. Joly, then by Maze followed by deputy IG Ting Kwei-tang between March and August 1943, and finally by American L. K. Little from August 1943. The Customs establishment was now bifurcated; the Chongqing Inspectorate, which scraped together a skeleton staff from those employees who remained in free China, ran parallel to the Kishimoto Inspectorate until the end of the war.

The Nationalist government's attempts to curb the autonomy of the Foreign Inspectorate were not halted by the war. In September 1942 the Chongqing Inspectorate was forced to comply with the 1938 Public Treasury Law, which required all government organisations to submit their revenues in their entirety to the Treasury. Whereas the Customs had previously worked out its own budget, which it appropriated directly from the Customs revenues, it was now issued with a budget and funds by the Ministry of Finance, meaning a complete loss of its financial semi-autonomy. This further blow to the Foreign Inspectorate's status came in the context of a broader disassembling of Western imperialism in China during the war. The Sino-British and Sino-American Friendship Treaties of January 1943 abolished extra-territorality and the remaining foreign concessions for good. Other wartime allies of China followed suit.[109] Not only did the future of the Inspectorate and its foreign staff look bleak. The intensification of the War of Resistance from December 1941 onwards and the growing economic, bureaucratic and political weakness of the Nationalist government meant that the Chongqing Inspectorate was working under increasingly trying conditions.[110] The Customs establishment survived the War of Resistance, just barely, but by this time the foreign staff had been dramatically reduced. By July 1944 only eighteen foreign nationals were active in the Service in unoccupied China. Although dozens returned after the war, they were entering a fundamentally changed working world. In this new environment, when the days of the foreign staff were obviously numbered, many were disillusioned with the what the Customs had to offer them.

Conclusion

The employment of extraterritorialised foreigners was supposed to render the Customs impervious to the political pressures that had supposedly caused the imperial bureaucracy to degenerate into a pit of intrigue and corruption. The Foreign Inspectorate was, however, such a contentious symbol of foreign power and its semi-autonomous status was so confusing that the Customs staff was simply not able to stand aloof. Foreign Customs officials were ideally supposed to act as intermediaries, yet instead of reconciling the foreign and Chinese worlds they were often pulled in two contradictory directions by Chinese and foreign actors who expected them to serve different interests. Furthermore this ambiguous status meant that foreigners and Chinese often encroached upon the indistinct boundaries of the Commissioner's sphere of jurisdiction. The perpetual stream of challenges to the Commissioner's authority demonstrates how imperial institutions, especially those on the edges of formal empire, had to engage in a series of conflicts, compromises and negotiations with other powerbrokers in order to maintain their influence. While it is true that the Customs, as a foreign-run organ of the Chinese government, was in some ways a special case, *all* colonial bureaucracies had to carefully maintain delicate power balances with other authorities. This was especially true of institutions operating on the edges of empire where a greater number of authorities competed for influence and the institutions and structures of colonial power were more fluid and heterogeneous. Like similar institutions elsewhere in empire the Customs had to contend with a burgeoning nationalist challenge from the 1920s onwards. Its position as a mainstay of foreign power at the very heart of the Chinese state made it particularly susceptible to attack. Indeed its answerability to the Chinese government meant that the Foreign Inspectorate was forced to make concessions to the nationalist movement more readily than other colonial institutions. Imperial bureaucracies, then, were not infallible.

Neither were the employees of colonial institutions. Many would-be expatriates failed to thrive overseas. In the Customs the work could be monotonous or, in some branches, dangerous, and the strict hierarchy maintained by the Inspectorate was stifling. In the tumultuous twentieth century there was always the risk of getting caught up in regional or national conflicts, as Edwards and Andreyanow found out to their cost. Many employees simply found China itself hard to bear. Estrangement

[120]

from the surrounding culture, loneliness and ill-health could hit junior members of staff hard. Foreign employees frequently complained about the Chinese diet, the relentless noise and the lack of recreation. These problems were also experienced by Chinese employees. In 1949, for example, a Chinese assistant, Li Hsung Han, wrote to Little asking for a transfer from Zhanjiang on the Leizhou Peninsula to either Kowloon or Taiwan. 'This is a foreign place to me,' he explained. 'I do not speak the native tongue. In fact, I feel that I am in a place which is more foreign to me than if I were in any part of your country.'[111] This sense of isolation was heightened in the case of the foreign staff by immense cultural differences, by their whiteness, and by their status as extraterritorialised foreigners. The example of working life in the Customs, which veered between tedium and danger, provides a necessary corrective to the assumption that Europeans and Americans in the empire world were able to take advantage effortlessly of the professional opportunities offered by the colonies. Expatriate life could also be hard, demoralising and alienating.

Notes

1   SHAC, 679(1) 3659, 'Breaker Point kidnapping incident', letter from Edwards enclosed in letter from Xiamen Commissioner, H. Hawkins, to Coast Inspector Hillman, 10 Mar 1932; SHAC, 679(1) 32371, 'Swatow semi-officials, 1933–34', memo enclosed in S/O no. 617, 30 Nov 1933.
2   SHAC, 679(1) 3659, 'Breaker Point kidnapping incident', telegram from commander-in-chief, British China Station, 29 Feb 1932, enclosed in letter from Coast Inspector Hillman to IG Maze, 5 Mar 1932.
3   SHAC, 679(1) 32370, 'Swatow semi-officials, 1931–32', Maze to Fletcher, 5 Apr 1932; Fletcher's diary account of the kidnapping, enclosed in S/O 572, 16 Apr 1932.
4   SHAC, 679(1) 32370, 'Swatow semi-official, 1931–32', S/O no. 575, 31 May 1932 and no. 585, 15 Oct 1932.
5   SHAC, 679(1) 32371, 'Swatow semi-official, 1933–34', S/O no. 591, 16 Jan 1933.
6   Veronica and Paul King, The Commissioner's Dilemma (London: Heath Cranton, 1932), 199.
7   For the ICS and Tropical African Services see Kirk-Greene, Imperial Administrators, 102–4 and 132–3. For the post-1932 Colonial Administrative Service training course see Kirk-Greene, Symbol of Authority, chapter 3, 42–59.
8   Bland papers, memoirs, chapter 1, 8.
9   SHAC, 679(9) 1303, 'Chinese examination of Indoor Staff', circular no. 1732, second series, 22 Oct 1910.
10 Kirk-Greene, Symbol of Authority, 70.
11 SHAC, 679(9) 2424, 'Mr H. E. Prettejohn's report on Out-door Staff reorganization and comments, May 1930'.
12 Fairbank, 'Synarchy under the Treaties', 222–3.
13 SHAC, 691(1) 15856, 'Stenographers and Typists, Swatow', memo from the Chief Secretary, 28 July 1931, and Shantou dispatch no. 6881, 12 Aug 1931.
14 LOC, MSS84834, Denby Family Papers, 1850–1911, letter from Edwin Denby (Beijing) to Graham Denby (Evansville IA), 9 Oct 1887.
15 Quoted in Herbert Croly, Willard Straight (New York: Macmillan, 1924), 116.

16 SHAC, 679(3) 1599, 'NRS dispatches, 1910', 'Memo of existing regulations', enc. in NRS letter to IG no. 3,773, 17 Aug 1910; SHAC, 679(3) 1603, 'NRS dispatches, 1914', 'Admission to the Customs Service: Out-door staff', enc. in NRS letter to IG, 24 Apr 1914.

17 SHAC, 679(1) 32517, 'Nanning semi-official, 1913–20', S/O no. 120, 27 Feb 1919.

18 SHAC, 679(1) 17142, 'Case of Mr. H. Wyatt, Chief Examiner, and formation of Customs out-door staff union, Shanghai, 1919', Shanghai Outdoor Staff Union's circular letter, 8 Feb 1919; letter from Aglen to Wyatt, 1 July 1919; Fuzhou S/O no. 207, 14 Mar 1919.

19 See Bickers, *Empire Made Me*, 245–6.

20 When the Marine Department was first created in 1868 a Marine Commissioner was appointed at its head. After the department was disbanded in 1870 and then reformed in 1881 its chief was renamed the Coast Inspector.

21 School of Oriental and African Studies (SOAS), London, MS 380628, 'Jack F. Blackburn letters, 1927–41', letter from Blackburn to his mother, 30 June 1935.

22 Tyler, *Pulling Strings in China*, 32.

23 Kirk-Greene, *Imperial Administrators*, 279.

24 This rule was officially inaugurated in 1869 at the same time as the confidential reports system was instituted. *Documents Illustrative*, vol. 1, circular no. 25 of 1869, 169.

25 *Origin and Organisation of the Chinese Customs Service*, 27.

26 SHAC, 679(9) 2339, 'Case of Mr. H. J. de Garcia, 1938', confidential letter from Cloarec to Maze, 16 Feb 1938; confidential letter from Maze to Cloarec, 12 Apr 1938; letter from Garcia to Maze, 7 July 1938.

27 For an analysis of Shanghai's distinctive commercial and economic culture see Wen-hsin Yeh, *Shanghai Splendor: Economic sentiments and the making of modern China, 1843–1949* (Berkeley: University of California Press, 2007).

28 Bergère, '"The Other China"', 34. Wen-hsin Yeh has also emphasised the importance of *global* forces in Shanghai's development: Yeh, 'Shanghai Modernity', 375–94.

29 For the Shanghai labour movement see Elizabeth J. Perry, *Shanghai on Strike: The politics of Chinese labor* (Stanford: Stanford University Press, 1993). For student protests see Jeffrey N. Wasserstrom, *Student Protests in Twentieth-Century China: The view from Shanghai* (Stanford: Stanford University Press, 1991).

30 Harumi Goto-Shibata, *Japan and Britain in Shanghai, 1925–31* (Basingstoke: Macmillan, 1995), chapters 4 and 5, 42–92.

31 Christian Henriot, *Shanghai 1927–37: Municipality, locality, and modernization* (Berkeley: University of California Press, 1993), 1.

32 SHAC, 679(1) 17616, 'Handing-over-charge memoranda, Shanghai, 1901–48', handing-over-charge memo, Commissioner Maze, 1 Oct 1929.

33 See Frederic Wakeman Jr, 'Shanghai Smuggling', in *In the Shadow of the Rising Sun: Shanghai under Japanese occupation*, edited by Christian Henriot and Wen-hsin Yeh (Cambridge: Cambridge University Press, 2004), 116–55.

34 Frederic Wakeman Jr *Strangers at the Gate: Social disorder in South China, 1839–1861* (Berkeley: University of California Press, 1966).

35 SHAC, 679(2) 1867, 'Swatow Customs: Dispatches and enclosures to IG, 1878–81', correspondence between Commissioner Huber and Hart, July–Aug 1881.

36 SHAC, 679(1) 17630, 'Handing-over-charge memoranda, Swatow, 1900–26', dispatch no. 4,021, Deputy Commissioner Currie to Commissioner Gilchrist, 17 May 1909.

37 SHAC, 679(1) 17630, 'Handing-over-charge memoranda, Swatow, 1900–26', dispatch no. 6,268, Commissioner Hedgeland to Commissioner Klubien, 23 Nov 1926.

38 SHAC, 679(1) 32082, 'Ichang semi-official, 1930–31', S/O no. 596, Commissioner Dawson Grove to Maze, 22 Feb 1930.

39 SHAC, 679(1) 32083, 'Ichang semi-officials, 1932–33', S/O letter, Commissioner Kurematsu to Maze, 28 May 1932.

40 SHAC, 679(1) 32088, 'Ichang semi-official, 1939', S/O from Yichang Commissioner to Maze, 28 Mar 1939.
41 See SHAC, 679(1) 17583, 'Handing-over-charge memoranda, Harbin', handing-over-charge memo, Commissioner Konovaloff, 30 Nov 1910 for a history of the early years of the Harbin Customs establishment.
42 See SHAC, 679(1) 17583, 'Handing-over-charge memoranda, Harbin', dispatch no. 2,010, handing-over charge memo, Commissioner Grevedon, 21 Oct 1919 for an account of the tribulations of the Harbin Customs in the aftermath of the Russian Revolution. For the history of nationalism in Harbin see James H. Carter, *Creating a Chinese Harbin: Nationalism in an international city, 1916–1932* (Ithaca: Cornell University Press, 2002).
43 SHAC, 679(1) 17583, 'Handing-over-charge memoranda, Harbin', dispatch no. 3,023 of 1924, Commissioner d'Anjou, 1 May 1924.
44 SHAC, 679(1) 31893, 'Harbin semi-official, 1929', S/O no. 827, acting Commissioner Barentzen, Harbin, to Maze, 22 Oct 1929.
45 For Harbin under Japanese rule see Søren Clausen and Stig Thøgersen, eds,. *The Making of a Chinese City: History and historiography in Harbin* (Armonk: M. E. Sharpe, 1995), Part 3, 109–23.
46 LOC, MSS84834, Denby Family Papers, 1850–1911, letter from Edwin Denby (Beijing) to Graham Denby (Evansville IA), 9 Oct 1887.
47 Houghton Library, Harvard University, MS Chinese 4, Sir Robert Hart Papers, letter from Hart to Edward Drew, 22 Aug 1875.
48 *Documents Illustrative*, vol. 2, circular no. 894, 5 May 1899, 193–212.
49 SHAC, 679(9) 1406, 'Staff Secretary's office: semi-official and confidential correspondence during 1939: to and from Chungking to Kowloon', confidential letter from Commissioner Forbes to Staff Secretary Hu Fu-sen, 17 Jan 1939.
50 Ristaino, *Port of Last Resort*, 67.
51 SHAC, 679(9) 1429, 'Staff Secretary's office: Semi-official and confidential correspondence during 1938; To and from C.I.-Kowloon', confidential letter from Staff Secretary Hu Fu-sen to Mengzi Commissioner Cloarec, 3 Feb 1938.
52 SHAC, 691(1) 31642, 'IG's confidential correspondence with port Commissioners', confidential letter from Commissioner Prettejohn to Maze, 21 Oct 1931.
53 SHAC, 679(1) 17583, 'Handing over charge memoranda, Harbin', dispatch no. 2144, 31 Mar 1930.
54 SHAC, 679(1) 31896, 'Aigun semi-officials, 1921–26', S/O no. 35, 8 Sept 1923 and S/O no. 38, 27 Nov 1923.
55 SHAC, 679(1) 14234, 'Staff Secretary's office: semi-official and confidential correspondence during 1936', enclosure in confidential letter from Staff Secretary Hu Fu-sen to Commissioner Barentzen, 20 Jan 1936.
56 The British Library (hereafter BL), Stella Benson Papers, Add. Mss. 59659, letter from Stella Benson to Stephen Hudson, 4 Jan 1926.
57 Ristaino, *Port of Last Resort*, 81–95.
58 For Customs correspondence about the affair see SHAC, 679(2) 666, 'Chinkiang Customs: Dispatches from IG, 1881–1892', Shanghai dispatch no. 2,319 and enclosures, 21 Sept 1891; minutes of a meeting at the Shanghai custom house re the Mason affair, 16 Sept 1891; letter from Mason to Robert Hart, 15 Sept 1891; Shanghai dispatch no. 2337, 28 Sept 1891.
59 For press reports on the case see *The North-China Herald*, 18 Sept and 2 Oct 1891.
60 For correspondence between the Zongli Yamen and Sir John Walsham about the case see TNA, FO228/1053, 'From and to Yamên, despatches, 1891', Zongli Yamen dispatches on 19 Sept, 23 Sept, 26 Sept, 8 Oct, 2 Nov and 21 Dec 1891.
61 Some of Mason's novels were ostensibly based on his experiences living in China and working for the Customs. See Julian Croskey, *The Chest of Opium* (London: Neville Beeman, 1896) and *The Shen's Pigtail, and Other Cues of Anglo-China Life* (New York: G. P. Putnam's Sons, 1894). The main character of his novel *'The S. G.': A Romance of Peking* (Brooklyn: Mason, 1900) was clearly based on Sir Robert Hart, who in the book has a love affair with a Eurasian woman during the Boxer

Uprising. For Mason's memoir about his involvement with the Gelaohui see *The Chinese Confessions of Charles Welsh Mason* (London: Grant Richards, 1924).

62 Scully, *Bargaining with the State from Afar.*
63 *The I. G. in Peking*, vol. 1, letter Z/59, Hart to Campbell, 16 Oct 1881, 390.
64 See *Archives of China's Imperial Maritime Customs*, vol. 1, letter A/24, Hart to Campbell, 8 Dec 1880, 581; letter Z/37, 30 Dec 1880, 590; letter A/32, 24 Apr 1884, 629.
65 SHAC, 679(2) 1515, 'Shanghai Customs: Dispatches from IG, 1883 (July–Dec)', IG dispatch no. 2,400 to Shanghai, 11 Sept 1883.
66 *Documents Illustrative*, vol. 1, circular no. 11 of 1870 (first series), 10 Dec 1870, 180.
67 SHAC, 679(1) 31642, 'IG's confidential correspondence with port Commissioners, 1931', letter from Macdonald to Maze, 13 May 1931.
68 *Documents Illustrative*, vol. 1, circular no. 8 of 1864 (first series), 39–40.
69 Hippisley papers, MS Eng c. 7291, 'Foreign matters, 1873–91', letter from Morse to Hippisley, 15 Feb 1898.
70 SHAC, 679(1) 17616, 'Handing-over-charge memoranda, Shanghai, 1901–08', Shanghai dispatch no. 14,308, Commissioner Unwin, 1914.
71 SHAC, 679(1) 31642, 'IG's confidential correspondence with port Commissioners, 1931', confidential letter from Commissioner Prettejohn to Maze, 21 Oct 1931.
72 TMA, W2-1-72, 'Outward semi-officials to postmaster general re. the local situation during the revolution', S/O no. 11, 19 Apr 1912.
73 SHAC, 679(1) 32390, 'Canton Semi-Official, 1925–27', S/O no. 314, Commissioner Hedgeland to officiating IG Edwardes, 1 Oct 1927.
74 SHAC, 679(1) 31643, 'IG's confidential correspondence with port Commissioners, 1931–32', confidential letter from Commissioner Chen Tso-chu to Maze, 16 Dec 1932.
75 SHAC, 679(9) 1795, 'Confidential reports of employees withdrawn from service in 1931', confidential letter from Klubien to Staff Secretary Lebas, 10 Feb 1928.
76 See Rana Mitter, *A Bitter Revolution: China's struggle with the modern world* (Oxford: Oxford University Press, 2004), chapters 3 and 4, 69–152.
77 For a discussion of the etymology of the work *hanjian* (traitor) and its specific application to Chinese who collaborated with foreigners see Frederic Wakeman Jr, 'Hanjian (Traitor)!: Collaboration and Retribution in Wartime Shanghai,' in *Becoming Chinese: Passages to modernity and beyond*, edited by Wen-hsin Yeh (Berkeley: University of California Press, 2000), 298–341.
78 SHAC, 679(1) 31639, 'IG's confidential correspondence with port Commissioners, 1929', translations of anti-Customs articles in confidential letter from Commissioner Basto, Jiangmen, to Maze, 10 July 1929.
79 SHAC, 679(1) 32370, 'Swatow semi-official, 1931–32', S/O no. 552, Commissioner Fletcher to Maze, 30 June 1931.
80 SHAC, 679(1) 22162, 'Disturbances at Swatow, 1925', dispatch no. 6118, Carey to Aglen, 23 July 1923.
81 To compare the divergent viewpoints on the success of Guomindang state-building efforts see Lloyd E. Eastman, *The Abortive Revolution: China under Nationalist rule, 1927–1937* (Cambridge, MA: Council on East Asian Studies, Harvard University, 1990), chapter 1, 1–30, in which Eastman argues that the government's efforts at institution-building and administrative centralisation largely failed. Contrast with Robert E. Bedeski, 'China's Wartime State', in *China's Bitter Victory: The war with Japan, 1937–1945*, edited by James Chieh Hsiung and Steven I. Levine (Armonk: M. E. Sharpe, 1992), 33–49, in which Bedeski contends that the Nationalist government was remarkably successful at building the foundations of a modern state considering the difficult circumstances in which it operated.
82 For the Salt Inspectorate's decline in status during this period see Julia C. Strauss, *Strong Institutions in Weak Polities: State building in Republican China, 1927–1940* (Oxford: Oxford University Press, 1998), 84–5.

83 For a summary of the consolidation and operation of the Nationalist state see Peter Zarrow, *China in War and Revolution, 1895–1949* (London: Routledge, 2005), 241–54.

84 See Brunero, *Britain's Imperial Cornerstone*, chapter 4, 79–100, for an account of the 1927–29 Customs succession crisis.

85 SHAC, 679(1) 31641, 'IG's confidential correspondence with port Commissioners, 1931', S/O 'special' letter from Stephenson to Maze, 31 Mar 1931.

86 SHAC, 679(1) 14237, 'Staff Secretary's office: semi-official and confidential correspondence during 1937: Kiungchow-Santuao', confidential letter from Staff Secretary Hu Fu-sen to Commissioner Forbes, Kowloon, 28 Sept 1937.

87 Miners, *Hong Kong Under Imperial Rule*, 85.

88 Houghton Library, Harvard University, bMS Chinese 4, Sir Robert Hart Papers, letter from Hart to Hannen, 30 May 1867.

89 SHAC, 679(1) 32229, 'Shanghai semi-official, 1936', enclosure in S/O letter, commissioner Barentzen to Maze, 12 Aug 1936.

90 SHAC, 679(1) 14235, 'Staff Secretary's office: semi-official and confidential correspondence: to and from Amoy-Chungking', confidential letter from Hu Fu-sen to all Commissioners, 21 July 1937.

91 SHAC, 679(1) 14236, 'Staff Secretary's Office: Semi-official and Confidential Correspondence during 1937', enc. in confidential letter from Coast Inspector Terry to Staff Secretary Hu Fu-sen, 7 June 1937.

92 Houghton Library, Harvard University, bMS Chinese 4, Sir Robert Hart papers, letter from Hart to Morse, 11 June 1906.

93 SHAC, 679(1) 31639, 'Confidential correspondence with port Commissioners, 1929', confidential letter from Howell to Maze, 29 July 1929.

94 SHAC, 679(1) 31639, 'Confidential correspondence with port Commissioners, 1929', confidential letter from Maze to Commissioner Howell, 21 Aug 1929.

95 SHAC, 679(1) 31639, 'IG's confidential correspondence with port Commissioners, 1929', confidential letter from Howell to Maze, 29 July 1929.

96 SHAC, 679(9) 1421, 'Staff Secretary's office: semi-official and confidential correspondence during 1933–35: to and from Shasi-Wuhu', confidential letter from Lawford to Hilliard, 16 Mar 1934.

97 TMA, W1-1-4322, 'Semi-official letters from IG, Jan–Dec 1932', letter from Maze to de Luca, 17 June 1932.

98 Bickers, *Britain in China*, chapter 4, 115–69.

99 *Documents Illustrative*, vol. 5, S/O circular no. 95, 'Manchurian customs: account of seizure of by "Manchukuo" authorities', 20 Apr 1933.

100 Clifford, 'Sir Frederick Maze and the Chinese Maritime Customs', 22.

101 TMA, W2-1-889, 'Semi-officials from Mr. D'Alton nos. 568–720', S/O no. 662 from D'Alton to postmaster general Stapleton-Cotton, 19 Nov 1934.

102 SHAC, 679(1) 14102, 'Staff Secretary's office: semi-official and confidential correspondence during 1936', letter from Morgan to Hu Fu-sen, 28 Jan 1936.

103 TMA, W2-1-889, 'Semi-officials from Mr. D'Alton nos. 568–720', S/O no. 698 from D'Alton to Postmaster-General Stapleton-Cotton, 10 Dec 1934.

104 SHAC, 679(1) 31971, 'Tientsin semi-official, 1934', S/O letter no. 982, Commissioner Bos to officiating IG Lawford, 6 June 1934.

105 SHAC, 679(1) 32082, 'Ichang Semi-Official, 1930–31', S/O letter from Kurematsu to Maze, 13 Oct 1931.

106 SHAC, 679(1) 32083, 'Ichang semi-official, 1932–33', S/O correspondence between Maze and Kurematsu, nos 689–92, 10 Mar–4 Apr 1933.

107 For Frederick Maze's negotiations with the Japanese, 1937–41, see Clifford, 'Sir Frederick Maze and the Chinese Maritime Customs'. Also see Bickers, 'Anglo-Japanese Relations and Treaty Port China'.

108 SHAC, 679(1) 1426, 'Staff Secretary's office: semi-official and confidential correspondence during 1938: to and from IG-Chungking', confidential letter from Commissioner Foster Hall to Staff Secretary Hu Fu-sen, 7 Dec 1938.

109 For the end of British dominance in Shanghai see Robert Bickers, 'Settlers and

Diplomats: The end of British hegemony in the International Settlement, 1937–1945', in *In the Shadow of the Rising Sun,* edited by Henriot and Yeh, 229–56. For the dismantling of the French concession in Shanghai see, in the same volume, Christine Cornet, 'The Bumpy End of the French Concession and French Influence in Shanghai, 1937–1946', 257–76.

110   For the increasing challenges faced by the Nationalist government after 1941 see Hans J. van de Ven, *War and Nationalism in China, 1925–1945* (London: Routledge, 2003), chapter 7, 252–93.

111   Little papers, FMS Am 1999.13, 'IG correspondence with Customs Commissioners and staff, May–Dec 1949', letter from Li Hsung Han to Little, 16 July 1949.

CHAPTER FIVE

Private lives, public reputations: the off-duty world of the Customs staff

The colourful diaries and letters of the British novelist Stella Benson offer a glimpse into the diverse and often dreary social worlds inhabited by Customs officers and their families over the course of a career. After marrying the Indoor man James 'Sheamus' O'Gorman Anderson in 1922 until her death in 1933, Benson accompanied her husband on a succession of postings. With brief interludes in Shanghai, Hong Kong and London, Benson and Anderson spent much of the decade in small outports, including Mengzi in the southwest border region with French Indochina, the Manchurian town of Longjing and the southern ports of Nanning and Beihai. Dripping with derision for the parochial concerns of her neighbours, Benson's writings paint an unflattering portrait of the petty-minded bureaucrats, traders, railway men and their equally unsophisticated wives who made up the small coterie of European residents in these provincial towns. 'I do not see how I can bear living the rest of my life in small outposts,' Benson wrote in an anguished letter to her friend and confidante Laura Hutton in 1925. Such was the lot of most Customs officers and their families. The social offerings of Mengzi and Longjing were a far cry from the hedonistic pleasures of Shanghai, and anyone who joined the Customs anticipating adventure and high living was apt to be sorely disappointed. Benson argued that small-port China was an even more trying environment for women, who found their social opportunities more tightly circumscribed by convention than those of their husbands. Indeed Benson was immeasurably happier when Anderson was transferred briefly to Nanning in Guangxi province in 1929. With 'practically no white neighbours' Benson basked in 'the glorious absence of social Duties or clubs', instead devoting her time to writing and exploring the surrounding countryside on horseback.[1]

Periodic scandals enlivened small-port life, providing a fecund source of gossip and entertainment. Adultery, pregnancies outside of marriage, mental illness and penury – nothing escaped the notice of the treaty port guardians of respectability. Several of these scandals involved Customs officers. Benson's letters wryly recounted the tribulations of the lovesick British Customs Commissioner at Mengzi, married with four children, and his passion for Madame David, a married Frenchwoman. After Benson was forced to suffer through a 'bombardment of tragic confidences from both sides' the Davids left Mengzi in 'a storm of melodramatics', leaving Benson and Anderson to endure 'hours of highly moral yap by the lonely Commissioner on the subject of his Love'.[2] A further noteworthy scandal occurred in 1925. The previous summer a Frenchwoman had appeared in Mengzi with her twin babies, penniless and apparently in delicate physical and mental health. The following year the Frenchwoman was 'recalled in fire and brimstone' by her husband, who lived in Indochina, after he heard talk that a Customs examiner had been spending every night at her 'dismal shack'.[3] A third scandal occurred during Benson and Anderson's short stay in Nanning. Anderson's only foreign colleague in the port, a Swede referred to obliquely as 'E.' in Benson's diaries, was suffering from advanced syphilis. In a dramatic escape from the beleaguered city, then in the throes of civil war, in May 1930, Benson and Anderson attempted to traverse the fighting to get E. to a hospital in Hong Kong.[4] On arrival in Hong Kong E. discovered to his dismay that the Customs had 'made arrangements with a mission hospital – in innocence – not knowing what E's trouble was', which E. refused to enter, 'knowing he would be preached at by missionaries'.[5]

Hong Kong was not much better than the outports, Benson discovered. In letters to fellow novelists Winifred Holtby and Stephen Hudson, Benson mercilessly mocked Hong Kong's pretensions to sophistication – or its 'best-hattiness', as she put it.[6] Keeping up appearances was, as it turned out, all the more essential in a formal colony such as Hong Kong where the boundaries between the British and Chinese communities, demarcated by cultural and social practices, were more strictly policed. 'It is a world of extreme REFANEMENT, and we have almost given up hope of ever being allowed to say or hear anything honest or individual,' observed Benson.[7] Her criticisms were born of more than frustration at the stuffiness and conceit of European society. Eager for an occupation on which to focus her intellectual energies, Benson had turned her attentions to investigating and publicising the plight of indentured prostitutes in the city's government-sanctioned brothels, which resulted in a report for the League of Nations. Her very public chastisement of Government House, which she accused of burying its head in the sand as regards this issue, raised the hackles of the colonial authorities and the Customs Inspectorate alike.[8] Customs wives were expected to enhance their husband's social and professional capital while refraining from 'meddling' in official affairs.

Tedium, squabbles with the neighbours and adultery were common enough in any provincial town from Mengzi to Maidstone. Benson's carping commentary on the tribulations of life in small-port China, however, is significant because it complicates and contradicts the romanticised ways in which colonial social life has been visualised and represented. Benson's writings evoke the sheer monotony of life for Customs officers and their families in China's outports, something which her contemporary W. Somerset Maugham also observed.[9] Shanghai's foreign concessions, imagined as a perpetual cavalcade of revelry and vice, have a seemingly endless allure for novelists, film-makers and writers of popular histories.[10] The reality for most Customs employees, stationed in the most far-flung corners of the country, was likely to be very different.

Benson's letters also hint at the private tragedies, troubles and indiscretions that punctuated the boredom of small-port life. The profusion of euphemistic commentary in the archives on the social faux pas and moral lapses of Customs employees reveals the Inspectorate's nervousness about its reputation. Policing the collective reputation of European communities preoccupied colonial authorities everywhere, given that their claims to legitimacy and privilege were predicated upon the presumption that Europeans represented a superior civilisation. Gregor Muller, using the example of the French seizure of the Cambodian judiciary in order to rein in the scandalous behaviour of French merchants more effectively, has gone so far to claim that 'it was less thirst for power than the fear of ridicule that served as a driving force for the advance of French rule'.[11] A main concern of this chapter is the Inspectorate's attempts to monitor and delimit the off-duty lives of its foreign employees in order to buttress the Service's good reputation and thus preserve its privileged position in China. The near obsession with reputation on the part of colonial communities and institutions exposes the perceived fragility of colonial power formations, which, it was imagined, could be undone by something as ephemeral as rumour and gossip. This was especially the case in China, where the absence of 'formal' colonial rule placed institutions of foreign power such as the Customs in an even more tenuous position.

This chapter also shows how expatriate Europeans and Americans on the edges of empire were expected to negotiate multiple overlapping sets of behavioural standards. The Customs staff were, for instance, accountable to at least three different authorities and interest groups: the Chinese government, the Inspectorate and China's foreign communities. As employees of the Chinese state, they were instructed to eschew the more objectionable practices and prejudices of other foreign communities. Yet they were also clearly creatures of the treaty port world. Customs officers lived in the foreign concessions, drank at European-only clubs, played tennis and took tea with foreign consuls. The ways in which they negotiated these two overlapping sets of behavioural standards and expectations reveal the tensions inherent in colonial communities, especially the heterogeneous populations on the outskirts of empire where a broad range of colonial projects and ideals coexisted and competed. All of this provides a necessary corrective to the common assumption, both then and now, that empire was as an unbounded arena of opportunity for Europeans, particularly men, who were apparently effortlessly able to reap the sexual, economic, social and professional rewards that accompanied 'white prestige'.[12] In reality the power to exploit these opportunities was constrained by a series of official, ideological and socio-economic constraints.[13]

Clubs, class, and socialisation into the treaty port world

Men in white, in evening dress, in flannels, skull-capped priests, long bearded missionaries and their frowsy wives, ladies from the first cabin, maids from the third, German stewards, Chinese, Singhalese, English, Americans, French, Africans, Arabs, all bickering and bargaining; from the Cockney clerk to the English diplomat, from the seedy French priest to Alexander Agassiz.[14]

Such were Willard Straight's quixotic impressions of the human diversity he observed during his passage from New York to China to take up a junior position in the Indoor Staff in 1901. For Straight this international scene onboard ship, where men and women of assorted national, racial and class backgrounds appeared to rub shoulders, was exhilarating. The voyage to China provided a tantalising foretaste of the treaty port world, where he imagined social and racial divisions would be distorted, reordered and sometimes overridden.

Yet Straight's starry-eyed visions of cosmopolitanism would have been dashed soon after going ashore in Shanghai. The treaty port social order was a complex beast, structured around a series of overlapping hierarchies based not just on race but also on nationality, gender and class. Although many Europeans saw an opportunity to become 'true gentlemen' in the colonies, their compatriots overseas were likely to trample on the ambitions of would-be social climbers.[15] If anything, the social pecking order was even more rigorously enforced in colonial communities than at 'home'.[16] Lower-class individuals and other marginals who led less than exemplary lives were deemed a menace to the stature of white settlers, and were consequently pushed to the shadowy peripheries of foreign society. Yet, while it was true that class hierarchies remained inflexible *within* white communities, it was equally the case that *all* Europeans and Americans overseas were expected to conspicuously occupy a higher status rung than most colonized subjects. These two seemingly contradictory impulses defined the social practices of expatriates in China.

Treaty port social institutions imparted both imperial and local ideologies and also taught newcomers the correct way to behave. Socialisation began on the long sea voyage to China for Customs employees recruited in London and the United States. Before even reaching dry land the first stirrings of Customs camaraderie could be felt among groups of new recruits travelling together. An assortment of old China hands returning from sojourns at 'home' introduced 'griffins' to treaty port folklore and provided an object lesson in the various substrata of the treaty port foreign world, and their relative social rankings. The boundaries between the largely middle-class Indoor Staff, who sailed first class, and the largely working-class Outdoor Staff, who sailed second class, were made clear by the style in which each group travelled. In the first-class lounge Indoor Staff recruits rubbed shoulders with high-ranking employees of Butterfield and Swire, managers in the Hongkong and Shanghai Banking Corporation, diplomats and consuls, sometimes making useful acquaintances which could enhance their social capital in the treaty port world. Paul King, for example, befriended William Keswick, head of Jardine, Matheson & Co. and an influential figure in China, on the voyage to Hong Kong in 1874.[17] In second class the Outdoor and Coast Staffs mingled with policemen, railway engineers and, to a lesser extent, missionaries, thus initiating them into the second-tier status they would occupy in China.

Many new Outdoor men were piqued to find that, in the words of L. C. Arlington, 'the Indoor Staff people were treated like Commissars, and the Outdoor like the proletariat', a situation that resulted 'in the complete social ostracism of the Outdoor people'.[18] Rasmussen, too, commented with rancour that 'caste among the Europeans, was a reality that no one could escape, and the outdoor staff in the Customs were almost like the untouchables in India, and nearly as low as the Eurasians'.[19] Rasmussen's and Arlington's comments were not just evidence of sour grapes; annual staff confidential reports were replete with class prejudice. 'Arriviste' upstarts in the Indoor Staff were mocked, Outdoor employees deemed to have got above their station were accused of harbouring a 'superiority complex' and the accents of those from the north of England were derided.[20] Across the empire world class intersected with concepts of race, gender and nationality to determine one's social position.[21]

Colonial communities were highly self-conscious and self-regulating entities, enforcing a strict code delineating acceptable and unacceptable social behaviour. Reputation was everything to European society, helping to secure and perpetuate foreign privileges, which explains why even the most trivial blunders took on an exaggerated importance. Fraternising with Chinese was the ultimate social taboo. European communities in the colonies believed that only by tirelessly replicating a distinct set of cultural behaviours, which set them aloof from, and by implication superior to, local communities could the fiction of white prestige be preserved. In China maintaining separateness was arguably even more essential given the informal and uncertain nature of foreign power, which prompted even greater anxiety about perceived threats to the inviolability of foreign society. Yet, contradictorily, the hybrid institutions that sprang out of this semi-colonial situation seemed on the surface to encourage the crossing of boundaries. Take, for example, Robert Hart's famous 1864 circular outlining the guiding principles of the Customs:

> Whatever other Foreigners resident in this country may deem themselves entitled to do, whether from their position, or fancied superiority to the Chinese, or in the way of showing their superior enlightenment by riding rough-shod over prejudices, and by evincing a general contempt for customs differing from their own, it is to be expected from those who take the pay, and are the servants of the Chinese Government, that they, at least, will so act as to neither offend susceptibilities, nor excite jealousies, suspicion, and dislike.[22]

In practice, however, there was no such clear-cut boundary between the world of the Customs and the world of other foreigners. As Paul King reminisced about his first posting in Shantou, there was 'a good deal of comradeship of an international nature, for in those days all white men on the coast held together and sank their separatist tendency'.[23] The two spheres overlapped and constituted part of a fluid continuum of imperial cultures.

As an organ of the Chinese government, whose position increasingly came under fire as the nationalist movement went from strength to strength in the late 1920s and 1930s, the Inspectorate was keen to cultivate the goodwill of the Chinese public. Yet this by no means gave a green light to social mixing with Chinese. While formal calls on local officials were required of high-ranking staff, they were usually viewed as a tiresome professional duty rather than a source of pleasure. 'I have had to endure 9 Chinese feasts – port wine in tumblers, beer in champagne glasses, and champagne in sherry glasses,' grumbled R. F. C. Hedgeland shortly after arriving at his new post as Nanning Commissioner in

1914 and making the obligatory round of visits to Chinese officials.[24] Closeness with Chinese individuals above and beyond the call of duty was viewed with unease. Annual confidential reports abound with insinuations about the problematic nature of employees who crossed this most deeply entrenched divide. Take, for example, the tidewaiter Thomas Holland who from day one of his employment was viewed with suspicion for being 'too intimate' with certain Chinese acquaintances. The examiner L. A. Hurlow's annual reports from 1922 to 1930 describe a man who, in the eyes of his superiors, was gradually sucked into an insular Chinese world, becoming deracinated in the process. 'He has married a Chinese woman whose brother acts as his servant (boy-cook), and I foresee that he will become increasingly Oriental in tastes and traits as time goes on,' reported the Lappa Commissioner disdainfully in 1926.[25] Foreigners were expected to be courteous and professional in their dealings with Chinese colleagues and the public, but nothing more.

A repertoire of social institutions and organisations, duplicated across the empire world, enforced this separateness and taught new expatriates social rules. Clubs, churches, Masonic lodges, volunteer corps and sporting teams structured the social worlds of European and American communities overseas. Membership of these associations was vigilantly patrolled and designed to keep 'undesirables' out. The linchpin around which European male society revolved was indisputably the club.[26] Ensconced within their teak-panelled interiors was an ambiance of white, masculine conviviality in which colonial folklore, ideologies and hierarchies were continually reproduced. This quintessential colonial social institution was replicated across the empire world, from Canton to Calcutta. In China every port had at least one.

Clubs did not simply reinforce social hierarchies; they also played an indispensable role in cementing and perpetuating European political and economic power.[27] In the secluded confines of the club, essential business was conducted and professional contacts made and cemented over tiffin or else over an after-work gin and tonic, out of sight of prying Chinese eyes. For this reason, lunchtime visits to the club were almost mandatory for Customs Commissioners in the larger ports if they wanted to maintain friendly relations with the heads of foreign trading companies. In 1922, for example, the Shanghai Commissioner, Lowder, claimed that special dispensation to leave the office and go to the Shanghai Club at lunchtime was essential to performing his duties. Indeed daily attendance was required 'for the sake of the prestige of the service'. In a margin note IG Aglen scribbled, 'is this necessary?' The Staff Secretary affirmed: 'Yes, strange as it may sound. Between 12.30 and 1 o'clock all the Taipans and several consuls look in at the

Club and very often important questions can be settled or vexatious controversies avoided by a friendly word said at the right moment.'[28] For ambitious new arrivals, then, regular attendance at European-only clubs was essential to gain access to professional and political networks which deliberately excluded, and thereby disadvantaged, Chinese.

Clubs were status-, race-, nationality- and gender-conscious entities.[29] Women, colonised people of all classes and working-class settlers and sojourners were deemed, to use Mrinalini Sinha's term, 'unclubbable'. As such, colonial clubs were not simply British imports, exact replicas of clubs at 'home'; they were responses to specific local contexts, particularly the perceived need to present an idealised image of an elite white ruling class through restrictive membership policies. As Sinha argues, '[T]he colonial expression of clubbability functioned precisely to ensure that the colonizer was seen as unique and exceptional, on the one hand, and that the colonized was seen as perpetually still-to-be-redeemed, on the other.'[30] One's club membership, then, loudly declared one's professional, racial, national and social status. The Customs, as a hybrid institution, had a more complex attitude towards racial exclusivity, yet the staff clubs established specifically to service the social needs of Customs employees were nonetheless scrupulously segregated along class and race lines. Seeing an invaluable opportunity to foster camaraderie, the Inspectorate was all too happy to sanction the development of recreational clubs in response to staff requests from the 1880s onwards.[31] By the 1920s Customs clubs had become fixtures on the treaty port social scene, serving a dual purpose of providing much-needed recreational facilities in small ports and enabling the Inspectorate to monitor the social activities of its employees and contain them within a distinctive Customs environment.

Yet, like their counterparts in the wider treaty port world, Customs social institutions zealously sought to maintain separate social worlds for low-status and elite expatriates, even in the tiniest ports. In Zhenjiang, with its foreign community of only thirty-five, Rasmussen reported that two clubs were established, 'one for the outdoor staff and one for the Consul, the indoor staff and the merchants'.[32] Both Indoor and Outdoor men were fiercely territorial when it came to their social institutions, which were so essential to shaping and maintaining their respective communal identities. This is perfectly illustrated by a furore caused by Indoor Staff use of the Outdoor Staff library in Shantou in 1884. A proposal to appoint an Indoor man to the library management committee was considered an egregious encroachment on their autonomy by many Outdoor employees at the port.[33] The Commissioner, Colin Jamieson, admitted that 'it is a matter of little moment to the Indoor Staff whether or not they belong to the Library', yet argued that

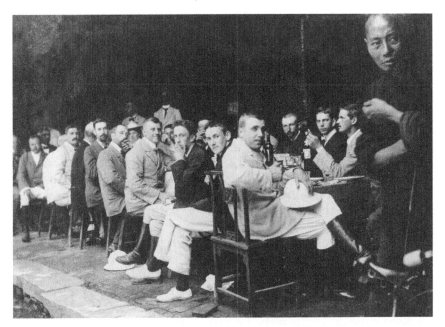

4   The Nanjing Customs staff during a meal, c.1899-1903. R. F. C. Hedgeland
is seated front right

'it is well to maintain this library "point of contact" between the two staffs'.[34] While this episode appears trivial on the surface, it encapsulates the social gulf between the two branches. The Indoor Staff's entrenched condescension towards their Outdoor counterparts meant that the Outdoor Staff had little inclination to share their leisure facilities. At best Indoor employees seemed to view their Outdoor colleagues as an exotic and inscrutable breed best kept at arm's length. Take, for example, A. G. H. Carruthers, Shantou Commissioner in 1917, whose attempts to gamely bridge this deeply entrenched divide by joining the Outdoor billiards club left him baffled. 'They [the Outdoor Staff] are always difficult to gain the confidence of and understand – and incidentally very poor billiard players,' he reported.[35]

The Inspectorate's uncharacteristic eagerness to channel money into staff recreation speaks to its desire to create separateness, not just between the Chinese and foreign staffs but also between foreign employees and the dangerous temptations of the treaty ports. Customs clubs provided a respectable sanctuary, which would shield impressionable foreigners from the insalubrious pleasures that lurked outside. This was the subject of a great deal of hand-wringing on the part of senior employees. For the Antung Commissioner in 1910, the formation of a Customs club at his port was a pressing concern. 'There is in the port absolutely no place where our men can find healthy recreation,' he complained in 1910, warning that 'the prominence of the most undesirable forms of amusement is such in this place that every counteracting influence possible should be striven for'.[36] In 1911 the Shanghai Commissioner argued that the club should be moved to a 'better neighbourhood' without delay because of the 'presence of numerous brothels in the immediate vicinity of the present club'.[37] Club rules, which invariably prohibited gambling and enforced strict opening times, also betrayed a preoccupation with promoting respectable behaviour.[38] While promoting the Customs as a proudly hybrid institution, the Inspectorate was nonetheless ever-fearful of the polluting effect of both Chinese and foreign societies.

Like their opposite numbers in the foreign community, Customs clubs set social parameters based on race. Although Chinese employees were not expressly forbidden from using the foreign staff clubs, until the 1940s clubs were segregated. While this partly reveals an unspoken intent to buttress the privileged position of the foreign staff by fashioning an exclusively foreign social sphere, it is equally true that there were also practical reasons for this separateness. Until the 1920s Chinese employees were usually appointed to a custom house in their home town or province, meaning that they belonged to a pre-established social sphere on joining the Service. Chinese employees, moreover, were often married and had more pressing family responsibilities than their foreign colleagues, who had abundant free time to spend in the club. Also, the gentlemen's or working men's club, a fixture of British society, was simply alien to Chinese culture. This situation changed as Chinese employees began to be regularly transferred between ports in the 1920s. In 1922 the Chinese staff based at the Inspectorate offices, led by a linguist named Charles Leung originally from Guangdong province, requested that a Chinese staff club be formed. Previously most Inspectorate staff were Beijing natives, Leung explained, but 'with the growth of the Linguists Staff appointed at the Inspectorate from various parts of the country . . . it has now become more or less a matter of necessity for us to have a suitable place for recreation, social intercourse, and intellectual development after office hours'.[39] It was now difficult to argue that the Chinese staff and foreign staff did not have similar social requirements – a place of refuge and relaxation which could foster camaraderie between men who were far from home. In any case dwindling foreign staff numbers by the late 1930s made maintaining foreigner-only clubs untenable.[40] In reality, of course, Service social spheres had never been quite as separate as the foreign staff liked to imagine. The Customs was at its core a hybrid institution, which attempted to fuse together the foreign and Chinese worlds while at the same time preserving a privileged position for the foreign staff. In their social lives its staff negotiated a path between these seemingly contradictory forces.

Tennis and tea parties: social life in the outports

Although a minority of employees took pleasure in the bucolic delights of a remote posting, in general nothing served to dampen the spirits of Customs men more than a transfer to a small outport where social life was at best dull and at worst non-existent. Many a Customs employee could attest to Stella Benson's frustrations with the stifling social environment of small-port China, especially in the nineteenth century when China's nascent foreign communities were only just taking root. Edward Bowra, who joined the Indoor Staff in 1863, was bitterly disappointed on his arrival in China to find himself transferred to Tianjin, a port which had been opened to foreign trade and residence only two years previously. Bowra described his new home as 'a dirty little hole of a town, with about six Europeans and a hostile population of half a million'.[41] 'How distance lends enchantment, or how charming the missionary ladies must have shown themselves,' scrawled Alfred Hippisley acerbically in the margin of an 1889 letter from Hart appointing him Commissioner at Lappa and extolling the virtues of his new port.[42] Willard Straight described Nanjing's non-existent social scene at the turn of the century in damning terms as 'a great barren sameness, a desert of Chinese character with tiffin and dinner and tea and an afternoon walk as the little green spots make life bearable'.[43] Like their counterparts in other colonial services, foreign Customs men were often forced to make their own entertainment, especially if they were intent on remaining separate from Chinese society – which most of them were.[44] Indeed many made valiant efforts to replicate a repertoire of social and cultural practices found in expatriate communities empire-wide. Amateur dramatics, musical evenings, tea parties and dances all served a practical purpose of creating a familiar and therefore comfortable social environment and sense of connection with 'home'. For when Customs men griped about the lack of social life, they were really complaining about the dearth of *foreign* society. Chinese society was all around them, threatening to inundate the tiny foreign communities unless they kept their guard up. The endless tennis matches and tea parties that structured expatriate social life were not just born out of nostalgia for home; they also served as a bulwark against 'going native'.

[137]

5   R. F. C. Hedgeland taking tea with the British consul and friends, Haikou, Hainan Island, August 1898

Even in the most rural settings, there was always the prospect of riding, shooting and sports to relieve the boredom. The ubiquity of these sporting pursuits, which cut across the class divide, speaks volumes about the way in which Europeans overseas imagined their purpose and position in empire. Hunting boar and snipe and horseback jaunts into the countryside were not only innocuous leisure pursuits designed to pass the time, although they did fulfil this function. By the late nineteenth century they were symbolically entwined with the colonial endeavour in the popular European imagination.[45] For Edward Bowra, sticking to a regimen of early morning rides demonstrated strength of character, as expressed through clean, hard living. In a letter home in 1864 he boasted that 'at 5 my horse is saddled and waiting and away I go for a scamper across country, astonishing the weak minds of the English students by leaping everything in my way and beating them as easily on horseback as I do at Chinese'.[46] Bowra's youthful bravado encapsulated a recurrent motif in colonial discourse: the effortless mastery of foreign landscapes by Europeans. The motif of European masculine physical prowess enabling and legitimising the conquest of hostile peoples and environments was central to a host of adventure stories and travelogues published in the late nineteenth

The Programme.
·I·M·C· College ·
·April·4th·1902·
· ♪ · ♪ · ♪ · ♪ · ♪ ·
1· Ouverture · ·
·Mr·Deveria
2·Quartette · ·
· ♪ · ♪ · ♪ · ♪ ·
3· Vocal·solo · ·
Mr·Aglen ·
4· Piano·solo · ·
Mr·Praschma ·
5· Vocal·solo · ·
Mr·Straight ·
6· Quartette · ·
· ♪ · ♪ · ♪ · ♪ ·
7· Vocal·solo · ·
Mr·Simpson ·
8· Reciept de Cuisine
Mr·Gory ·
9· Potpourri · ·
Mr·Straight·
10· Piano·Solo · ·
Mr·Deveria ·
11· Vocal·Solo · ·
Mr·Andes ·
12· Quartette ·
學個四

6   Programme for a Customs musical evening, Nanjing, 1902

and early twentieth centuries.[47] Europeans in China, consciously or
unconsciously, sought to emulate this masculine, imperial ideal in
their actions and narratives.

Team sports and athletics served a dual purpose of displaying
European, masculine physical strength and dexterity and fostering

[139]

community solidarity. The popularity of tennis, boxing, cricket and swimming in China's foreign communities speaks to the way in which the colonial discourse connecting athleticism with the qualities of an expert imperial administrator was absorbed into the very fibre of treaty port institutions.[48] To the selection boards of colonial civil services athleticism denoted leadership, team loyalty, good judgement, physical robustness, self-discipline and initiative – all deemed essential components of a good character.[49] What is more, by participating in team sports and athletics, colonisers and nationalists alike sought to associate themselves with manliness and by implication to effeminise either colonised peoples or the colonial oppressor.[50] In accordance with this ideal, foreign-staffed organisations in China often founded their own sporting teams; the SMP, for example, had its own rugby and football teams and a cricket eleven.[51] Paul King forged a particularly sporty path in the Customs, fondly reminiscing about cricket matches in Shantou, rowing in Shanghai and the Customs gym and boxing clubs he organised in Jiujiang, Shanghai and Tianjin.[52] Even those Customs men who were not so athletically inclined often doggedly persevered at fulfilling this sporty ideal. R. F. C. Hedgeland, for example, went to considerable lengths to develop a makeshift golf course in Nanning in 1914 – 'frolic golf, but good-fun' as he described it – despite the fact that only four foreigners lived in the port to take advantage of the facilities.[53] The athletic world of the Customs was at once typically British, typical of empire and intensely masculine. Furthermore, these athletic pursuits were open to *all* male inhabitants of treaty port foreign society, regardless of socio-economic class. Although they rarely played on the same athletic teams as their Indoor counterparts, Outdoor men were paradoxically able to pursue a range of quintessentially upper-class leisure activities, which would have been strictly off-limits in their home countries. Rasmussen recalled how almost all foreign men in early twentieth-century Zhenjiang owned a gun, a dog and a pony, and usually employed a groom, too.[54] Sporting activities, then, encapsulate one of the most glaring inconsistencies in imperial ideologies and the social formations shaped by them; expatriate communities were at once obsessed with demarcating social boundaries based on class, race and nationality, and at the same time were equally concerned with setting the *entire* foreign community apart through shared social behaviour.

Frequent vacations in the countryside, the mountains or the seaside also interrupted the monotony of life in the smaller treaty ports. Holiday resorts across the empire world were modelled on the hill stations of the British Raj. As Dane Kennedy has demonstrated, these mountain-top enclaves fulfilled both a practical and a symbolic role in British India, serving as 'sites of refuge and sites for surveillance'.[55]

7   The makeshift golf 'club house' at Nanning, c. 1919

Mountain sojourns to Beijing's Western Hills and Chengdu's Bailuding and holidays in twentieth-century seaside resorts such as Qingdao and Weihaiwei provided seasonal respite from the 'social and psychological toll of an alien culture'.[56] Some would also take their annual vacations in more far-flung locations such as Japan, a destination which was attractive to many foreign men chiefly because of its difference from China, its perceived 'cleanliness' and the sexual opportunities it offered. Especially for Customs officers and their families, who often lived in the most remote corners of China where foreign influence was minimal, such trips were considered essential to European mental and physical health. Spending too long submerged in a wholly Chinese environment raised the spectre of 'going native', the subject of multiple admonitory tales of treaty port life published in the 1920s and 1930s. Temporary seclusion in a largely European milieu guarded against that fate, causing one to remember one's race, and the cultural and social behaviours that defined it.

Private lives: sex and marriage on the China coast

'I have no desire whatsoever to interfere with men's private affairs,' Hart announced in 1873, 'but, as Inspector General, I cannot stand by, look on, and do nothing, when a man allows his private temperament to harm the official position held by him.'[57] This circular formed the

[141]

bedrock of the Inspectorate's policy towards its employees' personal lives until 1949. Yet there was no precise definition of what exactly constituted disreputable off-duty behaviour. Some situations, such as public displays of drunkenness or violence, were reasonably clear-cut. Others, such as sexual relationships with Chinese women, were more ambiguous. The Inspectorate's rather woolly guidelines on which private actions were deserving of punishment is telling of both the anxieties about reputation and the ideological inconsistencies that characterised colonial institutions.

The private lives of employees were also policed unofficially, through rumour and scandal. Kristen McKenzie has argued that gossip performed a vital regulatory function in colonial societies, defining and promulgating ideas about what constituted respectable and disreputable behaviour. Respectability was, moreover, intimately tied up with defining the status and social rank of individuals within nascent colonial communities, becoming 'a weapon to be wielded in the social competition whereby each would find their level in the new society'.[58] In China's cloistered treaty port communities the power of scandal and gossip was keenly felt. J. O. P. Bland, for example, recollecting the diplomatic community's reaction to his affair with a secretary at the Russian Legation, remarked that 'Peking society lived and moved in a big glass house, all girt about with watchful, Oriental eyes, and diplomacy had perforce its dignity to maintain *"in partibus infidelium"'*.[59] Preserving a spotless collective reputation was intended primarily for a *Chinese* audience. Foreign claims to power and privilege were built upon the assertion that China would benefit from the tutelage of a more advanced civilisation. Indecorous behaviour damaged these claims.

Providing communal living quarters for unmarried men enabled senior staff to keep a close eye on their subordinates. It also encouraged camaraderie and created aesthetic and cultural distance from Chinese society. However, while Customs lodgings in some ports were spacious and genteel, especially the Indoor mess, finding sufficient accommodations was a constant trial in the outports. Many Customs officers were not able to maintain the European style of living expected by treaty port foreign communities. Temples were often converted into makeshift staff quarters as a last resort, especially during the nineteenth century when European-style buildings were particularly scarce. Temporarily roughing it in a temple was usually regarded as a novelty, all part of the adventure of China, by junior employees. 'The living-room was spacious, but in the centre of one side stood a plaster idol nearly eight feet high,' in which there lived a colony of rats, commented Alfred Hippisley about a spell living in a 'tumble down temple' in Wenzhou in 1881.[60] Senior staff were more sensitive to the indignity of such situations. The Tidesurveyor at Leizhou in 1937, despite being one of the highest-ranking employees in the port, was lodged in a temple which had retained its religious function. He therefore had to endure worshippers traipsing through his living quarters for several days each month.[61] The judgement 'unfit for occupation by a European' peppered Customs correspondence about accommodations.[62] Slumming it in a Chinese temple undermined the aura of cultural exclusivity that foreign communities worked so hard to maintain.

The Inspectorate was much less concerned about the standard of living of Chinese employees. Whereas foreigners were paid a rent allowance or else were housed by the Customs, Chinese employees were forced to dig into their own pockets to pay the rent. In 1913 the Tianjin Commissioner tried to intervene on behalf of Chinese employees, who frequently had to spend between forty and one hundred per cent of their wages on rent for one or two rooms, which were home to as many as six additional family members. 'The result of these conditions is that many members of the staff are in poor health and that deaths of family members are frequent, which all tends to diminish the efficiency of the staff,' wrote the Commissioner, in a petition clearly calculated to appeal to the Inspectorate's concern with productivity.[63] The situation was even worse for female Customs employees, who subsisted on a fraction of the wages paid to male clerks. During the War of Resistance (1937–45), when rampant inflation combined with huge movements of refugees to create a housing crisis, it was all but impossible for them to find affordable lodgings. 'In spite of my city-wide search for adequate accommodations I have often been driven from pillar to post. Sometimes I just feel like a stray pup wandering in a strange place, forlorn and helpless,' wrote copyist Miratta Mao in a request for transfer from Luoyang to Chongqing in February of 1944.[64] Petitions such as these laid bare the unequal treatment of female and male employees, and the foreign and Chinese staffs, even at a time when Chinese and foreigners were ostensibly being placed on an equal footing. The result was acute hardship.

The scarcity of suitable accommodation could also cause considerable friction with local communities, which were often fiercely protective of land rights. The purchase of temples or sacred sites was guaranteed to provoke the ire of local communities. At Wuzhou in 1920 the Customs clashed with the local community over its plans to build on a hillside scattered with ancestral graves, and managed to resolve the issue only by agreeing to move the graves to a different location.[65] What is more, Chinese employees were usually extremely reluctant to violate religious taboo and inhabit such sites. 'No Chinese member of the staff is willing to occupy the ancestral temples for superstitious

8 The foreign assistants' quarters, Lappa (Macao), 1906

reasons,' complained the frustrated Liuzhou Commissioner in 1937.[66] In flouting Chinese convention these actions endangered the Customs' status as an institution emblematic of Sino-Western partnership, which was one of the key ways in which it legitimised its continued existence in the twentieth century. More so than other foreign organisations, the Customs could not afford to ignore Chinese sensibilities.

The occasional stay in rudimentary living quarters notwithstanding, the foreign staff, Indoor and Outdoor alike, undoubtedly enjoyed a better standard of living than would have ever been possible at home. A petition for higher wages from the Shanghai Outdoor Staff in 1916, giving precise details of each man's monthly expenditure, revealed that most petitioners considered children's 'school fees', 'rickshaws', 'club chits' and 'tailor' amongst their 'essential' monthly outgoings. *All* claimed that servants' wages were the most costly domestic necessity, accounting for up to one-fifth of monthly expenditure.[67] 'The custom of the China coast decreed that I must keep at least a cook, a boy, and a coolie,' wrote Rasmussen nostalgically.[68] Senior staff employed entire armies of servants, less out of practical necessity than as an ostentatious display of importance. Customs Commissioners needed to impress local Chinese officials, on whom they often depended when

9   R. F. C. Hedgeland's domestic staff outside the Commissioner's house,
Nanning, 1918

carrying out tricky operations such as anti-smuggling manoeuvres, and
also European consular agents and heads of foreign trading companies.
Large numbers of servants endowed Customs men with authority, in
Chinese and foreign eyes alike.

Servants also hinted at one of the most sensitive concerns for
treaty port communities: intimacy between Europeans and Chinese.
Employment of domestic servants at once denoted European mastery
over the Chinese population and alluded to a worrisome closeness,
particularly the potential for illicit sexual relations between European
men and Chinese women. Salacious tales of unconventional household
arrangements in French Indochina and the Dutch East Indies, where
female domestic servants and sexual partners were often regarded as
one and the same, both titillated and horrified foreigners on the China
coast. Ann Laura Stoler has observed that by 'conflating servitude and
sexual service, cohabitation and conjugality, domestic service and
motherhood, these colonial domestic arrangements continually raised
the possibility that some European men were indifferent to bourgeois
civility and not even aspiring to it'.[69] Yet at the same time as mixed-
race relationships were condemned for eroding European sensibilities

they were also grudgingly accepted. While sexual or romantic contact between European women and Chinese men was viewed with nothing short of horror, brief relationships between Chinese women and young, single European and American men of all classes on the China coast were largely accepted as a regrettable yet inevitable outlet for male sexual desire. This was especially true in the nineteenth century when foreign communities were tiny, and the female European population almost non-existent. Robert Hart himself had an eight-year relationship with Ayaou, a Cantonese woman with whom he had three children, which he began while stationed in Ningbo as a student interpreter with the consular service in the 1850s.[70] 'There were generally one or two [Chinese women] on the strength of the Customs Mess . . . amiable creatures withal, models of propriety and honest as this world goes,' observed J. O. P. Bland phlegmatically in his memoirs, although he claimed to have abstained himself.[71] Before the twentieth century, then, the Inspectorate was largely silent on the matter, providing these affairs took place behind closed doors. When they were made conspicuous, however, thus threatening the reputation of the Customs, the Inspectorate intervened. In 1884, for example, the Shanghai Tidesurveyor Fergus Gallagher was forced to resign after twenty-two years of service after he took a Chinese woman to watch the band play at the Astor House gardens, thereby making 'an immoral exhibition of himself'. By *publicly* crossing the race divide, Gallagher had committed the ultimate transgression. It did not help his case that he was clearly drunk at the time.[72] Most, though, avoided censure by conducting their relationships clandestinely.

These temporary relationships reveal not only the ever-present intimacy that subverted taboos about cross-racial contact but also the power differentials inherent in colonial sexuality. Foreign men could usually disentangle themselves from relationships with Chinese partners at will and without fear of consequences. Many such relationships were undoubtedly founded on genuine bonds of affection, but they were nonetheless envisaged as a transitory stage in a European man's life, something that years later could be chalked up to youthful exuberance and the intoxicating effects of submersion in alien, exotic surroundings. The vast majority of middle-class expatriates thus ended these attachments within a few years; acceptable relationships were impermanent and informal by their very definition. Although the Inspectorate was tolerant of youthful dalliances, conspicuous evidence of sexual intimacy with Chinese women was incompatible with positions of power and influence in the treaty port world. Hart, for example, severed his relationship with Ayaou three years after landing the job of Inspector General, apparently judging his private life to be irreconcilable with his new professional responsibilities, and in 1905 he took legal steps to disassociate himself further from his three Eurasian children.[73] While cross-racial intimacy represented a temporary transgression, the fact that middle-class men could effortlessly extricate themselves from these affairs demonstrated to Chinese and foreign observers alike that racial boundaries were still fundamentally intact.

Anxiety about the damage done to the reputation of the foreign staff by sexual and romantic relationships with Chinese women intensified in the twentieth century commensurate with hardening attitudes towards racial mixing empire-wide. As opposition to colonial rule swelled, maintaining the illusion of 'white prestige' by shoring up the racial exclusivity of European communities became ever more important.[74] Furthermore the growing number of marriageable white women across the empire world punctured the earlier rationale that mixed-race relationships were a necessary evil for isolated foreign men exiled to far-flung corners of the globe. This broader context certainly shaped the Customs' growing concern about the threat sexual scandals posed to its reputation, especially from the late 1920s onwards. The Inspectorate was particularly concerned to rein in the behaviour of the Outdoor and Coast Staffs, whose off-duty conduct had heretofore been largely ignored by the Inspectorate because of their marginal status in the treaty port world and because many such employees lived and worked in remote lighthouses or on board ship meaning that their behaviour largely went unnoticed. The Inspectorate's reaction to perceived sexual misconduct among these employees depended on the exact nature of the offence and the likelihood that it would draw public attention. As a general rule, Customs men stationed in remote and sparsely populated regions where news of scandals could be easily contained were dealt with leniently. In 1940, for example, officer Anderson, stationed with the River Inspectorate on the Middle Yangzi, was found guilty of having 'kept continuously a female on board his vessel', the daughter of a coal dealer who regularly supplied the Customs launches at Wushan with fuel, yet despite this being a clear violation of Customs regulations he only received a reprimand.[75] Similarly the lightkeeper P. U. Sorensen stationed near Qiongzhou on Hainan Island was accused in 1938 of 'annoying local girls' tending to cattle and buffalo in the fields surrounding the lighthouse, likely a euphemistic reference to sexual harassment or violence. Despite the serious nature of the accusations, which his Commissioner believed to be true, Sorensen kept his job and was hastily transferred to another port.[76] In contrast Commander Allton, stationed on the Customs steamer *Yunhsing* at Shanghai, was immediately dismissed in 1937 after being found 'guilty of action subversive of discipline and of abusing his official authority by ordering members of his crew to procure women for him'.[77] Allton's high-ranking position, his prominent location in Shanghai and the 'immoral' and public nature of his conduct, which connected the Customs with the city's vast sex industry, made him a liability. Clearly, this all combined to result in his dismissal. The Inspectorate's priority was to minimise the consequences rather than punish offenders.

The public, both foreign and Chinese, was well aware of the potential for sexual scandal to destabilise the Foreign Inspectorate's position in China. After Customs boat officer B. W. Bulbrook was murdered in Shantou by his servant in 1916, the Chinese newspapers printed a 'scurrilous paragraph that Bulbrook was shot by his Ningpo boy for reproving him for being too familiar with his woman, also Ningpo'. The Commissioner suspected that the killing was organised by opium smugglers, as a pattern of similar murders had emerged over the past few years, yet the papers' reporting of the case demonstrated a shrewd understanding of the potential for rumours about sexual contact with Chinese women to cast a shadow upon a foreigner's character.[78] Twenty years later, a British resident of Hong Kong, R. S. Pigott, displayed a similar astute awareness of the Customs' increasing nervousness about its reputation when he accused the Assistant Tidesurveyor at the small southern port of Sanshui, T. Thoresen, of duping, kidnapping and 'seducing' his wife while she was en route from her home village to meet her husband. In an outraged letter to the IG Pigott claimed that he was prepared to halt legal proceedings, which would have surely unleashed a very public scandal, if the Inspectorate agreed to dismiss Thoresen, thereby removing a 'definite dirty smirch . . . from the good record of the Customs Service'. Pigott closed one of his letters with a veiled threat to create an even more public hullaballoo, warning 'that even if it means personal intervention I will under no circumstances permit this swine to remain in Samshui as my wife's people – should they know – may not be so generous as I am'. Evidently alarmed by the possibility of a public altercation, the Staff Secretary expelled Thoresen from the Service as quietly as possible, by paying him off at the end of his leave.[79] In an age when anti-imperialist sentiment was mounting, the 'immoral' conduct of employees could be used as a weapon to manipulate the Service, and further weaken its already shaky position.

Even in an age when reputation was everything to the Customs, though, high-ranking *Indoor* men could still disassociate themselves from potential sexual scandals with ease. An illustrative case erupted in 1941 involving Irene Mok, a typist formally employed in the Guangzhou Customs office, and two British employees, the former Guangzhou Commissioner E. D. G. Hooper and Deputy Commissioner S. M. Carlisle. In a series of impassioned letters written that year from a Shanghai mental hospital, Mok, in somewhat vague terms, accused Hooper of using intimidation tactics in order to prevent her from disclosing a romantic entanglement with his friend, Carlisle, in the early 1930s.[80] Carlisle categorically denied the relationship, claiming that his knowledge of the alleged affair began only after receiving a series of postcards and letters from Mok in 1937, one of which he described disdainfully as 'a most erotic effusion, containing a lurid and no doubt entirely imaginary account of her whole life'. In response he asked Hooper to confront her and warn that Carlisle 'had every intention of taking action, legal and official, if there was any further hint of slanderous insinuations against my name'.[81] After the Inspectorate was brought in to adjudicate, Mok was invalided out of the Service on a diagnosis of 'mental imbalance' because, according to the Staff Secretary, this way 'the responsibility for the loss of her job would rest squarely on the medical decision, and to some extent the staff would be protected from her unpleasant insinuations by the very fact that she had been pronounced to be mentally unfit for the Service'.[82] Of course it is impossible to determine the real facts of this case, but the whole episode points towards the unequal values placed upon different sub-sectors of its staff by the Inspectorate, determined by whether an employee was high-ranking or low-ranking, male or female, foreign or Chinese. Whereas Hooper's and Carlisle's accounts were trusted implicitly, Mok's was dismissed as the delusional ramblings of a disturbed mind. Carlisle's description of her 'erotic' and 'lurid' communications was a further smear on Mok's character. It was almost impossible for a female, Chinese subordinate to impugn the testimony of a British Commissioner whereas, in contrast, the Customs was willing to go to great lengths to defend the good names of senior foreign staff.

Marriage conferred respectability on senior employees, provided it was with a 'suitable' woman, and helped to remove the taint of past sexual transgressions. Despite this, until the 1930s the Inspectorate did its best to make marriage difficult, if not impossible, for junior employees. '"Married Assistants". The IG Circulars are full of warnings and even threats to such misguided people,' wrote Paul King bitterly.[83] Misgivings about the ability of European women and children to withstand the supposed mental and physical dangers of life in the colonies, nineteenth-century colonial discourses that imagined colonial conquest and administration as an exclusively masculine endeavour and prosaic concerns about the extra costs incurred by the wives and families of officials all culminated in a series of restrictions on marriage in most overseas services. Depending on the service, these limitations ranged from stern discouragement to outright prohibition.[84] Until the 1930s the Inspectorate vacillated between summarily dismissing junior employees who married and devising various disincentives, such as denying them extra rent and passage allowances and requiring low-ranking employees to obtain their Commissioner's permission before marrying. The chief justification was that a wife and family would impede the mobility of employees and would saddle the Inspectorate with additional housing and travel costs.[85] Such restrictions were particularly onerous for Chinese employees, who often supported large extended families on their meagre wages. Parsimony may have been the official logic behind this stance, but family life and marriage also impeded the development of masculine camaraderie in the Customs mess, thereby disrupting the Inspectorate's idealised vision of its staff as a loyal cohort of men perfectly attuned to the needs and philosophies of the Service through a process of group socialisation.

By the 1930s, however, deflecting nationalist criticism of the Foreign Inspectorate was a more pressing concern. A settled family life kept a man out of trouble and the domesticating influence of a wife was deemed to be even more essential in small, frontier ports. In 1936, for example, the Wuhu Commissioner warned the Staff Secretary that a bachelor, 'unless he is a man of considerable character, is apt to deteriorate rapidly' as there was 'literally *nothing* to do whatever, nowhere to go and nothing to see'.[86] In the Inspectorate's eyes wives of the 'right sort' contributed to the smooth running of the Service by fashioning a soothing domestic space, providing much-needed companionship, and by presenting an image of conjugal respectability to treaty port society. As a result of these concerns, all restrictions on marriage were lifted in 1937, although because of the hardships imposed by the War of Resistance that broke out later that year the new regulations were not put into force until 1942.[87]

Wives of the 'wrong sort', on the other hand, were a liability. In the eyes of the Inspectorate, a suitable wife should either remain meekly in the background or else enhance her husband's professional standing with her social charms. Those who went against the grain were considered a liability and could damage their husbands' chances of promotion. Commenting on the Shanghai Commissioner, E. Rocher, in 1896, Hart lamented that 'he's handicapped by a wife that produces port storms and not family squalls'.[88] A wife could be deemed unsuitable because of her race, an attitude which played upon empire-wide fears of racial mixing that became prominent in the early twentieth century. Although in the eighteenth and nineteenth centuries concubinage, a form of unofficial marriage, was considered a useful means of increasing understanding of local cultures, by the turn of the century the empire world was riddled with anxiety about such arrangements. Formal marriages were unthinkable and in certain colonies, such as

German South-West Africa and East Africa, mixed marriages were banned outright.[89] Whereas short-term relationships between European men and native women were usually informal, fleeting and sometimes clandestine, marriages, by contrast, were official, enduring and public. They therefore represented an obvious and permanent contradiction to the ideology of white exclusivity.

By the early twentieth century the large mixed-race populations in the colonies were even more unsettling for metropolitan and colonial Europeans alike. Concern about the perceived racial dilution resulting from cross-racial sexual liaisons coupled with falling birth-rates in Europe led to increasing anxiety about the fate of European civilisations, which, it was argued, faced the prospect of being overwhelmed by more prolific races. In Europe this paranoia fed into public debate about immigration and an emergent discourse on preserving and improving the race, propagated in particular by the increasingly popular eugenics movement.[90] In the colonies these fears of racial degeneration found their tangible expression in various policies, ranging from unofficial prohibitions on marrying indigenous women enforced by colonial institutions and companies to the attempted assimilation of mixed-race children into white society in some settler colonies.[91] Short-term sexual relationships and practices of concubinage produced offspring, of course, yet children born of mixed *marriages* added another layer of anxiety to an already charged issue. Whereas European fathers could often easily cast off official ties to their 'illegitimate' children, as Robert Hart did with his Eurasian family, children born in marriage were legally recognised as the 'legitimate' offspring of their fathers and thus created a host of legal and discursive ambiguities.[92] Should nationality and citizenship be determined by race or by the status of one's father? Should race be defined by parentage or by an elusive concept of cultural and racial sensibility? In European societies in the empire world, whose very claims to govern rested upon their supposedly superior and exclusive qualities, questions such as these carried real weight. The existence of a permanent mixed-race community, many members of which had a European nationality and therefore enjoyed the legal privileges endowed by such a status, raised the spectre of a steady erosion of the fiction of 'white prestige'.[93]

In China's foreign communities attitudes were no different. As Henry Lethbridge has commented with regard to Hong Kong, 'Eurasians in a European social gathering created a climate of unease and psychological tension'.[94] Lacking formal governing authority in China, foreign communities were not able to enforce official restrictions on mixed marriages, yet they certainly made their disapproval felt. The way in which the Customs dealt with marriages between Chinese women and foreign

[151]

staff complicates this picture further. Foreign Customs employees worked for a *Chinese* organisation alongside Chinese colleagues who should be considered as brothers and who increasingly in the 1920s and 1930s occupied a similar professional status. To take a prohibitive stance on mixed marriages would have undermined this keystone of Customs identity. Furthermore as a Chinese state organ which also aimed to protect foreign economic interests, the Inspectorate was wary of offending the sensibilities of foreign and Chinese communities alike.

Such unions appear to have been very rare in the Indoor Staff ranks. Middle-class men were well aware of their assigned role as guardians of Europeanness and most had no desire to ostracise themselves from 'respectable' society by marrying Chinese women. A rare case involving a junior assistant in the Indoor Staff, W. Fitzgibbon, who was stationed at Changsha, came to Aglen's attention in 1911. Fitzgibbon had 'bought a girl betrothed under Chinese custom to one man, and who has cohabited for some years with another', and then secretly married her. The case, Aglen claimed, had resulted in a 'scandal most damaging to the good name of the Service' and served to prove that Fitzgibbon was 'deficient in some moral qualities which we have a right to look for in our Indoor Staff'. 'Continued unemployment is impossible,' he decided.[95] Not only did his 'immoral' actions threaten the Customs' reputation under the censorious gaze of foreign society; his flouting of marriage customs also had the potential to cause friction with the local Chinese community.

Working-class employees were subject to less censure. Lower-level employees were pushed to the margins of 'respectable' foreign society and therefore often mixed more freely with Chinese communities. There are no exact figures, but it appears that marriages between Chinese women and members of the Outdoor and Coast staffs were fairly common. Unlike their middle-class, Indoor Staff counterparts, employees in these branches envisaged putting down permanent roots in China. They were therefore much more likely to marry Chinese women and raise families in China. Such marriages became an official problem only if the men in question attained higher-ranking positions in the Service. In 1937, for example, the Commissioner at Nanjing reported that the newly appointed British Tidesurveyor was 'totally unsuited' to the position entirely because he was 'married to a Cantonese woman and for that reason is not exactly *persona grata* with Chinese and foreigners alike'.[96] Matters were made worse by the fact that Broderick's house was 'to all intents and purposes inside the British embassy compound', thereby placing a Eurasian family squarely in the middle of this British enclave. Not only did Broderick's marriage cause raised eyebrows among foreign residents; the southern origins of his wife were scorned by the residents of the Yangzi River city of Nanjing. For a man whose professional position required eliciting the respect of Chinese and foreigners alike, his marriage was doubly objectionable.

For the most part, however, the Inspectorate cared little about the race of a low-ranking Outdoor man's wife so long as it did not bring public opprobrium upon the Service. Yet, in the 1930s, interfering in the marital lives of employees, should they threaten to cause gossip, became the Inspectorate's modus operandi. Most noticeably, senior Customs officials, concerned that divorces would jeopardise the Service's reputation, began to adjudicate more frequently in the marital difficulties of employees. In a striking case from 1935, for example, the Shantou Commissioner reported that the Customs appraiser A. E. V. Nielsen, despite being married and a father to five children, had 'become very enamoured with the typist in the General Office' and insisted on showering her with expensive and conspicuous gifts, including a piano. The very public nature of Nielsen's infatuation was becoming a distinct embarrassment to the Shantou Customs establishment, especially after Mrs Nielsen (who was Chinese) lodged a complaint with the Danish consul about her husband's plans to send her and their children to live in his native Denmark 'so as to be free to follow up his "affaire du coeur"'. 'In view of the danger of a scandal and a break up of the Nielsen family and the slur this would cast on the Service', Nielsen was hastily transferred to Shanghai in the hope that his passion for the typist would subside if he were posted far from Shantou.[97] The Inspectorate's imperative was to avoid unwelcome publicity which endangered the wholesome image of the Customs at a time when it needed to revive confidence in the good character and dedication of its staff.

Debt, drink and disorderliness

Debt, drunkenness and violence were even more insidious problems in the foreign staff and were perceived as evidence of worrisome character deficiencies which threatened to undermine the influence of the Service. Cases of unruly conduct were more frequently reported among the low-ranking Outdoor and Coast staffs, employees who already occupied the lowest rung on the social and professional hierarchies of the China coast and therefore had the least to lose in terms of reputation. Indebtedness was a particular sore point for the Inspectorate, as it placed non-Customs agents in a position of power over employees. From the earliest years of the Service, staff handbooks enjoined employees to avoid borrowing money from 'any merchant or person transacting business at the Custom House' or from 'any subordinate member of the Service'.[98] Debts had the potential to undermine both internal staff hierarchies and the Customs' authority in the treaty port world. As with other aspects of private conduct, the Inspectorate exhibited heightened concern about the damaging effect of indebtedness on the Service's reputation in the 1930s. One ongoing saga, which was the subject of voluminous correspondence in the late 1930s, involved W. Mahan, Commander of a Customs vessel, the *Liuhsing*, stationed in Xiamen. In 1937 it came to light that Mahan had accumulated a host of debts, including a medical bill from a Hong Kong hospital and an unpaid balance of $500 at a British-owned wine merchant. Later in the year Mahan's impecunious behaviour caused his superiors even more embarrassment when two of his creditors at Fuzhou petitioned the British consul to intercede with the Customs on their behalf. Mahan's debts had thus ceased to be a private matter. Indeed his private behaviour was explicitly considered as a reflection on Mahan's professional abilities. 'The casual attitude he assumes with regard to his debts is reflected in the way he carries out his duties in general,' declared the Xiamen Commissioner. The fact that one of his debts was 'to a widow (now at home) exceedingly hard up' was a further blot on Mahan's character.[99]

At the same time as Mahan was accumulating arrears in the southeast, the disturbing prevalence of debt among the River Inspectorate staff was causing alarm. So many employees were found to owe money that the River Inspector, W. D. Fraser, was forced to issue a general warning to his staff. 'That I have been placed in the very embarrassing position of debt collector both for service and private accounts is due entirely to the utterly irresponsible behaviour of certain River Officers, who have recklessly run into debt in a most dishonourable manner, thereby bringing the service into disrepute,' he scolded. The debts of foreign employees damaged the prestige of the Service by casting doubt upon the character and dependability of the staff. 'Character, reliability and sense of responsibility are indispensable adjuncts to a successful career,' Fraser lectured, 'and the officer who through his own fault suffers from chronic impecuniosity has no proper place on the staff of the River Inspectorate'.[100] The inability of some employees to manage their finances successfully indicated that they did not possess the strength of character expected of a Customs man. What is more, employees who were beholden to non-Customs creditors and businesses diminished the trustworthiness of the Service in the eyes of the public. Such bonds seriously undermined the Customs' raison d'être: the creation of a scrupulously honest service able to manage foreign trade *impartially*.

Insobriety, the quintessential 'colonial condition', was similarly regarded as proof of a fundamental moral laxity. Colonial society, with its short working hours, club-centred social life, frequent lack of family responsibilities and loneliness, created an environment conducive to chronic over-indulgence. The Customs was no different in this respect, and reports of drinking problems amongst the foreign staff abounded from the Service's inception until the very end of its days. This was a particularly embarrassing problem for the Inspectorate given its pious stance on opium-smoking among Chinese employees. Indeed the widespread European perception of the Chinese imperial bureaucracy as enfeebled by endemic opium addiction helped to legitimise the very existence of the foreign staff, who, it was implied, would revitalise the organisation with wholesome European vigour. Insobriety while on duty and bouts of off-duty drinking that impaired employees' abilities to perform their work undermined this assumption and therefore usually led to instant dismissal for members of the Outdoor and Coast staffs. This was the single most common cause of dismissal in the lower ranks of the Service.

As with other indecorous aspects of off-duty conduct, intoxication in an employee's private life became a serious issue only when it elicited public complaints or otherwise undermined the authority of the foreign staff. There are countless examples of foreign employees – usually Outdoor men – making public spectacles of themselves while under the influence, something which was often linked to violent behaviour. In the nineteenth century most reports of drunken tidewaiters publically embarrassing the Service came from Shanghai, the port that was fast becoming known as a site of riotous, cosmopolitan decadence. Several months after being dismissed for public drunkenness in August 1864, the British tidewaiter M. Molineux was given a second chance in view of his long service and reinstated. This proved to be an error of judgement and in June 1865 Molineux was once again dismissed, this time for good, after being 'found intoxicated about the streets and put in prison by the Municipal Police'.[101] After the Austrian tidewaiter F. J. Hegrat's heavy off-duty drinking habits came to light in May 1883 he was pressured into signing a pledge to refrain from drinking alcohol for twelve months, with the caveat that he would be obliged to forfeit one month's salary to 'some charitable institution' should he break his promise. Unfortunately, this measure failed to curb his drinking and in February 1884 Hegrat was dismissed after throwing a tumbler at the Customs club 'Bar Boy' while drunk.[102] In the same year the Shanghai Commissioner received complaints from a Mr Yoshioga about the drunken late-night behaviour of his neighbour, the French tidewaiter E. Bonneau, who acted 'with a good deal of violence and in a most disorderly manner every night', and also made a habit of throwing stones and buckets of water at visitors to Yoshioga's house.[103] Bonneau was discharged from the Service four months later. All three of these cases demonstrate a keen concern with the reputation of the Shanghai custom house, which was the most commercially important in China and therefore very much in the public eye. Molineux's arrest by the Shanghai Municipal Police humiliated the Customs by undermining its reputation with the British-dominated authorities of the International Settlement. Hegrat's and Bonneau's violence, coupled with the racist overtones of their conduct, had the potential to provoke Chinese and Japanese resentment. In an age when the Customs tended to be regarded as a meddlesome interloper by Chinese and foreigners alike, the Inspectorate dealt swiftly and severely with such incidents.

By the late 1920s anxiety about inebriated employees shaming the Service had redoubled. The Inspectorate now cast a wider net in its efforts to suppress embarrassing off-duty behaviour, and reports on employee drinking habits flooded in from harried Commissioners in the outports. Boat officer Walters's drinking was an ongoing headache for the Inspectorate. His habit first came to light in 1929 when the Qiongzhou Commissioner reported that Walters was 'addicted to beer-drinking in such a manner as his intemperance will not interfere with his service duty but [is] sufficiently bad enough to spoil his reputation as a Boat Officer in the eyes of the native crew'.[104] Five years later the Ningbo Commissioner echoed the same concerns when he reported that Walters's off-duty conduct had severely undermined his authority, meaning he was regarded by his subordinates 'as a mere figurehead and a tool in their hands'. What is more, within Ningbo's foreign community Walters's raucous drunken behaviour had 'given rise to much criticism and complaint', to such an extent that the Commissioner was 'once placed in a very embarrassing position when a foreign lady asked me in a social gathering to chase him out of the room'.[105] Walters was subsequently paid off for unsatisfactory conduct. In addition to damaging the Service's prestige with the foreign community, Walters's personal habits made him an object of ridicule with his Chinese crew, thus undermining the strict professional and racial hierarchies that the Inspectorate worked so hard to maintain.

Violence was even more disconcerting. Aggressive behaviour unleashed by heavy drinking was expected, if not condoned, and violence in the line of duty was even championed. In 1880, for example, Hart vowed to fight the case of the Guangzhou tidewaiter Page, discussed in Chapter 3, who had shot and killed a Chinese smuggler, 'to the nth'.[106] Unprovoked violence, on the other hand, exposed the dark underbelly of the Service, which was far removed from the image of a principled and disciplined foreign staff that the Customs wished to cultivate. Violence was a core feature of all colonial societies, and the use of coercion and brutality to subdue colonised populations during the initial stages of conquest and consolidation and in the period of decline and decolonisation is well-documented.[107] Yet, although most historiography has focused on the use of violence in the creation and dissolution of the colonial state, it was also crucial to the maintenance of colonialism, and was thus endemic in colonial labour, policing and judicial systems.[108] The Customs, however, considered itself to be aloof from the squalid brutality of colonial society. As a service that was ultimately answerable to the Chinese government the Inspectorate's official line was that violence towards Chinese colleagues, servants or members of the public would not be tolerated.

In reality foreign employees, especially Indoor men, were often given second, or even third and fourth chances, after being found guilty of violence. This was especially true in the nineteenth century, a time when China's dealings with the outside world were punctuated and reinforced by frequent acts of violence. Many early Customs men were recruited from the remnants of foreign armies in China. Moreover, the broader context of conflict worked to normalise violent relations between foreigners and Chinese, something that is very much apparent in the Customs record. In 1864, for example, just four years after the end of the Arrow War, the British Indoor employee M. R. Mercer was reprimanded for beating his servant as punishment for forgetting to change his bathwater. Mercer was a thoroughly unpleasant character, the Shanghai Commissioner Thomas Dick reported, who had deliberately made enemies amongst the other non-British Customs employees in his quarters on the grounds 'that they were "foreigners"'. Furthermore, Dick reminded Hart, there had been two previous incidents 'of beating Chinese' in the Shanghai Customs in 1864 alone.[109] Mercer was, notwithstanding his violent conduct, permitted to stay in the Service until his resignation in 1871. A brutal attack perpetrated by three foreign Outdoor employees in Guangzhou, which left one Chinese man dead and two wounded, provoked a tougher response from the IG, probably because of the public outrage generated. All three were immediately dismissed and their superiors at Guangzhou were transferred to a different port.[110] Violence committed against Chinese by foreign Customs men underscores how the Inspectorate's efforts to style its foreign employees as benevolent tutors of China operated in tension with broader treaty port norms of racist violence.

Violence was not only committed upon Chinese bodies by foreign Customs officers. Within Service ranks there were inevitably bullies, who made a habit of tormenting their foreign colleagues and subordinates. One such person came to the Inspectorate's attention in 1886 when a fracas broke out in Shanghai between the British tidewaiters J. Roberts, T. J. Howell and B. Davis, who were accused of 'having behaved in a disorderly and disgraceful manner whilst on duty, and in uniform'. Davis was the main culprit, according to the Commissioner's report. His ceaseless harassment of Roberts and Howell had eventually provoked them to violence. Shortly after joining the Service the previous year, Howell recounted, Davis had asked him to provide assistance to a Mrs Sinnott, the widow of a recently deceased officer in the Outdoor Staff, who was attempting to establish a boarding house. Howell agreed, but soon after moving into the establishment he discovered that Davis was having an affair with Mrs Sinnott, that he frequently attacked her and her children, and that the boarding house was generally a hotbed of immorality. On one occasion, Howell reported:

> I heard Mr. Davis using filthy and disgusting language to Mrs. Sinnott in reference to a man he accused her of being intimate with, she denied it and he then made a rush at her she passed through a glass door and slammed it he raised his fist to make a hit at her and put his hand through the pane of glass . . . During the whole of this he was stark naked in the presence of the children (one of whom I would wish to state is a girl lacking three months of being fifteen years old). As a father of a family my feelings at such a sight were very much hurt and I should have left at once but both he and Mrs. Sinnott begged so hard that I would spare them the scandal that I consented to keep quiet and remain. Things for a while went on very well but after a few days he commenced his orgies again abusing both her and the children. In fact the sights that I have seen would never be credited without people could witness it.[111]

This lurid scene was hardly the image of respectable domesticity that the Service desired its staff to cultivate. Howell's detailed account of this episode, which was not directly related to the case in hand, demonstrates his awareness of the weight attached to maintaining a good reputation. His story impugned Davis's character in several interrelated ways, highlighting not only his violence but also the sexual immorality of his affair with recently widowed Mrs Sinnott and his shocking lack of decency in appearing naked in front of Sinnott's children. All of this amounted to evidence that Davis exhibited a dangerous lack of control over his violent and sexual impulses, traits that were apt to plunge the Customs into a scandal. Across the empire world violence revealed a fundamental tension in imperial ideologies. Coercion and brutality often underpinned the formation and maintenance of colonial systems, yet one of the principal legitimising rationales of colonialism was the insistence that Europeans brought cool-headed leadership, strength of character and discipline to precolonial societies. The Inspectorate used much the same rhetoric to validate the existence of the foreign staff, yet violence, drunkenness and debt pointed instead to hot-headedness, moral weakness and impulsiveness.

Conclusion

Although colonial arrivism was derided by contemporary commentators such as Stella Benson and W. Somerset Maugham, social life is what feeds much empire nostalgia. Images of cocktails at the club, tennis matches played in subtropical heat, tea parties on the veranda, and languorous summers spent at hilltop retreats pervade this rose-tinted view of empire, a world that is imagined as benign, opulent and administered entirely by upper-class Englishmen. This conservative imperial history has been retooled for a postcolonial age in works such as David Cannadine's *Ornamentalism: How the British Saw Their Empire*, which argues that the empire represented the British class system writ large.[112] In this view colonialism gave the increasingly anachronistic landed aristocracy a new lease of life, as expressed through the absurdities of colonial pomp and ceremony and the puffed-up honours system. The case of the Customs foreign staff *does* serve to remind us of the fixation with status in colonial communities. Yet in the archives of overseas services such as the Customs a rather more desperate tale is told, one which brings to light the social anxieties and failures of many colonial expatriates, something which is overlooked if one focuses solely on the ruling elite. What is more, the status system of empire was infinitely more complex than a simple 'extension of British social structures . . . to the ends of the world'.[113] An individual's status was not only determined by class but was also defined in relation to others of a different nationality, gender, and race. In particular, the centrality of race in constructing social hierarchies in the empire world cannot be underestimated. Even in a self-proclaimed hybrid, tolerant organisation such as the Customs professional and social status could be undone by social or sexual relations with Chinese. Furthermore, one's place in social and professional hierarchies was determined by the precise meanings that these signifiers of class, nationality, gender, and race took on in specific colonial contexts.

In many ways the obsession with status and making and maintaining reputations speaks to the pervasive disquiet about the long-term viability of colonial institutions and societies. The fiction of 'white prestige' could be sustained only by delineating strict status divisions and by pushing those who did not fit the archetype of the ruling elite – in other words, non-whites, women and marginal Europeans – to the peripheries of colonial society. Furthermore, in the treaty port world, where respectability was everything, the private became public. In part this was a symptom of the insularity of China's foreign communities, but it also speaks to the importance placed upon the domestic sphere as a site where imperial loyalties and ideologies were taught and strengthened across the empire world.[114] Of course, behind closed doors social, sexual and racial taboos could also be clandestinely broken. For both these reasons personal lives were a subject of intense scrutiny, by colonial authorities, imperial organisations and the self-appointed moral watchdogs of European society. This meant that Customs men were never entirely off duty.

The multilayered responses to the private conduct of Europeans overseas also expose the internal conflicts that pervaded imperial ideologies and institutions. Empire was often imagined as an exotic arena of sexual and social freedom for European men, yet colonial societies, institutions and authorities were intent upon reining in the impulse to exploit these opportunities. In the case of the Customs, unruly private conduct laid bare the gap between the Inspectorate's lofty vision of its staff as a loyal and principled cohort of men and the reality of attitudes and behaviour on the ground. Furthermore, although the Inspectorate insisted that foreign employees should consider themselves as the de facto countrymen of their Chinese colleagues, in reality it was intent upon preserving the elite standing of the foreign staff, especially after its position became increasingly shakier in the 1920s and 1930s. Disorderly behaviour unravelled the foreign staff's claims to a monopoly on civility, its principal raison d'être, and thus its legitimacy. Hence the Inspectorate's heightened fixation on private conduct and public reputations in the face of intensifying nationalist opposition to its existence.

Could rumour and gossip unseat colonial power in any tangible way? Although scandals could be used as ammunition by nationalists, it is doubtful that most colonised peoples cared particularly about the private antics of Europeans or acknowledged the white ruling elite as a model of civility and good character. The fixation on status and reputation is best understood as a reflection of the anxieties of colonisers themselves about the fallibility of colonial ventures, particularly as the privileged position of white communities began to be seriously challenged in the twentieth century. In an organisation such as the Customs these tensions and concerns were amplified owing to the hybrid character of the institution; neither the Chinese government nor the foreign diplomatic establishment had a clear vested interest in preserving the Foreign Inspectorate by the late 1920s and neither party was thus prepared to fight for its future. In this situation the Inspectorate had nothing but the time-honoured reputation of its foreign staff to justify

[160]

and ensure its survival. As such it imagined that something as illusory as a rumour could topple the entire edifice.

Notes

1 BL, Schiff Papers, Add Ms 52916 vol. 1 fos 55–96, letter to Sydney Schiff (al. Stephen Hudson), 6 Nov 1931; BL, Benson papers, Add Ms 59659 fos 201–21, letter to Winifred Holtby, 21 Apr 1930.
2 BL, Benson papers, Add Ms 59659 fos 1–161, letters to Laura Hutton, 29 Aug and 6 Sept 1924.
3 BL, Benson papers, Add Ms 59659 fos 1–161, letters to Laura Hutton, 29 Aug 1924 and 19 Feb 1925.
4 George M. Johnson, 'Stella Benson (6 January 1892 – 6 December 1933)', in *British Short Fiction Writers, 1915–1945, Dictionary of Literary Biography Vol. 162*, edited by John H. Rogers (Detroit: Gale Research, 1996), 28. The escape was fictionalised in Benson's short story 'The Desert Islander', first published in *Harper's Monthly Magazine*, June 1930, and later collected in *Hope against Hope and Other Stories* (1931).
5 BL, Benson papers, Add Ms 59659 fos 222–40, Benson's diary, 5–17 May 1930.
6 BL, Benson papers, Add Ms 59659 fos 201–21, letters to Winifred Holtby, 29 June & 27 Aug 1930.
7 BL, Schiff Papers, Add Ms 52916, vol. 1 fos 55–96, letter to Sydney Schiff (al. Stephen Hudson), 21 Mar 1931.
8 BL, Benson papers, Add Ms 59659 f 201–21, letter to Winifred Holtby, 29 Oct 1930.
9 See W. Somerset Maugham, *On a Chinese Screen* (London: Vintage, 2000; 1st edition 1922), 'The Fannings', 76–9.
10 See Dong, *Shanghai*; Christopher New, *Shanghai: A novel* (New York: Summit Books, 1985).
11 Muller, *Colonial Cambodia's 'Bad Frenchmen'*, 8–9 and 101–26.
12 See, for example, Ronald Hyam, *Empire and Sexuality: The British experience* (Manchester: Manchester University Press, 1990).
13 Eves and Thomas, *Bad Colonists*; Muller, *Colonial Cambodia's 'Bad Frenchmen'*.
14 Croly, *Willard Straight*, 56–7.
15 James Whidden, 'Expatriates in Cosmopolitan Egypt: 1864–1956', in *Settlers and Expatriates*, edited by Bickers, 44–73.
16 Harper, 'The British "Malayans"', in *Settlers and Expatriates*, edited by Bickers, 240–1.
17 King, *In the Chinese Customs Service*, 14.
18 Arlington, *Through the Dragon's Eyes*, 121.
19 Rasmussen, *China Trader*, 3.
20 SHAC, 691(9) 1797, 'Confidential reports of employees withdrawn from service, 1931', J. F. Laucournet's confidential report, Mengzi, 1929; J. H. Saunder's confidential report, Tianjin, 1928; H. Speakman's confidential report, Shanghai, 1915.
21 See, for example, James Whidden's argument that status in colonial Egypt was determined primarily by class rather than race: 'Expatriates in Cosmopolitan Egypt', 44–73.
22 *Documents Illustrative*, vol. 1, circular no. 8 of 1864 (first series), 36.
23 King, *In the Chinese Customs Service*, 18.
24 SHAC, 679(1) 32517, 'Nanning Semi-Officials, 1913–20', S/O no. 75, Hedgeland to Aglen, 13 Jan 1914.
25 Harper, 'The British "Malayans"', 240–1.
26 John G. Butcher, *The British in Malaya, 1880–1941: The social history of a European community in colonial South-East Asia* (Oxford: Oxford University Press, 1979), 147–57.
27 Mrinalini Sinha, 'Britishness, Clubbability, and the Colonial Public Sphere', in

Bodies in Contact: Rethinking colonial encounters in world history, edited by Tony Ballantyne and Antoinette M. Burton (Durham, NC: Duke University Press, 2005), 188–91.

28 SHAC, 679(1) 17616, 'Handing-over-charge memoranda, Shanghai, 1901–48', dispatch no. 17,690, 17 Apr 1922.

29 Bickers, *Britain in China*, 83; Butcher, *British in Malaya*.

30 Sinha, 'Britishness, Clubbability, and the Colonial Public Sphere', 193.

31 An early example of a staff request for a Customs club was submitted in 1881 when the Shantou staff petitioned to found a billiards club paid for by member subscriptions. SHAC, 679(2) 1867, 'Swatow Customs: dispatches and enclosures to IG, 1878–91', dispatch no. 52, 24 Apr 1881.

32 Rasmussen, *China Trader*, 12.

33 SHAC, 679(2) 1869, 'Swatow Customs: dispatches to IG, 1884–86', dispatch no. 91, 20 Sept 1884.

34 SHAC, 679(2) 1869, 'Swatow Customs: dispatches to IG, 1884–86', dispatch no. 93, 27 Sept 1884.

35 SHAC, 679(1) 32366, 'Swatow Semi-Official, 1915–17', S/O no. 255, Carruthers to Aglen, 7 July 1917.

36 SHAC, 679(1) 17062, 'Chinese and foreign staff clubs, Antung', dispatch no. 626, 15 June 1910.

37 SHAC, 679(1) 17084, 'Customs clubs, Shanghai', dispatch no. 11,707, Commissioner Merrill to Aglen, 22 Aug 1911.

38 SHAC, 679(1) 17062, 'Chinese and foreign staff clubs, Antung', Customs club rules enclosed in dispatch no. 626, 15 June 1910.

39 SHAC, 679(1) 17085, 'Chinese staff club, Shanghai, 1922–46', letter from Charles Leung to Aglen, 8 July 1922.

40 See, for example, SHAC, 679(1) 17097, 'Customs club, Swatow', dispatch no. 8,008, 6 Oct 1942, notifying the IG that the foreign and Chinese clubs had been amalgamated.

41 Quoted in Charles Drage, *Servants of the Dragon Throne: Being the lives of Edward and Cecil Bowra* (London: Peter Dawnay, 1966), 65.

42 Hippisley papers, MS. Eng. c. 7288, 'Correspondence, 1864–89', letter from Hart to Hippisley, 27 Apr 1889.

43 Quoted in Croly, *Willard Straight*, 63.

44 Kirk-Greene, *Symbol of Authority*, 164–79.

45 John MacKenzie, 'Hunting in Eastern and Central Africa in the Late Nineteenth Century, with Special Reference to Zimbabwe', in *Sport in Africa: Essays in social history*, edited by William J. Baker and J. A. Mangan (New York: Africana Pub. Co., 1987), 172–95.

46 SOAS, MS 201813. Bowra papers, box 3, letter from Edward Bowra to his mother, 20 Oct 1864.

47 Mary Louise Pratt, *Imperial Eyes: Travel writing and transculturation* (Abingdon: Routledge, 1992); Glenn Hooper, ed., *Landscape and Empire, 1770–2000* (Aldershot: Ashgate, 2004).

48 On sport in China: Bickers, *Britain in China*, 84; Frances Wood, *No Dogs and Not Many Chinese: Treaty port life in China, 1843–1943* (London: John Murray, 2000), 120–3.

49 Mangan, *The Games Ethic and Imperialism*; Anthony Kirk-Greene, 'Imperial Administration and the Athletic Imperative'.

50 Patrick F. McDevitt, 'Muscular Catholicism: Nationalism, masculinity, and Gaelic team sports, 1884–1916', in *Bodies in Contact*, edited by Ballantyne and Burton, 209–13.

51 Bickers, *Empire Made Me*, 137.

52 King, *In the Chinese Customs Service*, 25, 62–65, 80, 188–9; Patrick F. McDevitt, *'May the Best Man Win': Sport, masculinity, and nationalism in Great Britain and the empire, 1880–1935* (Basingstoke: Palgrave Macmillan, 2004), chapter 4, 58–80.

53   SHAC, 679(1) 32517, 'Nanning Semi-Official, 1913–20', S/O no. 75, Hedgeland to Aglen, 13 Jan 1914.
54   Rasmussen, *China Trader*, 26, 44–7, 49–65.
55   Kennedy, *Magic Mountains*, 1–18.
56   Kennedy, *Magic Mountains*, 1. See, for example, student interpreter W. H. Wilkinson's account of idyllic summers spent in the Western Hills near Beijing. W. H. Wilkinson, *'Where Chineses Drive': English student-life at Peking* (London: W. H. Allen & Co, 1885), 197–234.
57   *Documents Illustrative*, vol. 1, circular no. 24 of 1873 (first series), 'Commissioners and Superintendents; relations between', 18 Dec 1873.
58   Kirsten McKenzie, *Scandal in the Colonies: Sydney and Cape Town, 1820–1850* (Carlton: Melbourne University Press, 2004), 13.
59   Bland papers, memoir, 17–18.
60   Hippisley papers, MS Eng c 7286, memoirs.
61   SHAC, 679(1) 14237, 'Staff Secretary's office: semi-official and confidential correspondence during 1937, Kiungchow–Santuao', S/O, 9 Jan 1937.
62   SHAC, 679(2) 1932, 'Tianjin dispatches to IG', dispatch no. 182, Commissioner Hobson to IG Hart, 16 Dec 1883; SHAC, 679(1) 23119, 'Outdoor Staff quarters, Harbin', dispatch no. 1,903, 3 Apr 1919.
63   TMA, W2-1-72, 'Outward semi-officials to postmaster general', S/O no. 192, 2 Oct 1913.
64   SHAC, 691(1) 4335, 'Miss Miratta Mao's career', letter from Mao to acting IG Little, 28 Feb 1944.
65   SHAC, 679(1) 23202, 'Indoor Staff quarters, Wuchow', dispatch no. 2,876, 10 May 1920.
66   SHAC, 679(1) 14237, 'Staff Secretary's office: semi-official and confidential correspondence during 1937, Kiungchow–Santuao', S/O, 9 Jan 1937.
67   SHAC, 679(1) 16826, 'Commissioners' reports on outdoor staff petitions for increase in pay in reply to circular no. 2545', enclosure in Shanghai dispatch no. 122, 23 Oct 1916.
68   Rasmussen, *China Servant*, 78.
69   Stoler, *Carnal Knowledge and Imperial Power*, 136.
70   Lan Li and Deidre Wildy, 'A New Discovery and Its Significance: The statutory declarations made by Sir Robert Hart concerning his secret domestic life in nineteenth-century China', *Journal of the Hong Kong Branch of the Royal Asiatic Society*, 43 (2003), 63–87.
71   Bland papers, memoirs, chapter 2, 6.
72   SHAC, 679(2) 1585, 'Shanghai Customs: dispatches to IG, 1884 (July–Dec)', Shanghai dispatches: no. 207, 31 July 1884; no. 226, 15 Aug 1884.
73   Li and Wildy, 'A New Discovery and Its Significance', 63–87.
74   Kenneth Ballhatchet, *Race, Sex, and Class under the Raj: Imperial attitudes and policies and their critics* (New York: St Martin's Press, 1980), chapter 6.
75   SHAC, 679(1) 1001, 'Confidential coast inspector to commissioners and senior marine officers', Deputy Commissioner Tu Ping Ho, Yichang, to Coast Inspector Sabel, 23 Dec 1940.
76   SHAC, 679(1) 1000, 'Confidential Coast Inspector to commissioners and senior marine officers', Commissioner Groff-Smith, Qiongzhou, to Coast Inspector Carrel, 18 Feb 1938.
77   SHAC, 679(1) 1415, 'Staff Secretary's office: semi-official and confidential correspondence during 1937, Shanghai-Wuhu', confidential letter from Staff Secretary Hu to Commissioner Lawford, Shanghai, 17 July 1937.
78   SHAC, 679(1) 32366, 'Swatow semi-official, 1915–17', S/O no. 224, 22 Sept 1916.
79   SHAC, 679(1) 14103, 'Staff secretary's office: semi-official and confidential correspondence during 1936', confidential letters from Staff Secretary Hu to Sanshui assistant-in-charge Chan: 17 Feb 1936 (enclosing Pigott's letters of complaint); 31 Mar 1936; 21 May 1936.

80 SHAC, 679(9) 2398, 'Case of Irene Mok, Canton, 1938–41', letter from Mok (Shanghai) to Foster Hall (former Canton Commissioner), 6 Sept 1941.
81 SHAC, 679(9) 2398, 'Case of Irene Mok, Canton, 1938–41', letter from Carlisle to Staff Secretary Chiu, 2 Oct 1941.
82 SHAC, 679(9) 2398, 'Case of Irene Mok, Canton, 1938–41', Staff Secretary Chiu's comments on the case, 4 Oct 1941.
83 King. *In the Chinese Customs Service*, 70.
84 See, for example, Bickers, *Empire Made Me*, 153 and Kirk-Greene, *Symbol of Authority*, 184.
85 SHAC, 679(3) 1602, 'NRS dispatches to IG, 1913', dispatch no. 3,969, NRS Bruce Hart to IG Aglen, 12 Aug 1913; SHAC, 679(1) 17270, 'General regulations governing marriage of Customs employees', draft IG circular no. 3,306, 26 May 1922.
86 SHAC, 679(1) 14234. 'Staff Secretary's office: semi-official and confidential correspondence during 1936', S/O letter from Commissioner Lowder, Wuhu, to Staff Secretary Hu Fu-sen, 11 Sept 1936.
87 SHAC, 679(1) 17270, 'General regulations governing marriage of Customs employees', IG circular no. 5,517, 19 June 1937; IG circular no. 5,623, 18 Nov 1937.
88 *I. G. in Peking*, vol. 2, Letter Z/719, Hart to Campbell, 2 Aug 1896, 1076.
89 Philippa Levine, 'Sexuality, Gender, and Empire', in *Gender and Empire*, edited by Philippa Levine (Oxford: Oxford University Press, 2004), 138–42; Lora Wildenthal, 'Race, Gender, and Citizenship in the German Colonial Empire', in *Tensions of Empire*, edited by Cooper and Stoler, 263–83.
90 Anna Davin, 'Imperialism and Motherhood', in *Tensions of Empire*, edited by Cooper and Stoler, 87–151; Elisa Camiscioli, 'Reproducing the "French Race": Immigration and pronatalism in early-twentieth-century France', in *Bodies in Contact*, edited by Ballantyne and Burton, 219–33.
91 For an analysis of the Australian case see Fiona Paisley, 'Childhood and Race: Growing up in the Empire', in *Gender and Empire*, edited by Levine, 240–59.
92 See Jean Elisabeth Pedersen's discussion of paternity suits in early twentieth-century France and the empire. '"Special Customs": Paternity suits and citizenship in France and the colonies, 1870–1912', in *Domesticating the Empire: Race, gender, and family life in French and Dutch colonialism*, edited by Julia Ann Clancy-Smith and Frances Gouda (Charlottesville: University Press of Virginia, 1998), 43–64.
93 Lionel Caplan, *Children of Colonialism: Anglo-Indians in a postcolonial world* (Oxford: Berg, 2001), chapter 3, 59–90; Stoler, *Carnal Knowledge and Imperial Power*, chapter 4, 79–110.
94 Lethbridge, *Hong Kong: Stability and Change*, 177.
95 SHAC, 679(1) 32828, 'IG semi-official letter books to commissioners, diplomats, etc', IG Aglen to Commissioner Wakefield, Changsha, 20 Jan 1911.
96 SHAC, 679(1) 14237. 'Staff Secretary's office: semi-official and confidential correspondence during 1937', Commissioner Hilliard, Nanjing, to Staff Secretary Hu, 2 Apr 1937.
97 SHAC, 679(9) 1421, 'Staff Secretary's office: semi-official and confidential correspondence during 1933–35', letter from Commissioner Asker, Shantou, to Staff Secretary Hu, 15 June 1935.
98 *Provisional Instructions for the Guidance of the In-Door Staff* (Shanghai: Statistical Department of the Inspectorate General, 1877), 12.
99 SHAC, 679(1) 999, 'Confidential Coast Inspector to and from staff', confidential letters: Commissioner Barwick, Xiamen, to Coast Inspector Terry, 25 Feb and 27 Feb; Commissioner Lowder, Fuzhou, to Carrel, 28 Feb; Carrel to Mahan, 11 Dec 1937.
100 SHAC, 679(1) 1000, 'Confidential Coast Inspector to and from Commissioners and senior Marine officers', River Inspectorate circular, 22 Mar 1937.
101 SHAC, 679(2) 1557, 'Shanghai dispatches to IG, 1861–6', dispatch no. 43, 1 June 1865. Molineux had previously been dismissed for the same offence, but had later been reinstated.

102 SHAC, 679(2) 1584, 'Shanghai Customs: dispatches to IG, 1884', dispatch no. 65, 29 Feb 1884.
103 SHAC, 679(1) 1674, 'Shanghai Customs: General letters received, 1881–4', letter from Mr Yoshioga to Shanghai Commissioner, 30 May 1884.
104 SHAC, 679(1) 31639, 'IG confidential correspondence with port Commissioners, 1929', letter from Commissioner Kurematsu, Qiongzhou, to IG Maze, 27 Feb 1929.
105 SHAC, 679(1) 14101, 'Staff Secretary's office: semi-official and confidential correspondence during 1933–5', letter from Ningbo Commissioner to IG Maze, 8 Feb 1934.
106 *Archives of China's Imperial Maritime Customs*, vol. 1, letter Z/37, Hart to Campbell, 30 Dec 1880.
107 See, for example, David M. Anderson and David Killingray, 'Consent, Coercion and Colonial Control: Policing the empire, 1830–1940', in *Policing the Empire*, edited by Anderson and Killingray, 1–13; David Anderson, *Histories of the Hanged: The dirty war in Kenya and the end of empire* (New York: W. W. Norton, 2005).
108 On colonial police forces and violence see Norman Miners, 'The Localisation of the Hong Kong Police Force, 1842–1947', *Journal of Imperial and Commonwealth History*, 18:3 (1990), 296–315. For a discussion of the use of violence in colonial labour systems in British Africa see Jock McCulloch, 'Empire and Violence, 1900–1939', in *Gender and Empire*, edited by Levine, 220–39.
109 SHAC, 679(2) 1557, 'Shanghai Customs: dispatches to IG, 1861–6', dispatch no. 54, 8 Sept 1864.
110 SHAC, 679(1) 26892, 'IG's circulars, second series, vol. 3, 1882–85', circular no. 233, 29 Aug 1883.
111 SHAC, 679(2) 1589, 'Shanghai Customs: Dispatches to IG, 1886 (Jul–Dec)', dispatch no. 453, 8 Sept 1886, enclosing statements from Howell and Roberts.
112 David Cannadine, *Ornamentalism: How the British saw their empire* (Oxford: Oxford University Press, 2001).
113 Cannadine, *Ornamentalism*, xviii.
114 See Leonore Davidoff and Catherine Hall, *Family Fortunes: Men and women of the English middle class, 1780–1850* (Chicago: University of Chicago Press, 1987); Anne McClintock, *Imperial Leather: Race, gender, and sexuality in the colonial contest* (New York: Routledge, 1995), 1–17.

CHAPTER SIX

Leaving the Service: home, identity and post-Customs lives

In 1953, four years after the Chinese Communist Party came to power and the Foreign Inspectorate was subsequently dismantled, a former officer in the Marine Department, A. M. Troyan, wrote to the last foreign Inspector General of the Service, Lester Knox Little. His letter, written in Kaohsiung in Taiwan, sheds light upon the complex question of belonging in the empire world while also hinting at how an individual's sense of self could be changed by a career in China. Troyan took this opportunity to bring Little up to date on his movements since leaving the Service and the whereabouts of other ex-CMCS men he had encountered in the course of his travels. The foreign staff had scattered to the four corners of the globe after 1949, Troyan reported, but rather than returning to their home countries many had instead chosen to begin new lives in other outposts of empire and the British Commonwealth. In Australia, New Zealand and Hong Kong his former colleagues in the Marine Department had managed to parlay their Customs experience into new professional positions, including marine surveyor, ship's master and manager of a shipping company. The former Commissioner J. K. Storrs, who had stayed on in the Communist-run Customs for a few months after the Chinese Revolution in October 1949, was now partner in a 'Whale-boats business, running them like the Preventive Fleet, of good old days'. As for Troyan, he had found work as master of a Hong Kong-based ship flying a Panamanian flag of convenience, transporting cargoes to New Zealand, Africa and Australia. There was also sad news to impart; several former Commanders in the Customs had died soon after leaving mainland China. The Britons C. C. Warren and G. Flynn made it only to Hong Kong, Singapore was the final resting place of J. G. Skinner, and the Yugoslavian P. I. Tirbak died shortly after emigrating to the USA.

All of these men had made the empire world their home. For many a stint in the Customs was just one stage in their empire careers. Indeed working for the Customs gave them the professional skills, cosmopolitan mindset and contacts necessary for international mobility. Troyan's peripatetic lifestyle, however, was not a choice. A 'White' Russian who had fled the Bolshevik Revolution for China in 1920, he described himself as 'still stateless, i.e. "person without personality" – existing but not existing legally'. To add to the murkiness surrounding his political status, his nationality is listed in the Customs service lists as Chinese and Troyan himself referred to China as his 'second Mother Land'. The former Customs men who had congregated in Hong Kong after 1949 occasionally met to reminisce about 'the "good olde days" and happy life in the Customs Service; they all keep the good old tradition of Customs brotherhood'. Troyan's nostalgia ran deeper than most, however. Leaving China, where he had hoped to settle permanently, was a second exile. 'I left Russia because of communism in 1920; left China by the same cause in 1948; left the best Service I ever got – the Customs – in 1949, and now all my hopes are resting on "disunited" Nations, who at last MUST be United – to survive,' he wrote despondently. Indeed, lacking a recognised national status, Troyan was unable even to establish legal residency in Hong Kong and was thereby unwillingly forced into a perpetually itinerant lifestyle. Many former Customs employees, particularly the British, were able to exploit confidently the professional pathways that connected different sites of empire. By contrast Troyan was constantly buffeted from all sides by destabilising forces.[1]

In this chapter *Empire Careers* comes full circle by exploring the reasons why people left the Service, what they did afterwards and how their personal, professional and national identities were changed by a career in the Customs. The modes in which people withdrew from service – by resignation, dismissal or invaliding – speak volumes about their initial expectations of expatriate life and the extent to which their professional aspirations were fulfilled over the course of a career. Customs career trajectories were diverse; some were fleeting while others endured for over thirty years, some employees achieved positions of power and influence while others suffered ignominious professional failures, and some were contented with Customs work whereas others fantasised about moving on to bigger and better things. The endpoint of Customs careers reveals a broad spectrum of professional successes and failures. Although most Europeans and Americans migrated to the empire world in search of enhanced opportunities, many failed to exploit them successfully and left defeated.

The post-Service lives and destinations of foreign Customs employees also hint at the broader question of belonging, an issue which encircles wider debates about the nature of identity in the empire world.

White settler communities, migrants moving to the metropole or between colonies and imperial officials felt the pull of home from multiple locations – from their local communities, from their place of birth, from their adopted country of residence and, most importantly, from the empire world.[2] This chapter shows how the experience of living and working overseas actively transformed personal identities and national allegiances. For instance, empire careers sometimes intensified national loyalties and sometimes sidelined them in favour of local identities. Conflicting allegiances were even more pronounced within the Customs' multinational staff. Most studies on the multiple meanings of home in the colonial world have focused on the British case, but this chapter emphasises how the potency of nationalist sentiments and the desire to return to one's place of birth were partly determined by nationality and political status, as Troyan's story shows. Ultimately, this chapter argues that, although nostalgia for a national homeland exerted a powerful emotional pull on most expatriates, the sentimental desire to return home was often supplanted by the practical rewards, such as an enhanced standard of living, of life in the colonies. Customs men were first and foremost citizens of the empire world.

Leaving the Service

Resignation was by far the most common mode of leaving the Service in all branches of the foreign staff, amounting to 4,166 or 38 per cent of all foreign withdrawals over the course of the Inspectorate's lifespan. Reasons for resigning were manifold, including homesickness, inability to acclimatise to life in China, family commitments or a more lucrative employment offer. Many were simply unsuitable for Customs work. The Frenchman E. Cousturier, for example, who reached the position of Deputy Commissioner in the 1930s, suffered from 'a kind of nervous affliction that takes the form of dread of the water' that left him unable to cross the harbour – a particularly unfortunate phobia for someone who worked for the Maritime Customs Service.[3] The careers of others were stymied when they failed to pass their Chinese examinations and some found the cosmopolitan composition of the staff overwhelming and disorienting. Much as their professional and social experiences diverged, patterns of leaving the Service were different for the Indoor and Outdoor branches. While the Indoor Staff often stayed for lengthy careers, the Outdoor Staff were especially receptive to the lure of other employment options in China, which often far outshone the Customs, and the majority resigned after a short stay in the Service. In the service lists 326 employees are rather ominously recorded as having 'disappeared' and another seventy are recorded as having 'left without permission'. Indoor employees only accounted for seventeen of these 396 'unofficial' withdrawals. Low pay was the main reason why Outdoor officers felt little loyalty towards the Inspectorate. Under present pay and conditions, the Shanghai Commissioner warned in 1886, the only willing candidates would be 'the utterly needy who arrive here nobody hardly knows how and who disappear after a few months as mysteriously as they arrived'.[4] Considering that a major lure of work in the empire world was the enhanced pay and prestige bestowed upon white Europeans and Americans, it is unsurprising that most Outdoor officers soon moved on to more promising ventures.

Ill-health, both physical and mental, plagued the Customs staff and was a major cause of withdrawals from service, either through death, invaliding or resignation. Tuberculosis, chronic bronchitis, heart trouble, rheumatism, a variety of 'nervous' disorders, alcoholism and sexually transmitted diseases such as syphilis were the most common ailments.[5] With characteristic parsimony the Inspectorate was reluctant to invalid employees because of the high pension costs involved. In 1931 Maze warned Commissioners not to recommend those who were 'so seriously ill that their death was momentarily expected' for invaliding; otherwise the Inspectorate would be saddled with paying pro rata retirement benefits to the deceased employee's dependants.[6] Only 268 foreigners (two per cent of the total foreign staff) and 245 Chinese employees (two per cent of the total Chinese staff) were invalided out of the Service from the very first invaliding case in 1888 until 1949. The proportion of employees who died while working for the Customs was appreciably higher: 988 foreigners (nine per cent of the total foreign staff) and 1,008 Chinese (nine per cent of the total Chinese staff) are recorded as 'deceased' in the service lists. The high rate of fatal illness was due to both exposure to disease and woefully inadequate medical care. In an attempt to alleviate this problem nineteen Customs medical officers were appointed 1862–1900 to provide free consultations to employees and their families. An early Customs surgeon, Patrick Manson (in the Service 1866–89), even played a leading role in pioneering the field of tropical medicine in Europe, later becoming medical adviser to the Colonial Office and a founding member of the School of Tropical Medicine in London.[7] After 1900, rather than appointing medical officers directly, the usual practice was to outsource the medical care of Customs personnel to a foreign doctor resident in each port for a fixed fee.[8] The skills of the foreign doctors who ended up in the outports were, however, usually less than exemplary, leading to many misdiagnoses and botched treatments. Furthermore, access to hospitals was tricky in the more remote regions. For instance, the Portuguese examiner A. E. dos Santos stationed at Hekou on

Table 6.1 Numbers of staff recorded as deceased per decade (percentage of the total number of foreign or Chinese staff employed by the Service during each decade in parentheses)

	Foreign staff	Chinese staff
1850–1859	0	0
1860–1869	76 (7)	0
1870–1879	84 (8)	5 (2)
1880–1889	110 (8)	58 (10)
1890–1899	140 (6)	106 (11)
1900–1909	193 (6)	220 (8)
1910–1919	182 (6)	198 (10)
1920–1929	118 (5)	199 (6)
1930–1939	70 (3)	180 (4)
1940–1949	14 (1)	42 (1)

Source: Data extrapolated from service lists database of employees withdrawn from service

the border with French Indochina died from liver failure after being shunted between doctors and hospitals in Mengzi, Kunming, Hanoi and Macao before a diagnosis was finally reached.[9] Still, as Table 6.1 shows, the mortality rate *did* improve dramatically over the decades in tune with advances in medicine, public sanitation and improved access to doctors.

Despite the fact that serious illness was, if anything, more prevalent among the Chinese staff (see Table 6.1), Customs commentary on ill-health among foreign employees was couched in a colonial discourse that saw a 'correlation between the heat of the tropics and disease, decay, and death'.[10] The high incidence of disease among Westerners in China, especially in the nineteenth century when medical and sanitation facilities in the treaty ports were rudimentary, partly justi-fied these fears. In 1858 alone, for example, there were 29,990 cases of disease (a ratio of 2,653.9 per 1,000) and 706 deaths (a ratio of 62.5 per 1,000) among the 11,300 Britons on the China coast, many of whom were soldiers fighting in the Arrow War.[11] However, the way in which employees described their illnesses and the treatments recommended by Customs medical officers are also telling of underlying anxieties about contact with China. As discussed in Chapter 5, empire-wide assumptions about the debilitating effect of Asian and African envi-ronments on the European constitution also served to denigrate indigenous society, which was portrayed as insalubrious and lacking modern methods of sanitation, medical care and public health. Popular theories of environmental determinism gave credence to the concept of a hierarchy of civilisations; put simply, a 'tropical' climate stunted development while more temperate climes enabled advancement. Concerns about the enervating effects of long-term exposure to a 'tropical environment' also revealed doubts about the viability of colonialism, particularly long-term European settlement. These anxieties were at the forefront of mid-nineteenth-century debates about the suitability of the treaty ports as sites for European settlement. The hinterlands of Shanghai and Tianjin, in particular, were often portrayed as emanating a poisonous miasma while the proximity of the foreign settlements to supposedly unsanitary Chinese cities was a further cause of disquiet.[12] This range of concerns explains why 'leaving the East' or, if the patient could not afford to return to Europe, a sojourn in Japan or to a northern seaside resort in China, was the usual treatment prescribed by Customs doctors for chronic ailments.

This broader colonial discourse also explains why diagnoses of 'debility' or 'neurasthenia' were so common among the foreign Customs staff. These catchall labels referred to a nebulous collection of symptoms, including ennui, exhaustion, insomnia, anxiety and melancholia. The medicalisation of this psychosomatic malaise lent scientific authority to the deep-seated worry that Europeans were fundamentally unsuited to life in Asia and Africa.[13] In the Customs mental breakdowns were routinely attributed to the debilitating conditions of life in China, especially during the nineteenth century when foreign communities were still tiny and Customs work was therefore particularly isolating. Take, for example, the suicide of the American Statistical Secretary E. C. Taintor, who shot himself at Shanghai in 1878 after years of depression brought on by deafness resulting from an illness he contracted while stationed in Taiwan. Unable to follow conversations, his bad hearing left Taintor feeling increasingly isolated. Taintor's doctor ordered an immediate departure for America, which he duly obeyed, although his symptoms redoubled on his return to China. 'He grew morbid: imagined that laughter caused was at his expense: and melancholia followed – a terrible disease which, in China, usually culminated in suicide or homicide,' his colleague Alfred Hippisley recounted in his memoirs. The effects of depression were, Hippisley implied, amplified in the China context.[14] The mental collapse of other prominent staff in the 1860s and 1870s, such as Commissioner Kleczkowski, a Belgian count and former chargé d'affaires at the French Legation who threw himself down a well in Xiamen in 1867 'while labouring under mental delusion', served as confirmation of the incapacitating effects of long-term residence in the treaty ports.[15]

In the twentieth century mental illness was, if anything, reported even more frequently. By this time the Customs was established in dozens of provincial river ports and the stultifying conditions of a lifeless backwater could take their psychological toll. In May 1914 a junior assistant stationed at Nanning, John Thorburn, committed suicide after only two years of service during a vacation to Guangzhou. Although he was outwardly cheerful, it appeared that Thorburn had been desperate to leave China for some time, hatching various unsuccessful plans to find a new position in Britain. 'I am quite determined to go home early next year . . . I have had my 40 days in the wilderness and now I want to be back in the thick of things,' he wrote in a letter home. A failed marriage engagement, which Thorburn was hoping to make official in Guangzhou, seems to have precipitated his suicide. In a tragic twist of fate his erstwhile fiancée, Miss Baker, died the next month in the *Empress of Ireland* disaster.[16] Even outbursts of violence were often explained away as an unfortunate by-product of small town life. The Commissioner at Sanshui, a small southern port, pleaded mitigating circumstances for an American assistant in the Indoor Staff, Philip Hiram Everhart, who was in trouble for assaulting a Chinese clerk during an office argument in 1919. Everhart had been stationed in Sanshui for four years, far too long even for foreigners with the stoutest constitution, the Commissioner explained. Indeed, the town's oppressive environment had directly led to Everhart's violent conduct: 'He has suffered from sleeplessness caused largely by the intolerable noises at night coming from the harbour and foreshore under his bedroom window. When so afflicted he has been irritable and very suspicious, and I fear that has affected his good relations with the staff, so that I have had to intervene several times.'[17] To the Commissioner the link between Everhart's nervous trouble, his violent behaviour and his immersion in a wholly Chinese environment – with its 'intolerable noises' – was self-evident. Similarly, in 1933, Norwegian chief assistant E. J. Schjoth stationed at Kunming was pronounced 'un homme anormal et dangereux' who was 'livré à des actes de violence injustifiés qui auraient pu facilement dégénérer aux scandals publics' by the port doctor.[18] It was well known in the port that Schjoth was given to flying into rages and beating his wife. Because Schjoth's mental state was considered too dangerously unstable to cope with a sudden decision to invalid him, he was instead quietly transferred to Shanghai and then sent home under the pretence of going on leave. The public nature of Schjoth's mental breakdown, which had become a subject of gossip among Chinese and foreign alike, was the most disconcerting aspect of his behaviour for the reputation-conscious Inspectorate. The presumption that life in a small port made Europeans more susceptible to erratic and violent behaviour was, meanwhile, taken for granted. These examples suggest that the difference and distance that Europeans and Americans self-consciously cultivated between themselves and indigenous peoples and cultures did not only serve to enhance 'white prestige'; it also gave rise to deep feelings of alienation and unease about their place in the colonial world.

Growing tensions between China and Japan in the 1930s gave rise to a spate of mental breakdowns among the foreign staff, especially among the national contingents most vulnerable to wartime pressures. The stateless position of Russian émigrés, which meant they lacked extraterritorial protection, left them particularly anxious about the deteriorating international situation. In the archives there are several cases of Russians who suffered from paranoid delusions that they were being hunted down by either the Japanese or the Soviets. In 1937, for example, the Staff Secretary, Hu Fu-sen, forewarned the Kowloon Commissioner that the Assistant Tidesurveyor P. E. Pogodin, about to be transferred from Shanghai to Kowloon, had recently experienced a relapse of a 'nervous condition' provoked by the difficult wartime conditions in Shanghai. 'He now imagines that the Japanese are after him,' Hu explained, an idea which had 'got such a firm hold in his mind that he actually tendered his resignation in order that he might get out of China'.[19] Japanese employees were also hard hit by the impending conflict, especially those who had worked for the Inspectorate for years and yet suddenly found themselves hated enemies. The Qingdao Commissioner unhappily reported in May 1937 that so far that year he had already been obliged to send four Japanese employees on sick leave owing to the trauma caused by local political conditions. 'The strain has probably told more heavily on the Japanese members of the staff in that they have had to face more direct threats,' the Commissioner surmised, adding that three more 'had reached a stage when they would stand no more and were in danger of breaking up'. A fourth man, junior assistant Yamagata Akira, had been hospitalised after 'telephoning wildly to the Deputy Commissioner and various members of the staff that they, or the Custom House, were about to be attacked'.[20] Expatriate life could be hard and alienating in the best of circumstances, but the stress of wartime pushed many to breaking point.

Mental illness was worrisome, not just because of the broader stigma attached to this condition but also because it destabilised the Inspectorate's carefully crafted image of the foreign staff. Foreign employees were supposed to be indefatigable, level-headed and possessing of strength of character. Mental breakdowns instead presented an image of weakness. After all, if foreign employees could not even control themselves, how could they be trusted with positions of responsibility within the Chinese government? Anxiety about the public image of the Customs also permeated the Inspectorate's handling of misconduct and corruption. Twenty-one per cent of all foreign employees who served between 1854 and 1950 were dismissed or discharged from service after being found guilty of various offences ranging from slovenliness, insobriety and immorality to insubordination, fraud and taking bribes.[21]

This is strikingly at odds with a foundational myth at the heart of the Foreign Inspectorate's perception and justification of its role in China: the insistence that the foreign staff was a bastion of integrity able to set an inspirational example for corrupt Chinese bureaucrats. Robert Ronald Campbell, son of the former Customs Non-Resident Secretary at the London Office, James Duncan Campbell, summarised the prevailing view of the Service's crowning achievement:

> In a vast country . . . notorious for the bribery and corruption of the official classes, it [the Customs Service] shone out incorruptible like a beacon of pure light until, as port after port was opened to foreign trade and its sphere of activities gradually increased, there were few places where you could not truthfully say, 'Here the Customs Service did good.'[22]

The incorruptibility of the foreign staff was taken as a given in the Inspectorate's own literature and in multiple biographies and histories of the Service. The perception that China sorely needed Europeans and Americans to straighten out its bureaucracy rested on the widely held assumption that the Chinese government apparatus was rotten through and through. To a degree Western perceptions of endemic bribery and corruption in the late Qing bureaucracy were correct. Local government under the Qing was headed by a succession of inexperienced magistrates, meaning that long-serving clerks were easily able to manipulate government affairs, extorting bribes and defrauding tax revenues to supplement their meagre salaries in the process.[23] The widespread nature of bribe-taking notwithstanding, it is important to understand that this was simply *not* viewed by most people as a social problem. As Henry Lethbridge has pointed out in regard to corruption in Hong Kong, 'all parties involved in this dyadic relationship, the giver and taker, normally got what they wanted and no one was aggrieved'.[24] The identification of dishonesty as an intrinsic and serious problem of Chinese officialdom, then, said as much about political changes in the West as about corruption in China. In Britain the prevalence of 'old corruption' in the form of over-taxation, electoral bribery and political patronage had come under attack from many quarters in the period 1780–1830, leading to a series of reforms designed to increase efficiency.[25] Although in reality remnants of the old system persisted in British politics until as late as 1914, the nineteenth-century climate of political reform led to unfavourable comparisons between China and Britain after 1842. Moulding an honest and professional administrative service went hand-in-hand, in the Foreign Inspectorate's eyes, with

Table 6.2   Aggregate dismissals and discharges from the foreign staff
1854–1950

Rank on appointment		Dismissals		Discharges	
	Total number appointed	*Total*	*Percentage of staff appointed*	*Total*	*Percentage of staff appointed*
Assistants/clerks	1,188	46	4	92	8
Watchers/tidewaiters	5,983	657	11	1,002	17
Lightkeepers	528	50	9	127	24

Source: Data extrapolated from service lists database of employees withdrawn from service. Percentages calculated against the total number of foreign employees initially appointed to the specified rank on joining the Service

the creation of a quintessentially British bureaucratic apparatus on Chinese soil. As corruption was so ingrained in the system, the employ-ment of a cohort of foreign administrators well versed in the ways of conscientious government was vital to show Chinese administrators the correct way to behave.

Yet, judging by the relative proportions of foreign and Chinese employees dismissed or discharged from service between 1854 and 1950 – 21 and 12 per cent respectively – misconduct was actually higher among the foreign staff. It is possible that the more sophisti-cated integration of Chinese employees into local smuggling networks made corruption more difficult to detect, yet the fact remains that the foreign staff were hardly a model of honesty. As Christopher Munn has observed with reference to Hong Kong's colonial administration, 'Europeans needed no lessons in corruption from "the Asiatic genius"'.[26] This contradicts the common assumption that imperial administrators formed a loyal and honest corps of men and women dedicated to serving empire. Differences in motivations, status and aims among employees of imperial institutions meant that certain groups and individuals were less than enthusiastic about preserving the standards of colonial government. While an elite administrator in the ICS, committed from the outset to a lifelong career in colonial administration, may well have been virtually incorruptible, a badly paid colonial policemen or railway engineer had less incentive to forgo illicitly profiteering from their position. This pattern was clear in the Customs staff. As Table 6.2 shows, dismissals and discharges were far more common in the Outdoor and Lights staffs. Unlike the Indoor Staff who spent their working days confined to the office, tidewaiters and examiners worked on the docks liaising with ship captains and crews, thus providing

them with more opportunities for making dishonest deals. Their salaries, moreover, were so low that many could not resist a chance to
augment their income through taking bribes. 'While individuals may
not be naturally dishonest,' the Shantou Deputy Commissioner, E. A.
Pritchard, speculated in 1931, 'many are too weak to resist when they
see certain of their colleagues building up large bank balances with but
little fear of detection'. The main cause of the problem was that seizure
rewards – the bonuses awarded to Customs officers who successfully
intercepted smuggling operations – were paltry compared to the gains
to be had from colluding with the smugglers.[27] The Inspectorate,
however, usually insisted on seeing corruption in the outdoor branches
as a sign of moral failing and a vindication of the view that only men of
middle-class stock possessed the hereditary strength of character necessary to elevate the Service's public reputation. 'Unfortunately the class
from which the Out-door Staff is recruited, with the exception of an
occasional Bluejacket, is not trained as to make simple duty an incentive,' sermonised the Statistical Secretary, F. E. Taylor, in response to
a petition calling for higher Outdoor Staff salaries in 1916.[28] Salaries
were never raised significantly, and the Outdoor Staff's reputation for
dishonesty thus persisted.

Levels of misconduct and malpractice fluctuated according to the
Foreign Inspectorate's evolving responsibilities and in response to
changes in the external political climate. As Table 6.3 shows, rates
of dismissals and discharges among the foreign staff were especially
high in the nineteenth century, a testimony to the large numbers of
incompetent and otherwise unsatisfactory men – 'bad hats', as Hart
labelled them – who joined the Service in its early decades, before it
had developed a sufficient reputation to attract a higher quality of personnel.[29] The only decade when the number of Chinese dismissals and
discharges rose above that of the foreign staff was 1900–10. This apparent spike in misconduct among Chinese employees can be explained
by the Inspectorate's takeover of the Imperial Post Office in 1896 and
nineteen Native Customs stations, which calculated and levied the
lijin inland transit tax, after 1901. Thus this turn-of-the-century purge
can be explained by the incorporation into the Customs Inspectorate
of bureaucracies that already harboured high levels of corruption and
incompetency within their ranks. It was, however, the Nationalist
ascent to power in the late 1920s that amplified anxiety about corruption. Although levels of dismissals and discharges dropped off in
this period, this was not an indication of lower levels of misconduct
but rather a result of the Inspectorate's inability to police its staff in a
period of political upheaval. Maze himself admitted in a 1929 circular
that 'during the latter years of the Revolution the ancient discipline

Table 6.3 Five-year averages of dismissals and discharges 1871–1940 (percentage of average number of annual Chinese/foreign withdrawals in parentheses)

	Chinese staff		Foreign staff	
	Dismissed	*Discharged*	*Dismissed*	*Discharged*
1871–1875	0	0	0	11 (28)
1876–1880	0	2 (25)	7 (10)	22 (31)
1881–1885	1 (7)	3 (20)	6 (11)	14 (25)
1886–1890	1 (3)	6 (21)	8 (11)	18 (25)
1891–1895	0	9 (31)	8 (9)	17 (19)
1896–1900	3 (8)	7 (19)	25 (15)	26 (15)
1901–1905	17 (13)	32 (24)	19 (9)	41 (19)
1906–1910	35 (16)	56 (25)	19 (10)	29 (15)
1911–1915	1 (2)	11 (17)	16 (8)	23 (12)
1916–1920	1 (2)	6 (12)	12 (8)	15 (9)
1921–1925	9 (11)	15 (18)	19 (13)	18 (13)
1926–1930	10 (11)	6 (7)	7 (8)	4 (4)
1931–1935	8 (7)	9 (7)	23 (28)	4 (5)
1936–1940	6 (7)	8 (9)	2 (3)	2 (3)

Source: Data extrapolated from service lists database of employees withdrawn from Service

of the Service has been in some instances necessarily relaxed'.[30] The following year Maze lamented that 'bribery and corruption amongst the Staff appear to be on the increase, the dismissal of certain employees not having had the desired effect of stamping out this evil'. The Inspectorate would henceforth take a zero tolerance approach to malpractice, he warned.[31] China's recovery of tariff autonomy 1928–30 directly contributed to the rise in corruption after this date. Whereas previously, according to the terms of the 1842 Treaty of Nanjing, the import tariff had been set artificially low at five per cent, the government was now free to charge higher duties. Bribing Customs officers was a cost-effective way for merchants and brokers to circumvent the new tariffs. In the period 1931–35 dismissals among the foreign staff shot up to 28 per cent of all withdrawals from service.

The upsurge in corruption in the 1930s came at a politically inopportune time. As it came under increasing scrutiny from the new, determinedly anti-imperialist government, the Foreign Inspectorate urgently needed to defend its self-cultivated image as a model of efficiency and honesty. The Inspectorate needed to be seen to be taking action. As a result, it began to examine suspicions of corruption among the foreign staff with much more rigour after 1927. Offences ran the gamut from petty theft and one-time bribe-taking to organised fraud. Malfeasance on the part of senior, long-serving foreign staff was an especially worrying trend. In a rare case of corruption among the Indoor Staff, a Danish assistant in Tianjin, S. A. Klubien, was found guilty in 1928 of stealing a deposit paid towards the duty on a large shipment while head of the Appraising Department the previous year. Although the evidence against him was mainly circumstantial, Klubien's 'highly suspicious' answers to the investigating committee's questions swung opinion against him, especially after he refused to allow the committee access to his bank account records. He was eventually dismissed.[32] In 1938 a chief examiner in Shanghai, Oliver Hall, who had served in the Customs for twenty-eight years, was accused of defrauding the revenue along with his accomplice, assistant examiner Chang Hsuan, who had been in the Outdoor Staff for fourteen years. The investigation began when the Commissioner discovered that Hall had received a crate of beer and some oranges from a Chinese broker, Yah Cheng Chong. On further investigation it appeared that Hall had been consistently under-declaring the weight of Yah's cargoes of sea cucumbers. Both Hall and Chang were discharged, despite their long service.[33]

From these cases and others it became disturbingly obvious to the Inspectorate that high-ranking foreigners often took a leading role in initiating corruption rackets. It stands to reason that well-seasoned officers who had an intricate knowledge of Customs work, had built up contacts among the merchant community and who occupied positions of responsibility would be able to find loopholes in the system and, moreover, easily cover their tracks. Furthermore, rather than setting an example of incorruptibility for their lower-ranking and Chinese colleagues to follow, senior foreigners sometimes actively suborned their juniors. This was apparent in the Hall case; his co-conspirator Chang Hsuan appears to have played a minor role, acting under Hall's direction. Customs veterans could also initiate 'griffins' into corrupt practices. A high-profile incident in 1922, reported widely in the treaty port press at the time, involved the British boat officer James Doyle, in the Customs since 1909, and the tidewaiter Alan Palamountain, who had joined the Service two years earlier. Doyle worked with a network of Chinese informants who alerted him to ships docked in port carrying illegal cargoes of opium. He would then don his Customs uniform in order to gain access to the ship and extort backhanders from the smugglers. Doyle was clearly the ringleader and Palamountain a reluctant junior accomplice who accompanied him on just one occasion.[34] Several more incidents of this type came to light after 1927. A particularly alarming case uncovered in 1930 at Tanggu near Tianjin implicated no fewer than twenty foreign and forty-two Chinese employees – almost the entire Outdoor Staff at the port – in a corruption syndicate, which operated on the principle of extracting bribes from merchants in exchange for lower duties, pooling the profits and sharing them among all members of the ring. The extent of the fraud was revealed by a recently dismissed tidewaiter named Wong Yo Pei, who 'wished to unburden his conscience' about his role in the ring.[35] The acknowledged architect was a British boat officer, R. J. Redd, who had been discharged earlier that year in Shanghai for accepting bribes.[36] According to Wong's account, and those of other members of the ring who were later interviewed by the Staff Secretary, Hugh Prettejohn, the scheme began when Redd called a meeting with the express purpose of initiating as many Outdoor employees as possible into the syndicate. Even in spite of the incontrovertible evidence that Redd and other high-ranking foreigners had masterminded the scheme, Prettejohn gave many foreigners who admitted to taking bribes the benefit of the doubt while Chinese employees were subject to special censure. Certain of the foreigners had probably been 'forced' into accepting payments and should therefore be regarded as 'more as sinned against than sinning'. The Chinese staff's refusal to admit to wrongdoing was interpreted as obstinacy and a clear sign of guilt. 'The only way to make them speak would be to use Chinese methods and let them go before a Chinese Court,' Prettejohn commented darkly.[37] Well-worn assumptions about the innate venality of Chinese public servants were a long time in dying. In the end only the ringleaders – three foreign tidewaiters – were dismissed. While the Customs wanted to be seen to be cracking down on malpractice, to dismiss all sixty-two of those involved would have caused a public scandal.

The Tianjin case was unsettling because it exposed the systemic corruption in the Outdoor Staff, Chinese and foreign, that the Inspectorate had closed its eyes to for decades. Tianjin was not a special case. Wong also testified that the Outdoor Staff in Zhenjiang, where he had previously been stationed, was thoroughly dishonest. The foreigners in the port had amassed $150,000 in bribes between them in just a couple of years, Wong claimed. The Tianjin Commissioner, Edward Howell, concluded dejectedly that 'the clean-handed men among Service employees amount to only one per cent; the large majority are greedy for bribes'.[38] This pattern of endemic corruption was exacerbated by the War of Resistance against Japan (1937–45) and the civil war that followed until 1949. Numbers of dismissals and discharges fell to an all-time low, but this was more to do with the Inspectorate's inability to police staff conduct in the face of wartime turmoil. In reality malfeasance thrived, encouraged by salary depreciation resulting from inflation, a flourishing underground market in contraband and porous boundaries between territories controlled by diverse authorities. L. K. Little, appointed as IG in 1943, reminded staff that 'the basis of the Customs organization is the personal honesty of the individual employee. If it were understood that the Inspector General and his Commissioners were willing to shut the eye to malpractice, this basis would crumble, and dishonesty and corruption would spread like a cancer throughout the Service.'[39] Little's exhortations to return to the venerable tradition of scrupulously honest service at the heart of the Foreign Inspectorate's self-image were to no avail. In truth the foreign staff had never entirely lived up to this model of honesty, not even during its late nineteenth-century 'golden age'.

The Inspectorate largely failed on the public relations front, too. Customs scandals were gleefully reported in the treaty port press and the image of the corrupt tidewaiter was popularised by contemporary writers such as W. Somerset Maugham. His travel book *The Gentleman in the Parlour* (first published in 1930) contains a portrait of a former acquaintance from Maugham's days at medical school, given the pseudonym Grosely in the text, who had evidently evolved into a slippery character. Over twenty years of working for the Outdoor Staff, Grosely had amassed a surprisingly large fortune for a tidewaiter. 'He could not have come by it honestly, and little as I knew of the details of his trade, by his sudden reticences, by his leers and hints, I guessed that there was no base transaction that, if it was made worth his while, he jibbed at,' wrote Maugham. Now that Grosely had left China for retirement in Haiphong and squandered his ill-gotten gains on opium he looked back nostalgically on his prosperous years as a tidewaiter.[40] Portrayals of institutional corruption such as this were damaging to any government service, but they were especially destructive to colonial administrative services. As Clive Dewey has observed with regard to the ICS, imperial administrators were expected to be 'hard-working in a debilitating climate, incorruptible in a society riddled with bribery, celibate until middle age in a subcontinent which married at puberty'.[41] Malpractice thus undermined a principal ideological justification for colonial rule: the notion that Europeans and Americans brought enlightened and ethical rule to societies blighted by government rapacity. In the Chinese Customs Service professional reputation was doubly important. Lacking both wholehearted support from the Chinese government and the backing of foreign gunboats, expounding upon the model conduct of the foreign staff was increasingly the only way to ensure the continued existence of the Foreign Inspectorate. Furthermore evidence of seditious collusions between foreigners and Chinese spoke to deep anxieties and ideological ambivalences at the heart of the institution. While the Inspectorate continually reiterated the principle that foreign officers should work alongside their Chinese colleagues in a spirit of brotherhood, the very idea that the foreign staff formed a special and separate elite was at the core of the Customs' self-legitimising myths. The perception that foreigners could be willingly drawn into a morally murky Chinese world, where corruption reigned, fundamentally undermined this assumption.

War, nationalism and revolution

Resignations, dismissals, deaths and invaliding were routine endpoints to a Customs career, but for an internationally important organisation on which the interests of multiple foreign powers converged, fluctuations in the composition of the Customs staff were also highly attuned to global economic and political currents. The mass resignations and dismissals during the First World War were especially dramatic. On the eve of the conflict in August 1914, 1,595 foreign employees were recorded as working for the Service, yet 943 foreign nationals left between August 1914 and October 1918, most of whom then joined the armed forces. This number includes 146 Germans and Austrians who were dismissed as enemy nationals after China entered the war on the side of the Allies in 1917. For the individuals concerned this was life-changing. Most Germans in China were eventually repatriated – although those who had served for over twenty years in the Customs were permitted to stay in China – returning to their homeland jobless and sometimes penniless. In the months after the dismissals the Inspectorate received a deluge of letters from angry and desperate German former employees still resident in China whose hopes of a long-lasting career had been dashed by their dismissal. 'We, and those depending on us, are left thereby more or less destitute and are compelled to live in a manner not becoming men who have for long years served you and our Service most faithfully and loyally,' declared a petition from six German former Customs men submitted in 1917. It was only fair, they argued, that the Customs should issue compensation for their unexpected dismissals.[42] Those who had been stationed at Qingdao, a German colony, where looting German homes was routine practice after the city fell to the Japanese in 1915, bore the brunt of the hardship. The Chief assistant C. Pape reported that everything he owned was 'lost at Tsingtao [Qingdao], where my own house was burned down, and practically the whole of my household effects, furniture, curios, clothing etc. was lost through the repeated plundering of my Service house'.[43] The simple fact of suddenly losing their employment placed many in dire straits, especially for those who had envisaged a lifelong career in the Customs. The Customs was 'the life career of us all' claimed several German and Austrian former

Commissioners writing to then-IG Aglen in October 1917.[44] All that Aglen managed to secure in the way of compensation, however, was a relief fund, established in 1923, to assist former German and Austrian employees still resident in China who were unable to find new careers as a result of ill-health or old age.[45] The vast majority of German and Austrian ex-Customs men, however, left with nothing.

After the Guomindang rise to power in 1927, when the Customs was brought more closely under the aegis of the central government, the Inspectorate became much more ruthless about removing 'dead wood' from the foreign staff. The suspension of foreign recruitment in 1927 caused considerable alarm, but Maze's decision to weed out all foreigners who did not pull their weight as part of the 1929 staff reorganisation prompted real outrage at the dubious ethics of discharging long-serving employees.[46] Seventy-five foreigners were paid off in 1930–31, forty-nine of whom had served for over twenty years. As the privileged position of the foreign staff was eroded in the 1930s, many foreign employees were predictably sceptical about the continuing ability of the Service to provide a secure career. Morale suffered as a result and senior staff gloomily forecast that foreign juniors would soon jump ship.[47] The takeover of the Manchurian Customs stations by the Manchukuo authorities in 1932, which resulted in long-serving foreign staff being encouraged to take early retirement, further fuelled anxieties about the imminent dissolution of the foreign staff.[48] Yet this panic eventually proved ill-founded; foreign staff numbers diminished gradually during the 1930s, in tune with the usual pattern of retirements and resignations.

All this changed in 1941. The Japanese takeover of the Inspectorate in December effected an immediate and dramatic change to the profile of the foreign staff. In a mass dismissal, which echoed the elimination of Germans and Austrians in 1917, the names of all British and American employees in occupied China – 221 in all – were removed from the service list on 13 December. This decision was met with incredulity. The marine assistant Owen Gander queried 'why the position of foreigners in the Service should have been affected by the political situation' when previous upheavals had 'made no difference to the situation in respect of Customs employees, foreign or Chinese'. There was, he wrote, a widespread feeling that the foreign staff had been 'sold down the river' by the Customs.[49] But the situation of the Foreign Inspectorate had irrevocably changed since the late 1920s. Besides, the Customs had always been at the centre of political shifts and controversies. Worse was to come for those employees of Allied nationality who decided to stay in occupied China, or else could not get out. Most were interned after 31 January 1943, and in July 1943 eighty-six interned British and American employees were compulsorily retired by the Chongqing Inspectorate, most of whom did not realise they were unemployed until their release in 1945.[50] As a result the foreign staff was dramatically reduced; by July 1944 Little was responsible for a foreign staff of only eighteen, alongside 4,500 Chinese, in the whole of free China.[51]

After the war betrayal was the word on the lips of those who, unbeknownst to them, had been paid off while in captivity. 'May I picture in a nutshell how we see things at present. We stuck to our posts; as a result we have lost *everything* we possess, we have endured 3 ½ years of hell, some of us have learned we were paid off during the height of our misery,' wrote the former Commissioner E. A. Pritchard in a letter to Little. 'I am simply horrified and amazed that my services are so lightly esteemed by China.'[52] Little replied that he was doing all he could, but that he could not force the government's hand. Customs Japanese fared even worse; all Japanese staff – over one thousand in all – were paid off en masse at the end of the war.

Staff numbers did temporarily rebound; 479 foreign nationals are recorded as having worked for the Service 1945–50. Foreigners who had resigned to serve in the armed forces prior to 1941, and therefore avoided internment, were re-employed with seniority after reporting for duty in China and dozens more were employed on short-term contracts as technical experts.[53] Still, there was no disguising the fact that the Foreign Inspectorate's days were numbered. The power and prestige of the foreign staff had been irreversibly diminished and loyalties had been lost in the process. Many began to look for an escape hatch from the Service. Seven Commissioners submitted a collective petition in 1946 requesting that the entire foreign staff be paid off.[54] As Chinese replaced English as the official language of the Service, many foreigners were left floundering, especially those in the Outdoor Staff who had never received much language training. A 1946 petition made the case for a fundamental change in the foreign Outdoor Staff's role. Foreigners should be henceforth employed in 'consultative, advisory and instructive' roles, the petitioners argued, a solution that would preserve a leadership position for foreigners while placing the everyday running of the Service in Chinese hands.[55] Without the perks of 'white prestige' to sweeten the bitter pill of career insecurity, the Customs quickly lost its appeal. By the time of the communist revolution in October 1949, most foreigners had already left.[56] Hart's vision of one day relinquishing control of the Service to the Chinese had finally come to fruition, but few wholeheartedly embraced this transformation. Those who had flourished under the old system of foreign privilege left the Customs angry at what they perceived as the Chinese government's ungratefulness. A few remained temporarily. The Shanghai Commissioner W. R. Myers disgusted L. K. Little by working for the communists while simultaneously drawing a Customs pension from the Nationalist government *and* 'intriguing' with the Hong Kong authorities. Myers's actions smacked of duplicity. 'When a man in your prominent position, so well known by so many of the leading figures in the Nationalist Government (from which Government he is drawing a comfortable pension) throws in his lot with the enemy, you can imagine the reaction,' Little wrote contemptuously.[57] Such blatant opportunism stood in stark contrast to the idealised conception of the Foreign Inspectorate as a politically disinterested service dedicated to serving China.

Life after the Service

Where was home for Europeans and Americans in the empire world? It is too simplistic to assume that *all* expatriates equated 'home' with their country of citizenship. Over the course of a long career overseas people developed new affiliations and feelings of belonging that were not anchored in their birth country. People who moved between *multiple* sites of empire, moreover, felt the pull of home from several different places.[58] The identities of Chinese Customs Service employees were deterritorialised even further than those of their counterparts in other imperial administrative services. Exhorted by the Inspectorate to serve China, Customs officers were sometimes considered as deracinated, especially in its early years. Yet most also retained a strong sense of national identity and, more importantly, a sense of belonging to the empire world. This chapter now explores how working for the Customs changed people – their identities, their loyalties and their livelihoods. The Customs did not keep records of the post-Service destinations of their employees and no veterans' associations existed to help ex-CCS staff stay in touch. This means that our understanding of post-Service lives is necessarily hazy and incomplete, but a rough picture can nonetheless be reconstructed from the memoirs and correspondence of former employees.

For most the *idea* of returning to one's home held an enduring allure. For men and women who lived most of their lives overseas, the dream of one day returning 'home' provided an emotional mooring point. As Elizabeth Buettner has shown in her study of British-Indian families, concepts of home 'united what were often highly idealized understandings of the nation, family intimacy, and domesticity'.[59] It was as a sentimental construct that the aspiration to return to one's country of citizenship had the most power. To many colonial administrators an ultimate return home signified an end to the itinerancy and family separations that characterised colonial life and the chance to build a stable domestic haven. It also symbolised a return to one's national roots; after years submerged in an alien culture, going home offered a chance to reconfirm a sense of belonging to a nation. Most went to considerable lengths to sustain connections with home over the course of an overseas career. Many expatriates followed a career pattern of temporary sojourns overseas punctuated by long stays at home.[60] The periodic long leave granted to employees of colonial services, including the Customs, provided an extended opportunity to refresh their sense of national identity and reinforce a sense of difference from indigenous society. Letters helped to bridge the distance between employees and their family and friends and also kept them in touch with personal and cultural developments at home.[61] The culmination of decades of maintaining emotional and material links to one's country of citizenship was a permanent return home.

Many Customs employees did just that. Adjusting to life at home was, however, often a fraught process. Establishing a new social, domestic and professional life in a country which must have seemed foreign after so many years in China could be a daunting prospect, doubly so for those who were born overseas. Many felt as if they no longer quite belonged at 'home'.[62] Furthermore, returning emigrants suffered a humiliating blow to their social standing. After years of enjoying a higher status and standard of living in China, Customs men and their families inevitably felt like real nonentities without the factor of 'race prestige' to set them above and apart from the majority of the population.[63] Material hardships also weighed against returning employees; Customs men were simply unable to afford the extravagant lifestyle they had enjoyed in China.

Many deliberately chose to forgo a retirement at home. After a near lifetime of working overseas, new ties and loyalties sometimes supplanted the draw of one's homeland. On the eve of his retirement in 1933 Commissioner Luigi de Luca informed Maze that he intended to settle in Beijing or Tianjin, and that his sister, the widow of former Commissioner C. N. Holwill, and her daughter would be joining him as they found 'life difficult in America'. De Luca was simply *used* to China; his father had been the Italian minister in Beijing in the 1880s and he had consequently spent his childhood in China, joining the Customs Service in 1898. 'As for me, having spent the greater part of my life, boy and man, in China and having no very close ties in Italy, I don't feel inclined to leave this country and start at my age a new life elsewhere,' he confessed.[64] De Luca's decision to remain in China was an unusual one for a Commissioner; it was much more common for low-ranking staff to settle permanently. As discussed in Chapter 5, tidewaiters and lightkeepers were much more likely to form enduring relationships with Chinese women than their middle-class counterparts in the Indoor Staff. Often they married and raised families on the China coast. China was home for these men, and there was minimal incentive for them to return to their place of birth. Also, men with Chinese wives and Eurasian children had little desire to face the racial prejudice they would most likely encounter in Europe and North America.

For others return migrations were simply not a viable option. Although senior employees, who had lengthy and stable overseas careers, were able to retire fairly comfortably at home, more marginal Europeans and Americans faced significant material impediments. The tribulations of two former British tidewaiters, A. H. Kaye and P. W. Poutney, discharged from the Service in 1921 for misconduct, provide a case in point. Both were marooned in China because they could not afford return passages to Britain and could find no other employment in the treaty ports. As the pair were both British ex-servicemen they eventually turned for help to the United Services Association, which in turn appealed to the British consul in Shanghai, Fraser, on their behalf. In the opinion of Colonel Johnson of the United Services Association the Customs was 'very hard on this type of man, i.e. one who had no technical qualifications, that he should be liable to be thrown on his own resources in a foreign country at any time if he misbehaves himself'. Aglen grudgingly agreed to re-employ Poutney, and Kaye presumably found his own way home.[65] Their story was all too common. Unemployed foreigners who could not afford to return, or else had no incentive to, formed a European underclass of indigents and beachcombers in the treaty ports. Relief organisations such as the United Services Association and the Salvation Army worked to keep them off the streets.[66] Some were repatriated by consular authorities, travelling home by steerage. Many more were left in China, scrambling to make a living any way they could.[67]

Much of the literature on imperial migration flows assumes that white men and women were highly mobile, able to move easily between different sites or empire and the metropole. Yet mobility was often circumscribed by socio-economic or political constraints. As Troyan's case shows, Russians émigrés often struggled to find a place to settle after retiring from the Service. Unable to return 'home' because of their political beliefs, many chose to settle in China or else dreamed of emigrating to Europe. The emergent Russian Revolution discouraged the Commissioner N. A. Konovaloff, who resigned in 1916, from returning 'home' and he decided instead to retire in Beijing. A Commander in the Coast Staff, N. V. Potoloff, who was reluctantly invalided out of the Customs in 1933 after thirteen years in the Service, harboured dreams of settling down with his wife 'in an obscure French village, where a vegetable garden and a few chickens will probably feed us until "something happens"'.[68] The post-Service lives of many Russians were nomadic in character. Worse was to come after 1949, when the communist government set about expelling foreign nationals; now even settlement in China was off-limits to those without a definite homeland.

Indeed since the late 1930s mainland China had ceased to be a desirable retirement destination. Years of wartime deprivation took their toll and by 1945 the glamour of the treaty ports had long since faded. With the loss of extraterritoriality and other perks of white privilege China rapidly lost its charms. As the Commissioner A. L. Newman wrote in a 1946 letter to Little about the changing position of the foreign staff, 'foreigners are disappointed at the readiness with which foreign institutions, firms and people are maligned'. The wives of foreign Customs men were, moreover, 'disappointed and disillusioned because life in China nowadays does not provide the compensations to make up for the deficiencies which it did before, and shows little hope of doing so'. As a result many Customs officers were contemplating whether to 'cut their losses and start again in their own country or the Dominions'.[69] In 1958 C. F. A. Wilbraham, an ex-Commissioner who regularly kept L. K. Little up to date with the whereabouts of his former staff after the Foreign Inspectorate was disbanded, reported that G. Ellis, a former printer in the Statistical Department, was still living in Shanghai and was probably 'the last foreigner of the CMC still there'. Most Customs officers who wished to stay in Asia, however, moved to Hong Kong, including Chinese fleeing the nascent communist regime. Wilbraham, himself a Hong Kong resident in the 1950s, noted that he was 'continually dropping across ex-CMC-ites', foreign and Chinese alike, including the former Staff Secretary Hu Fu-sen.[70] Hong Kong was at once comfortingly Chinese and colonial. The Inspectorate's efforts at cultivating camaraderie had sometimes fallen on deaf ears while the Service still existed, but, in the period of dislocation that followed its dissolution, maintaining contact with ex-colleagues who had shared similar life and career experiences in China created a reassuring sense of belonging.[71]

Several ex-CCS officers migrated to African colonies, particularly Kenya and Nigeria, in the 1940s. It was the British Dominions, however, that presented an unparalleled chance to make a new start. In his letters to Little during the 1950s Wilbraham reported that he knew of seven ex-CCS men who were trying their luck in Australia. 'I occasionally hear from both Abbott and McNeale [former Chief Tidesurveyors], the former in Perth and the latter Sydney, and they say that all of the ex

C.M.C.s down there are doing quite well,' he reported.[72] Australia was a popular destination for European men and women travelling through or leaving China, partly owing to its relative proximity to East Asia. A sizeable number of former Shanghai Municipal Police, for example, emigrated there.[73] Diasporic groups who had previously fled to China sought sanctuary in Australia after the communist takeover in 1949. Jewish refugees who had escaped to China from Eastern Europe in the 1930s migrated in large numbers, as did Russian émigrés.[74] Former Customs employees were ideal candidates for settlement considering that the Dominions were increasingly seeking skilled and professional migrants in the 1940s, rather than the unskilled demographic they had previously attracted.[75] The attraction of life in Australia, New Zealand and Canada also worked on a symbolic level, especially for Britons. As Kathleen Paul has shown, white residents in the Dominions were clearly considered as the compatriots of the British, bound together with Britain in a 'single family' through perceived cultural and racial ties.[76] Imagining the Dominions in this way softened the transition of settlement; emigration both signified a new start and authenticated one's membership of a transnational British community. Furthermore a return to the austerity of post war Britain was an uninviting prospect, especially for those accustomed to the higher standard of living that often accompanied life in China. The Dominions provided a chance to retain a colonial style of living.

What did former Customs employees do professionally after resignation, discharge or dismissal? The foreign staff was comprised of a diverse assortment of individuals and their post-Customs occupations were equally eclectic, ranging from farmer and blacksmith to US Member of Congress.[77] B. L. Simpson's Customs credentials helped him into employment as a political adviser to the Chinese government. More dubiously, A. H. F. Edwardes, who lost out on the top job to Maze in 1929, later worked as adviser to the Japanese puppet state of Manchukuo.[78] It is clear, however, that the majority of those who resigned early on in their careers went on to staff the institutions of foreign China. Despite the Inspectorate's insistence that the Customs staff stood aloof from other foreign communities, they had little compunction about leaving to work for treaty port institutions. The Customs provided a convenient foot in the door to China coast society. It enabled young men to earn their stripes in China before moving on to more lucrative and satisfying employment. As discussed in Chapter 3, the nineteenth-century Customs heavily relied on poaching student interpreters from the legations, but this personnel stream flowed both ways. Several men who were disillusioned with the drudgery of Customs work left to join the diplomatic establishment in China.

Paul von Möllendorff joined the Customs in 1869 only because the German government had promised him a consular appointment after he had been in China for five years.[79] Others went on to work for the non-official foreign establishment. Many joined China coast firms or banks such as HSBC and Butterfield & Swire. After resigning in 1920 A. H. Rasmussen worked with Arnold, Karberg and Co. in Zhenjiang and Tianjin for twenty-seven years before he again uprooted, this time to London.[80] Several ex-CCS men found work as hacks for the treaty port rags that shrilly defended settler interests, or else as China correspondents for European and American newspapers. The China coast firebrands B. Lennox Simpson (Putnam Weale) and J. O. P. Bland both worked as journalists while the American Willard Straight became a Reuters correspondent and later enjoyed a long career in the US consular service after resigning from the Customs in 1904. E. L. Lépissier, in the Indoor Staff 1869–1912, had a successful side career as editor of a French-language Shanghai newspaper, Le Progrès.[81]

Many were offered new positions in the treaty ports because they were considered China experts by dint of their experiences working for the Chinese government. But to what extent did experience of Customs work prepare them for careers outside of China? Ex-CCS men rarely stayed in the customs line of work. Wilbraham reported optimistically in a letter about the post-Service careers of Customs men that 'the old Haikuan training was so varied that they are able to hold their own with anyone'.[82] Yet, while the technical skills developed while working for the Coast Staff and Marine Department could be easily parlayed into a seafaring career, employees in other branches pursued an extremely broad range of careers in their post-Customs lives. Various Outdoor men who had emigrated to Australia after leaving the Customs, Wilbraham informed Little, were trying their hand at farming, others had gone into business, and one had become a blacksmith. For others their Customs training proved useful. One man simply switched to working in the Australian customs and former Assistant Staff Secretary King's experience of work in China enabled him to secure a post in the Far Eastern branch of the Australian Foreign Office. Clerical and managerial work appears to have been the occupation of choice for those who had returned to Britain, and two former Commissioners had found posts working for the colonial authorities in Nigeria.[83] Post-Service careers were usually not illustrious, but then neither were their positions in the Customs.

While it is true that numerous former employees went on to enjoy stable alternative employment and that a stint in the Service often acted as a stepping stone to a more lucrative imperial career, many others found that working overseas did not enhance their social, professional and economic status in the slightest. What is more, the fortunes of those who left the Customs under a cloud plummeted. The boat officer E. M. Popov, paid off for stealing revenue moneys during the Spring Festival holiday in 1940, wrote to the IG protesting that the 'stigma attached to my name' meant that he could not find work.[84] Of the foreign employees found guilty of malpractice discussed earlier in this chapter, only S. A. Klubien successfully rebounded, becoming a successful writer of children's books, one of which featured a Chinese Customs officer. While Klubien was able to escape his dubious reputation by returning to Denmark, those who were forced to remain on the China coast found it practically impossible to eradicate the taint of dismissal. Oliver Hall, who had a Chinese wife and eight children to provide for, was reduced to penury. In 1939, 'after six months misery in trying to get employment', Hall swallowed his pride and wrote to Maze begging to be reinstated.[85] Even Hall's children wrote heart-rending letters to the IG. 'Next month, if nothing is done we will only have one meal per day,' one wrote. 'Surely you can forgive and forget?' Maze refused to reply to these entreaties.[86] Not only did misconduct endanger the Customs' reputation; it also irreparably damaged the future employment prospects and livelihoods of those responsible.

As the pleas from Hall's children suggest, sudden withdrawal from service and the consequent loss of salary could affect many other lives besides those of the employees in question. Until 1920, when an official pension scheme was introduced, employees were expected to save for their own retirement. Every five to ten years of service, depending on rank, the Inspectorate issued a sum of money to each foreign employee equal to between six months' and one year's pay. They were instructed to invest it as they saw fit.[87] Those who squandered their extra pay through 'individual extravagance' only had themselves to blame, admonished Hart.[88] This rudimentary retirement scheme left the dependants of employees who left the Service abruptly, either because of death, invaliding or dismissal, in a predicament. The Customs archives are peppered with desperate missives from the destitute wives and children of former employees. Sometimes the Inspectorate was moved to help out on compassionate grounds. The Shantou Commissioner in 1882, for example, forwarded a letter from the widow of the deceased lightkeeper J. H. Green, who had served for eight years, to the IG. Although Mrs Green was 'a native', and therefore regarded as 'able to earn a living in China' herself, the fact that she had three young children to care for persuaded the IG to grant an allowance.[89] In the nineteenth century the IG would often offer a job to the eldest son of a deceased employee in order that he could support his mother and siblings.

The letters received from the family of the deceased after the death of a Customs man reveal how China was integrated into global financial webs, through which expatriates remitted money to family members across the globe. An obligation to support relations was often, in fact, the primary motivation for seeking professional opportunities overseas, although many Customs employees found that their ability to do so was circumscribed by the high standard of living that Europeans and Americans were expected to maintain on the China coast. As Gary Magee and Andrew Thompson have shown in their analysis of remittance flows between the UK and Australasia, North America and South Africa, rather than showing individuals renouncing ties to their homelands, 'such streams of money pay testimony to the capacity of British migrants to construct complex webs of association stretching across the English-speaking world from their place of settlement all the way back to their place of origin'.[90] Even middle-class employees were often required to support down-at-the-heel relations. 'I am less glad for my own sake than for yours, as I can now send you at least a hundred a year,' wrote the junior assistant Edward Bowra to his mother on receiving a pay rise in 1863, which increased his annual salary to the equivalent of £600.[91] Edwin Denby, son of the American minister to China, also periodically helped his parents out financially. Customs wages, then, travelled thousands of miles to support international networks of beneficiaries.

The death of a Customs benefactor, therefore, dealt a severe blow to the livelihoods of dependants. After a more generous retirement scheme was introduced in 1920, the Inspectorate was inundated with letters from the families of deceased employees who had previously received financial support and now sought to stake their claims to Customs pension benefits. If the relative in question could prove that they had been supported by the deceased, the Inspectorate grudgingly agreed to pay out his contributions to the retirement fund. After chief assistant K. W. Power died in 1929 his mother wrote to the London Office 'very much harassed about financial matters, as her son, who had no private means, contributed to her support; and she is now deprived of that support'.[92] After receiving proof of Mrs Power's meagre income the Inspectorate granted an allowance. Similarly, in the same year the Inspectorate issued pension benefits to the Konovaloff family, which had multiple ties to the Customs. N. A. Konovaloff, a former Customs Commissioner who had resigned from the Service in 1916, submitted a petition on behalf of his brother, A. A. Konovaloff, and his family of three children, who had been supported by another brother in the Customs, chief assistant S. A. Konovaloff, who had recently died in Shanghai. 'The late S. A. Konovaloff has been supporting them, as well as an orphan niece of ours, for a number of years until his death when, owing to the conditions in Russia, A. A. Konovaloff became practically destitute,' he explained.[93] Most work on remittances has focused on flows of money from the colonies to Britain. Customs wages, however, provided a lifeline for family members around the world, in Europe, America, the Dominions, Russia and on the China coast itself. It thus fostered a global network of dependants whose livelihoods were influenced by Customs fortunes.

Wartime created rising panic about the future livelihoods of the foreign staff. By the late 1940s it was clear that most would not receive the retirement benefits promised to them in 1920. Post war currency depreciation meant that the contributions deducted from staff salaries were unlikely to amount to the sum necessary to purchase the promised annuity by the time of retirement. Those British and American employees forced out of the Service in 1941 and the foreign employees who were compulsorily retired in 1943 while interned were dismayed to find in 1945 that they would receive only half the pension they were promised in 1920. Little received a deluge of letters from disgruntled former employees who had pinned their hopes of a comfortable retirement on their Customs pension. The former Deputy Commissioner Flanagan, who served in Tianjin from 1939 until his dismissal in December 1941, pronounced the Customs guilty of 'little short of base ingratitude'. 'I have been insulted time and time again in the Tientsin Office [by the Japanese wartime authorities] and have taken it smilingly for the sake of the Service and the Chinese Government and now that very Government turns around and throws me out with a totally inadequate pension at an age when it will be well nigh impossible to obtain suitable employment,' Flanagan raged.[94] Little was apologetic, yet admitted that Flanagan's prediction that he would receive a derisory sum as a pension was 'pretty close to the truth'.[95] Since 1945 Little had, in fact, been subjecting the Ministry of Finance to a continuous barrage of letters requesting that the pensions of employees dismissed in 1941 and 1943 be released yet, despite his best efforts, the cash-drained government replied that it simply did not have the funds.[96] Little did, in June 1947, eventually manage to get the staff reduced pensions. Nevertheless, as their Customs days were drawing to a close in the late 1940s, those men who had joined with expectations of a long career were sorely disappointed at the poor dividends they received in return for years of loyal service.

Those who had anticipated a lifelong career in the Customs experienced an abrupt change in their life trajectories in the 1940s. Of course the employees of all major overseas services experienced a degree of anxiety in the age of decolonisation, but the Customs staff suffered more than most for the premature loss of their careers. The 700 British officers still serving the Indian Civil Service in 1947, for example, were presented with the option of continuing their careers in the successor civil services established in India and Pakistan, taking up a post in the Dominions or choosing early retirement with compensation.[97] Even former Shanghai policemen were helped by the Foreign Office into jobs in the Hong Kong police force or else into temporary positions in the War Crimes Commission.[98] Eminent figures in the foreign staff experienced few problems finding alternative employment. Commissioner B. E. Foster Hall was offered a lucrative second career with an American insurance company in Hong Kong in 1948, although he had to study for two years before he could qualify for a position.[99] The former Commissioner Everitt Groff-Smith also stayed in Asia after the war working for the financial department of the South Korean military government.[100] The American Coast Inspector F. Sabel, who stayed until the end after rejoining the Service in 1945, moved seamlessly from working for the Customs to advising the UN on navigational matters in the 1950s.[101] The former IG L. K. Little was certainly not short of job offers after 1950. He put his Customs expertise to good use in the early 1950s in various positions, acting as adviser to the Philippines Customs, the Japanese Customs Service and the Chinese Ministry of Finance in Taiwan, was offered and turned down the job of commissioner of the US Customs, and worked for the US Information Agency, 1955–60.[102] 'After forty years of service under a foreign government, it has been a privilege to have served my own government for five years,' he wrote on his eventual retirement in 1960.[103] Men who had served in the highest echelons of the Customs were marked as experts on international matters, and in the post war period of reconstruction and occupation they were able to segue smoothly into consultancy positions.

Distinguished positions such as these were not available to most, however. Most remaining foreigners in 1949 were Customs veterans nearing retirement age who were unwilling or unable to begin a new career. Reporting on the activities of former Customs employees resident in Hong Kong in 1958, Charles Wilbraham surmised: 'the trouble is that the majority of them having been in the Service for 20–30 years are now in the neighbourhood of 50, and at that age it is most difficult to obtain a post unless one happens to be a specialist, and how many can be classed as that, in a business sense?'[104] The futures of these employees were fraught with uncertainty. In the midst of evacuations from Shanghai in 1942, the marine assistant Owen Gander, dismissed in December 1941 after twenty-seven years of service, dithered over whether to leave China. Gander professed to prefer 'life in the East', and decided that 'if I leave China with nothing after spending over 28 years of my life here the reasons must be strong and urgent ones'.[105] Above and beyond his attachment to China, 'the idea of arriving in England with no money, no means of support for my family, is horrible. It seems to be highly undesirable to make definite arrangements to leave Shanghai until I have money or some definite assurance that will take the place of money,' he wrote in his diary. The cost of Gander's prevarication was internment for him and his family in Yangzhou camp early in January 1943. His concerns about returning home penniless were echoed by many. In 1946 the Non-Resident Secretary in London B. Foster Hall wrote to Little on behalf of ex-tidewaiter S. Halliwell and ex-lightkeeper H. Mitchell, dismissed in 1942 and now in London, 'both of whom have no funds whatever in this country and are living off relations until I am authorised to pay them'.[106] Most senior Indoor staff, too, were not unscathed by the war. On his release from internment in 1945 the former Commissioner E. A. Pritchard catalogued 'losses at £7000–£8000 excluding sentimental values which are inestimable'.[107] Flanagan, another ex-Commissioner, also emerged from his Customs career in an impoverished and embittered state. 'With 90% of my personal belongings in the bottom of Hong Kong harbour, three insurance policies about to be cancelled, a large proportion of my pension lost in Shanghai and my savings used up in keeping my family in London during the war in full expectation that I would be re-employed by the Customs,' he fumed. 'What an end to what I had hoped was going to be an honourable career.'[108] Of course they were at least alive, as were most Britons who had stayed in China for the duration of the war. Yet with the loss of their material possessions senior Customs men also lost some of their standing and respectability, their expectations of a secure career and comfortable retirement dashed.

Conclusion

Throughout their careers foreign employees were imbued by the Inspectorate with a sense of pride in their service's cosmopolitan character. Their post-Customs destinations were revealing of whether Customs men really *were* true cosmopolites, individuals who in the words of Robin Cohen and Steven Vertovec were 'prone to articulate complex affiliations, meaningful attachments and multiple allegiances to issues, people, places and traditions that lie beyond the boundaries of their resident nation-state'.[109] In many ways they fit this description. Post-Service destinations reveal how attachment to China and the Customs vied with nostalgia for a national homeland and the enticement of opportunities in the wider empire world in the minds of the foreign staff. The uneasy coexistence of these multiple loyalties meant that withdrawals from service and post-Customs life trajectories followed no clear patterns. In this respect the experiences of the foreign Customs staff present us with a useful lesson in the history of informal empire. The breadth of global and local allegiances in evidence amongst the Customs staff is telling of the range of loyalties and affiliations among foreign societies on the edges of empire more broadly. Whereas imperial administrators were expected to sustain clear loyalties to the Crown, the identities of those who lived and worked on the peripheries of empire were often much more ambivalent and heterogeneous. The networks of the empire world gave people mobility, especially white Europeans and North Americans. These movements around the world in turn fostered a global identity, which coexisted with national and local ties.

The modes by which people left the Service speak to the sheer diversity of experiences of working overseas. The foreign staff had its long-serving employees and its transients, its model workers and its reprobates, and the diversity of its personnel was reflected in patterns of leaving the Service, whether by resignation, dismissal or retirement. External political events also shaped career trajectories. The mass dismissals of the 1940s and the eventual dissolution of the foreign staff, for example, fundamentally changed the character of withdrawals from Service. Those whose careers were prematurely terminated in the early 1940s found themselves unemployed and forced to begin a new life elsewhere. In addition to offering opportunities for a better life, the empire world also spoke of dislocation, poverty and uncertainty. It is important to bring to light tales of colonial failure because they provide a necessary corrective to the common caricature of the upper-class Englishman overseas. Individual stories of personal triumphs and disasters bring to light the human stories of real weight that lay behind colonial stereotypes of the Putnam Weale adventurer, the dipsomaniac and the thug, and the upright Customs official.

Notes

1   Little papers, BMS Am 1999, box 1, folder 4, 'Miscellaneous correspondence, 1953', letter from A. M. Troyan to L. K. Little, 23 Aug 1953.
2   Some examples of discussions of colonial migration and identity are: Marina Carter, *Voices from Indenture: Experiences of Indian migrants in the British Empire* (London: Leicester University Press, 1996), chapter 5, 183–227, and Alison Blunt, '"Land of Our Mothers": Home, identity, and nationality for Anglo-Indians in British India, 1919–1947', *History Workshop Journal*, 54 (2002), 49–72.
3   SHAC, 679(1) 31684, 'IG's confidential correspondence with port Commissioners, 1934', confidential letter from Commissioner Forbes, Amoy, to officiating IG Lawford, 20 July 1934.
4   SHAC, 679(2) 1588, 'Shanghai Customs: dispatches to IG, 1886', dispatch no. 400, Commissioner Fitz-Roy to Hart, 15 May 1886.

5   For details of staff illnesses see the following files on invaliding cases: SHAC, 679(1) 15545–15590. Maze was also reluctant to invalid employees suffering from ailments caused by 'their irregular mode of living', a reference to alcoholism and sexually transmitted diseases. SHAC, 679(1) 16757, 'General regulations governing superannuation and retirement, 1921–47', circular no. 3,987 of 11 Oct 1929.

6   SHAC, 679(1) 16757, 'General regulations governing superannuation and retirement, 1921–47', circular no. 4,209, 11 Apr 1931.

7   Douglas Haynes, *Imperial Medicine: Patrick Manson and the conquest of tropical disease* (Philadelphia: University of Pennsylvania Press, 2001).

8   See SHAC, 679(1) 16677, 'Medical attendance: Tientsin, 1909–49', dispatch no. 11,014, 20 Aug 1937, for an example of the regulations governing the employment of medical officers.

9   SHAC, 679(1) 15608, 'Foreign Out-door employees deceased, 1929', Mengzi dispatch no. 4,490, Commissioner Kremer to Maze, 16 Oct 1929.

10 Kennedy, *Magic Mountains*, 19.

11 Kerrie L. Macpherson, *A Wilderness of Marshes: The origins of public health in Shanghai, 1843–93* (Hong Kong: Oxford University Press, 1987), 19. For the broader picture of European mortality rates in the tropics see Philip D. Curtin, *Death by Migration: Europe's encounter with the tropical world in the nineteenth century* (Cambridge: Cambridge University Press, 1989).

12 For Shanghai see Macpherson, *Wilderness of Marshes*, especially chapter 2, 15–48. For Tianjin see Ruth Rogaski, *Hygienic Modernity: Meanings of health and disease in treaty-port China* (Berkeley: University of California Press, 2004), 76–103.

13 Kennedy, *Magic Mountains*, 30.

14 Hippisley papers, memoirs, 93 and 155–6.

15 SHAC, 679(2) 84, 'Amoy Customs: Dispatches to IG, 1862–8', dispatch no. 62, 15 Aug 1867.

16 SHAC, 679(1) 32517, 'Nanning semi-official, 1913–20', S/O no. 79, 11 May 1914, and S/O no. 80, 30 June 1914; SHAC, 679(3) 1494, 'Nanning dispatches, nos. 611–700', dispatch no. 669, 11 May 1914.

17 SHAC, 679(1) 10839, 'Mr. Philip Hiram Everhart's career', report by acting Commissioner W. Macdonald, 21 Nov 1919.

18 SHAC, 679(1) 31644, 'IG's confidential correspondence with port Commissioners, 1932–3', confidential letters from Commissioner Peel to IG Maze, 9 May 1933 and 23 May 1933.

19 SHAC, 679(9) 14237, 'Staff Secretary's office – semi-official and confidential correspondence during 1937, Kiungchow-Santuao', confidential letter from Staff Secretary Hu Fu-sen to Commissioner Forbes, 16 Dec 1937.

20 SHAC, 679(9) 1415, 'Staff Secretary's office: semi-official and confidential correspondence during 1937', confidential letter from Commissioner Campbell to staff secretary Kishimoto Hirokichi, 19 May 1937.

21 SHAC, 679(1) 26890, 'IG's circulars, vol. 1, first series, 1861–75', circular no. 25 of 1869 (first series), 'Port requirements and reorganisation', 1 Nov 1869.

22 Robert Ronald Campbell, *James Duncan Campbell* (Cambridge, MA: Harvard University Press, 1970), xvii.

23 Qu Tongzu, *Local Government in China under the Ch'ing* (Cambridge, MA: Harvard University Press, 1962), 36–55; Madeleine Zelin, *The Magistrate's Tael: Rationalizing fiscal reform in eighteenth-century Ch'ing China* (Berkeley: University of California Press, 1984), chapter 6, 220–63.

24 Henry J. Lethbridge, *Hong Kong: Stability and Change* (Hong Kong: Oxford University Press, 1978), 227.

25 Philip Harling, *The Waning of 'Old Corruption': The politics of economical reform in Britain, 1779–1846* (Oxford: Clarendon Press, 1996).

26 Christopher Munn, *Anglo-China: Chinese people and British rule in Hong Kong, 1841–1880* (Hong Kong: Hong Kong University Press, 2009), 291.

27 TMA, W1-1-4321, 'Semi-official letters from IG, 1930–1', memo from Pritchard to Maze, 7 Sept 1931.

28 SHAC, 679(1) 16826, 'Commissioners' reports on Out-door Staff petitions for increase in pay in reply to circular no. 2,545', Statistical Secretary no. 2,807, 13 July 1916.

29 Fairbank et al. eds, *Robert Hart and China's Modernization*, Hart's journal entry for 18 Mar 1864, 73.

30 SHAC, 679(1) 16100, 'Instructions regarding conduct and discipline of Customs Staff, 1929–49', circular no. 3,899 (second series), 22 Apr 1929.

31 SHAC, 679(1) 26909, 'Inspector General's circulars, vol. 19, second series, nos. 3,801–4,100, 1928–30', circular no. 4,094 (second series), 27 June 1930.

32 SHAC, 679(1) 16922, 'Fraud on Revenue, Mr S. A. Klubien, Tientsin, 1928', Tianjin dispatches nos 8,655 & 8,776, 17 May 1928 and 8 Nov 1928.

33 SHAC, 679(1) 16953, 'Shanghai Fraud Case, 1938, involving Messrs. O. Hall, Senior Chief Examiner A and Chang Hsuan, Assistant Examiner A', Shanghai no. 29,413 to IG, 1 June 1938.

34 See report in *The North-China Herald*, 23 Dec 1922, 819–21.

35 SHAC, 679(1) 16919, 'Enquiry into corruption in Tientsin Out-door Staff arising out of the R. J. Redd case, 1930', dispatch no. 9,072, 14 Jan 1930.

36 SHAC, 679(1) 12033, 'Mr. R. J. Redd's Career'.

37 SHAC, 679(1) 16919, 'Enquiry into corruption in Tientsin Out-door Staff arising out of the R. J. Redd case, 1930', Prettejohn's report on the investigation, 8 Feb 1930; Tianjin Commissioner Howell's report on the investigation, dispatch no. 9,089, 10 Feb 1930.

38 SHAC, 679(1) 16919, 'Enquiry into corruption in Tientsin Out-door Staff arising out of the R. J. Redd case, 1930', minutes of interview with Wong Yo Pei, 16 Nov 1929; letter from Howell to IG, 13 Dec 1929.

39 SHAC, 679(1) 16100, 'Instructions regarding conduct and discipline of Customs Staff, 1929–49', circular letter from Little to deputy IG K. T. Ting, 4 Oct 1945.

40 W. Somerset Maugham, *The Gentleman in the Parlour* (first published 1930), in *The Travel Books* (London: Heinemann, 1955), 161.

41 Dewey, *Anglo-Indian Attitudes*, 5.

42 SHAC, 679(1) 15655, 'Questions relating to German and Austrian members of Service upon declaration of war on Germany and Austria-Hungary by China, 1917', petition forwarded in Canton dispatch no. 10,272, 14 Sept 1917.

43 SHAC, 679(1) 15655, 'Questions relating to German and Austrian members of Service upon declaration of war on Germany and Austria-Hungary by China, 1917', letter from C. Pape to IG Aglen, 22 Sept 1917.

44 SHAC, 679(1) 15655, 'Questions relating to German and Austrian members of Service upon declaration of war on Germany and Austria-Hungary by China, 1917', letter from K. Hemeling, H. E. Wolf, E. O. Heis and Wilzer to IG Aglen, 14 Oct 1917.

45 SHAC, 679(1) 15655, 'Questions relating to German and Austrian members of Service upon declaration of war on Germany and Austria-Hungary by China, 1917'.

46 See, for example, SHAC, 679(1) 31639, 'IG confidential correspondence with port commissioners, 1929', confidential letter from Shanghai Commissioner Myers to Maze, 31 Oct 1929.

47 SHAC, 679(1) 31639, 'IG's confidential correspondence with port Commissioners, 1929', letter from Tianjin Commissioner Howell to Maze, 29 July 1929.

48 For an account of the takeover see *Documents Illustrative*, vol. 5, semi-official circular no. 95, 'Manchurian Customs: Account of seizure of by "Manchukuo" authorities', 20 Apr 1933.

49 Imperial War Museum Archives, London, 86/44/1, Owen D. Gander papers, manuscript diary (hereafter Gander papers, diary), vol. 1, diary entry on 28 Jan 1942.

50 Little papers, FMS Am 1999.3, 'L. K. Little, personal correspondence, 1946', circular no. 610, 20 Sept 1943.

51 Little papers, FMS Am 1999.1, 'L. K. Little, personal correspondence, 1941–44', *The Chinese Maritime Customs Service*, 6 July 1944.

52 Little papers, FMS Am 1999.2, 'L. K. Little, personal correspondence, 1945', letter from E. A. Pritchard, Hong Kong, to Little, 20 Sept 1945.

53 See SHAC, 679(1) 15656, 'General questions concerning staff interned during the Pacific War', for a list of employees who had not been interned and were re-employed after 1945.

54 Little papers, FMS Am 1999.3, 'L. K. Little, personal correspondence, 1946', petition from seven foreign Commissioners, 4 Nov 1946.

55 Little papers, FMS Am 1999.4, 'L. K. Little, personal correspondence, 1946', personal letter from Commissioner Newman, Amoy, to IG Little, 15 Sept 1946, enclosing a petition from the Amoy Outdoor Staff.

56 For an account of the final years of the foreign presence in China, and of the fate of foreign nationals resident there, see Beverley Hooper, *China Stands Up: Ending the Western presence, 1948–50* (London: Allen & Unwin, 1986), especially chapter 5, 71–84.

57 TNA, FO 371/83394, letter from Little to Myers, 7 Dec 1949.

58 See Marilyn J. Barber, '"Two Homes Now": The return migration of the Fellowship of the Maple Leaf', in *Emigrant Homecomings: The return movement of emigrants, 1600–2000*, edited by Marjory Harper (Manchester: Manchester University Press, 2005), 197–214.

59 Buettner, *Empire Families*, 190.

60 Dudley Baines, *Emigration from Europe, 1815–1930* (Cambridge: Cambridge University Press, 1995), chapter 5, 35–8.

61 Buettner, *Empire Families*, 110–45.

62 Elizabeth Buettner, '"We Don't Grow Coffee and Bananas in Clapham Junction You Know!": Imperial Britons back home', in *Settlers and Expatriates*, edited by Bickers.

63 For a detailed discussion of the drop in social status and material hardships experienced by Anglo-Indian families returning to Britain in the nineteenth and early twentieth centuries see Buettner, *Empire Families*, chapter 5, 'From Somebodies to Nobodies: Returning home to Britain and perpetuating overseas connections', 188–251.

64 SHAC, 679(1) 31644, 'IG's confidential correspondence with port Commissioners, 1932–33', personal letter, Commissioner de Luca, Tianjin, to IG Maze, 7 Feb 1933.

65 TNA, FO 228/3497, letter from Colonel Marr Johnson, United Services Association, to Shanghai consul-general E. Fraser, 11 June 1921; letter from Aglen to British minister to China Sir Beilby F. Alston, 26 July 1921.

66 Bickers, *Empire Made Me*, 235–38.

67 For a discussion of how poorer settlers could not afford to make return migrations see Eric Richards, 'Running Home from Australia: Intercontinental mobility and migrant expectations in the nineteenth century,' in *Emigrant Homecomings*, edited by Harper, 77–104.

68 SHAC, 679(9) 1419, 'Staff secretary's office: Semi-official and confidential correspondence during 1933–35', letter from Potoloff to Coast Inspector Hillman, 21 Nov 1933.

69 Little papers, FMS 1999.4, 'Personal correspondence, 1946', letter from Newman to Little, 15 Sept 1946.

70 Little papers, BMS 1999, box 1, folders 6 and 7, 'Miscellaneous correspondence', letters from Wilbraham to Little, 23 Mar 1958 and 15 Oct 1956.

71 See Buettner, *Empire Families*, 209–38, for a discussion of the comparable efforts of British-Indian efforts to maintain a sense of community after their return to Britain.

72 Little papers, BMS 1999, box 1, folders 6 and 7, 'Miscellaneous correspondence', letters from Wilbraham to Little, 23 Mar 1958 and 15 Oct 1956.

73 Bickers, *Empire Made Me*, 223–50.

74 Antonia Finnane, *Far From Where?: Jewish Journeys from Shanghai to Australia* (Carlton, Vic.: Melbourne University Press, 1999).

75 Constantine, 'British Emigration to the Empire-Commonwealth', 16–35.

76 Paul, 'Communities of Britishness'.

77 Edwin Denby, in the Customs 1887–97, was first elected to Congress in 1904 and became Secretary of the Navy in 1921.

78 Bickers, 'Purloined Letters', 10.
79 *I. G. in Peking*, vol. 1, 136, n. 5.
80 Rasmussen, *China Trader*.
81 *I. G. in Peking*, vol. 1, 18, n. 2.
82 Little papers, BMS Am 1999, box 1, folder 7, 'Miscellaneous correspondence, 1959–60', letter from Wilbraham to Little, 23 Mar 1958.
83 Little papers, BMS Am 1999, box 1, folder 6, 'Miscellaneous correspondence, 1956–58', letter from Wilbraham, Hong Kong, to Little, 15 Oct 1956.
84 SHAC, 679(1) 16955, 'Case of theft of revenue moneys, Shanghai, 1940, involving Messrs. M. W. Hallums, E. M. Popov, and others', letter from Popov to Maze, 15 Mar 1941.
85 SHAC, 679(1) 16953, 'Shanghai fraud case, 1938, involving Messrs. O. Hall, Senior Chief Examiner A and Chang Hsuan, Assistant Examiner A', letter from Hall to Maze, 28 Feb 1939.
86 SHAC, 679(1) 16953, 'Shanghai fraud case, 1938, involving Messrs. O. Hall, Senior Chief Examiner A and Chang Hsuan, Assistant Examiner A'.
87 *Documents Illustrative*, vol. 1, circular no. 25 of 1869 (first series), 'Service re-organisation, regulations and explanations', 1 Nov 1869, 157 and circular no. 26 of 1870 (first series), 'Retiring allowances, retention in Service, rules regarding', 31 Dec 1870.
88 *Documents Illustrative*, vol. 1, circular no. 5 of 1876 (second series), 'Retiring allowances: new rules', 5 June 1876, 362–3.
89 SHAC, 679(2) 1868, 'Swatow Customs: Dispatches and enclosures to IG, 1882–3', dispatch no. 38, 6 Mar 1882.
90 Gary B. Magee and Andrew S. Thompson, 'The Global and Local: Explaining migrant remittance flows in the English-speaking world, 1880–1914', *The Journal of Economic History*, 66:1 (2006), 177–8.
91 SOAS, PP MS 69, Bowra papers, box 3, file 3, letter from Bowra, Tianjin, to his mother, 30 May 1863.
92 SHAC, 679(1) 15606, 'Foreign Indoor employees deceased, 1929–30', S/O letter, NRS Stephenson to Commissioner Myers, Shanghai, 24 June 1929.
93 SHAC, 679(1) 15606, 'Foreign Indoor employees deceased, 1929–30', letter from N. A. Konovaloff to Maze, 22 Nov 1930.
94 Little papers, FMS Am 1999.4, 'L. K. Little, personal correspondence, 1946', personal letter from H. R. J. W. Flanagan, Hong Kong, to IG Little, 9 Feb 1946.
95 Little papers, FMS Am 1999.4, 'L. K. Little, personal correspondence, 1946', letter from Little to Flanagan, 21 Feb 1941.
96 See, for example, Little papers, FMS Am 1999.2, 'L. K. Little, personal correspondence, 1945', personal letter, IG Little to minister of finance, O. K. Yui, 7 May 1945.
97 See Kirk-Greene, *Imperial Administrators*, chapter 9, 261–73.
98 Bickers, *Empire Made Me*, 322.
99 Little papers, FMS Am 1999.9, 'L. K. Little, personal correspondence, 1948', letter from B. Foster Hall, Kent, to Little, 19 Mar 1948.
100 Little papers, BMS Am 1999.4, 'L. K. Little, personal, 1946', letter from Little to Groff-Smith, 8 June 1946.
101 Little papers, BMS Am 1999, box 1, folder 6, 'Miscellaneous correspondence, 1956–58', letter from Little to Howard Abbott, Perth, 10 Jan 1957.
102 See Little papers, BMS Am 1999, box 1, folder 1 for Little's recommended reforms for the Japanese Customs Service, 1950; folder 2 for correspondence concerning Little's mission to the Philippines, 1951; folder 3 for Little's work with the Advisory Committee on Undeveloped Areas, 1952–52; and folder 5 for correspondence regarding his post with the Chinese Ministry of Finance (resigned 1954).
103 Little papers, BMS Am 1999, box 1, folder 7, 'Miscellaneous correspondence, 1959–60', letter from Little to George V. Allen, US Information Agency, 1 Aug 1960.
104 Little papers, BMS Am 1999, box 1, folder 7, 'Miscellaneous correspondence, 1959–60', letter from C. F. A. Wilbraham, Hong Kong, to Little, 23 Mar 1958.

105 Gander papers, diary, vol. 1, entry on 22 Mar 1942.
106 Little papers, FMS Am 1999.4, 'L. K. Little, personal correspondence, 1946', letter from Foster Hall, London, to Little, 9 Jan 1946.
107 Little papers, FMS Am 1999.2, 'L. K. Little, personal correspondence, 1945', letter from E. A. Pritchard, Hong Kong, to Little, 20 Sept 1945.
108 Little papers, FMS Am 1999.4, 'L. K. Little, personal correspondence, 1946', letter from Flanagan, Hong Kong, to Little, 9 Feb 1946.
109 Robin Cohen and Stephen Vertovec, 'Introduction: Conceiving Cosmopolitanism', in *Conceiving Cosmopolitanism: Theory, Context and Practice*, edited by Cohen and Vertovec (Oxford: Oxford University Press, 2002), 2.

CHAPTER SEVEN

Conclusion

> In one of your recent letters you express the fear that I will become, or am now, foreignized, by which I suppose you mean Anglicized, surrounded as I am by Englishmen and women. There might be danger of this for one who loved his country and his countrymen less than I do, but I assure you I have grown more uncompromisingly American every day. My greatest friends here have always been American . . . So have no fears on that score. I will only cease to be an American, an ardent enthusiastic American, when the clods of an American grave are trodden down above me.[1]

Edwin Denby's words were intended to reassure his mother that he had not lost sight of his national roots on immersion in the multinational environment of the Customs Service. This issue preoccupied Denby throughout his short Customs career. On taking up his appointment in 1887 he was concerned that his family would think 'I had done a wrong thing in expatriating myself' by joining the Chinese government's employ. Furthermore, the cosmopolitanism of the Customs had the potential to dampen nationalist feeling, although Edwin assured his mother that, while he got on well with the English, 'they do sometimes stir up the old Revolutionary spirit in me'.[2] In mapping the life trajectories of the Customs staff this book has primarily aimed to uncover the personal and professional ramifications of working within a different state's administration. Denby's fervent insistence that he was still a true American reveals deep-seated worries about the personal implications of serving the Chinese government and working alongside men of multiple nationalities. His anxieties were shared by many other foreigners in the Customs and were especially acute in the late nineteenth century when nationalist feeling was running high. While the Customs staff was viewed as a convenient vehicle for augmenting the influence of multiple foreign powers, its employees were also eyed suspiciously as people whose loyalties were suspect and who did not sail under their true colours. Prominent figures in the Customs who

[201]

were at ease with Chinese culture and adept at forming alliances with Chinese officials and entrepreneurs, such as Robert Hart and Gustav Detring, were regarded distrustfully as being too comfortable in China. In an age of imperialist competition between nascent nation-states, multinational co-operation was equally objectionable.

Fears of deracination were palpable in these nervous discussions. Such anxieties were common across the empire world, but were redoubled in the case of the Customs, an organisation that operated under the auspices of the Chinese state in which foreigners worked alongside Chinese counterparts. Even the Inspectorate, ostensibly established to serve China, experienced deep ambivalences about its 'hybrid' status. On the one hand, foreign employees were exhorted to act as the countrymen of their Chinese colleagues but, on the other hand, their very existence rested on the conviction that Europeans and Americans possessed certain intrinsic qualities that set them apart from their Chinese colleagues. Closeness with Chinese individuals and communities, whether exhibited through marriage, friendship or collaboration in seditious activities, undermined this legitimising rationale. This also explains why colonial societies and institutions were so unsettled by white pauperism, as evinced by the alarm with which the Inspectorate viewed indebtedness among the foreign staff. Insobriety, mental illness, violence and a lack of domestic 'respectability' were simultaneously viewed as predictable problems resulting from submersion in a Chinese environment and evidence of personal lapses that jeopardised the entire fiction of white prestige. As Richard Eves and Nicholas Thomas have commented, colonists soon found that 'one cannot depend on one's whiteness'; failure to uphold European behavioural and cultural standards could easily weaken an individual's claim to a place within 'white' society.[3] The parameters of 'Europeanness', then, were not fixed and neither were they based entirely on race. Fears about the dilution of racial sensibility also permeated the Chinese staff, especially during the anti-imperialist fervour of the 1920s. The Customs provided an opportunity for social and professional mobility for many Chinese, but at the same time employment in the Foreign Inspectorate marked them as 'running dogs' of the imperialists. In the early twentieth century, when Chinese national identity increasingly hinged upon ideas about common racial descent, fears of deracination through collaboration with foreigners became much more acute.[4]

Concern about the dangers of expatriate life starkly illuminates some of the ideological contradictions inherent in imperial expansion and colonial rule. Empire-building in the modern age scattered millions of people around the globe, bringing them into contact and conflict with people of different nationalities and different races. Furthermore

Europeans who moved overseas to staff the machinery of colonialism often acquired a heightened sense of belonging to the empire world, which coexisted with national and local identities. Yet the crossing of national, racial and cultural boundaries enabled by imperial expansion also sparked fears of the erosion of national and racial sensibilities. It thus resulted in corresponding efforts to police these boundaries more stringently. The Customs case, then, shows how the imperial experience could at once transcend the nation and simultaneously heighten nationalist sentiments. There are clear parallels with contemporary globalisation here. Dire predictions about the imminent dissolution of the nation-state in the face of globalising forces and the supplanting of national identity with a new global sensibility have similarly prompted a backlash, apparent in attempts to reassert the powers of the nation-state by, for example, more vigilantly guarding national borders.[5]

Empire Careers has attempted to situate China within the webs of commerce, patronage, capital and personnel that criss-crossed the world during the age of imperialism. In particular the case of the Customs' foreign staff expands our understanding of the transnational impulses that drove the migrations of people around the globe to staff similar organisations, and the connections they made in the course of these journeys. Men and women from all corners of the world were able, to varying degrees, to insert themselves into imperial networks in order to join the Customs and travel to China. *Empire Careers* shows how an overseas career could weaken or strengthen ties to one's homeland, and how new connections were formed in the process of working for a cosmopolitan institution. Furthermore, the knowledge, ideas and ideologies that circulated around the empire world influenced how Customs employees understood their status, role and place in China. After leaving the Service, as Chapter 6 demonstrates, former employees were able to exploit their experiences in China and in the Customs to begin new lives in the Dominions and elsewhere. The Customs' links to the empire world notwithstanding, it must be remembered that China's connections to imperial networks were often more fragile than those that held together sites of 'formal' empire. The presence of multiple foreign powers and China's partial retention of sovereignty ensured that imperial networks were less firmly rooted. Yet these very circumstances enable us to identify the ways in which multiple trajectories overlapped and converged in China, where people from Britain, Norway, Russia, Australia, the United States, India and a host of other countries vied for position.

Networks are generally understood to be fluid and dynamic in character. This definition has its advantages; for one, it encourages recognition of the layers of informal and personal connection that glued together the empire world. Yet the role of institutions in facilitating, controlling and limiting long-distance connections often goes unacknowledged, despite a recent resurgence of interest in the lives and careers of the staff of imperial administrative services.[6] In addition to the personal and informal webs of communication and exchange that the Customs personnel participated in, the Inspectorate self-consciously created and managed *institutional* connections with the broader empire world. The Inspectorate itself was well aware of the political and economic advantages of belonging to these networks and thus self-consciously sought to gain recognition as an archetypal institution of the empire world. First and foremost, as an organisation charged with regulating imports and exports, the Customs oversaw China's participation in global commercial webs. Because of its economic importance to multiple interest groups – including China – the Inspectorate was able to form connections with several different governments and diplomatic establishments around the world. Furthermore, the Inspectorate self-consciously and vigorously sought to embed itself in empire-wide circuits of knowledge production and exchange. Rather than being consistently informal, then, institutions could create imperial networks that were more rigid and official.[7] Neither were networks necessarily liberating and democratic. The language of 'breaking down borders', a central motif in the rhetoric of contemporary globalism, evades the discriminatory and sometimes violent nature of networks. But, as Frederick Cooper has commented, 'One should not assume that transnational networks are all warm and fuzzy.'[8] Organisations such as the Customs could limit as well as broaden access to networks by, for instance, selectively bestowing patronage and excluding those of the 'wrong' race, nationality or class.

In the West, China has usually been considered as an outpost of empire at most, despite the enduring importance of 'semi-colonialism' to Chinese understandings of the country's modern history. By shedding light upon China's significance to the empire world this book provides a corrective to the oft-reiterated assumption that China was peripheral to the 'real' story of colonialism. Indeed the dividing line between 'informal' and 'formal' empire is blurred at best. As James Hevia has argued, 'colonial apparatuses strove to achieve, while never actually realizing, complete domination'. Therefore, 'we might consider all the entities produced in the age of empire as forms of semi-colonialism – especially that patchwork of patchworks, British India, notwithstanding its canonical status as the colony of colonies'.[9] Study of 'hybrid' organisations like the Customs, which served both foreign power and the Chinese state, can contribute to our understanding of the

[204]

distinction – or lack thereof – between 'informal' and 'formal' empire in meaningful ways. The Customs experience demonstrates that there *was* something distinctive about imperialism in China. The institution answered to several different masters and its racism was tempered by the oft-reiterated mantra that Customs employees were servants of China first and foremost. The ambivalences and ambiguities intrinsic to all colonial endeavours were thus magnified in the Customs. Yet the prejudices and pastimes of foreign communities in the treaty ports were nonetheless shaped by the ideas and cultures of the broader empire world. Differences in the mechanics of colonial rule notwithstanding, political projects in 'informal' and 'formal' empire had a shared aim of augmenting imperial prestige and power. Indeed the Foreign Inspectorate's raison d'être, to modernise China's bureaucracy through a period of foreign tutelage, was a quintessentially colonial project. Together, then, these personal, cultural and political projects in China articulated a broader sense of belonging to the empire world. Besides, Chinese people who came into contact with institutions such as the Customs certainly felt colonised, as popular nationalist opposition to the Foreign Inspectorate in the 1920s shows.

Re-envisaging China as a site of colonialism adds to our understanding of the contours of European communities in the empire world in important ways. In China and in other sites of empire where no single colonial power held sway, the composition and structure of foreign communities was particularly fluid and heterogeneous. In his memoir Rasmussen described the foreign staff as a motley assortment of characters:

> The Customs Service at that time was the Foreign Legion of the Far East. There were men from every imaginable stratum of society: remittance men, drunks and sober men, gentlemen and rascals, ignorant and highly educated men. Love of adventure had attracted some of them to the Service; others were probably fugitives from justice, hiding under assumed names, and some like me had joined from dire necessity.[10]

China and the Customs, then, provide an insight into the human diversity of the empire world, which created deeply entrenched divisions in addition to the much-lauded cosmopolitan co-operation of the Foreign Inspectorate. 'White solidarity' was frequently destabilised by entrenched class hierarchies transported from the metropole and reconfigured or intensified in the colonies. Moreover, in the multinational environment of the China coast nationality played an important role in determining social and professional status, a factor which is often neglected in discussions of the impact of race, gender and class on the contours of colonial societies. There were huge disparities, for example, between the prestige attached to British nationality and the distaste with which Russian émigrés were viewed in China.[11] In the Customs staff, encompassing men and women of over twenty nationalities amongst its ranks, the full range of people for whom the empire world spoke of opportunity was represented.

Although the scope of this study is in many respects wide, it inevitably has its limitations. The most obvious omission is a consistent comparison with the experiences of the Chinese staff, which were clearly very different from those of their foreign colleagues. By the same token Japanese employees, the experiences of whom were in some ways similar to those of the other foreign staff but in many ways distinct, deserve a study in their own right. Furthermore, much work remains to be done on other institutions of 'informal' empire – those which operated, for instance, in Egypt and the Middle East. We know much for, for example, about men like Cromer, but far less about his subordinate staff in the Egyptian service.[12] The conclusions reached in this study of the Customs foreign staff provide a methodological framework for exploring many of the issues they would have faced during their careers.

It is important to understand the ideological and practical worlds of these organisations because their personnel formed a frontline of contact with local communities and officials. Therefore they constituted the visible face of colonial power. Exploration of the world of the Customs staff also exposes the fallibility of colonial institutions. Rather than exercising limitless power, their personnel had to engage in endless compromises and negotiations with other power-holders and with the public in order to maintain their influence. Disquiet about the professional and private reputations of the foreign staff, which, it was believed, had the power to unseat the Foreign Inspectorate, also point towards the perceived fragility of foreign authority. In the Customs these anxieties were amplified because of the Inspectorate's answerability to the Chinese government, but they also plagued other colonial institutions.

Studies of these organisations also offer insights into the connections between present-day globalisation and the 'proto-globalisation' of the past. There are, of course, clear problems with using the very contemporary concept of globalisation as an analytical tool to understand the age of imperialism. Not least, the globalisation paradigm, with its focus on interconnectedness and reciprocal long-distance connections, risks whitewashing the harsh realities of inequality and violence across the empire world.[13] Nonetheless, exploration of the world and worldview of the employees of transnational organisations – the agents of 'globalisation' both then and now – can clarify our understanding of globalising impulses. After all, transnational corporations operating overseas are one of the most controversial facets of contemporary globalisation. American oil firms in the Middle East, German electronics companies in China and private security firms in Iraq – all of these operations generate expatriate communities, which differ only in degree from those established in the colonial era.[14] Like their colonial counterparts, these present-day settlers and sojourners embarking upon overseas careers still form a frontline of contact with local communities, still operate in two different worlds, local and foreign, and still maintain distinctive cultures. Now just as in the past, Europeans and Americans seek work overseas using ever-multiplying global webs of transport, communication and commerce. Like the foreign staff of the Chinese Custom Service, which disbanded over sixty years ago, these present-day expatriates still negotiate overlapping and sometimes contradictory identities: national, global and local.[15]

Notes

1   LOC, Denby family papers, letter from Edwin Denby to Martha Denby, 29 Jan 1889.
2   LOC, Denby family papers, letters from Edwin Denby to Graham Denby (9 Oct 1887) and Martha Denby (29 Jan 1889).
3   Eves and Thomas, *Bad Colonists*, 72. Also see Stoler, *Carnal Knowledge and Imperial Power*, especially chapters 2, 4 and 5. See John Fitzgerald, *Big White Lie: Chinese Australians in white Australia* (Sydney: University of New South Wales Press, 2007), for a discussion of how culturally defined notions of race were used to justify anti-Chinese exclusion laws and the White Australia Policy.
4   Zarrow, *China in War and Revolution*, chapter 3, 53–74. See Wakeman, 'Hanjian! (Traitor)', for an analysis of the racial connotations of the label 'traitor' in China, often applied to those who collaborated with hostile foreigners and thereby betrayed their race.
5   On the demise of the nation-state see Kenichi Ohmae, *The End of the Nation State: The rise of regional economies* (New York: Simon & Shuster, 1995).
6   As Simon Potter has argued in 'Webs, Networks, and Systems'.
7   As Zoë Laidlaw has pointed out, in the British Empire informal networks built on personal connections between colonial governors were replaced by more formal and impersonal bureaucratic structures in the 1830s. Laidlaw, *Colonial Connections*, 5.
8   Frederick Cooper, 'Networks, Moral Discourse, and History', in *Intervention and Transnationalism in Africa: Global-local networks of power*, edited by Thomas Callaghy, Ronald Kassimir and Robert Latham (Cambridge: Cambridge University Press, 2001), 44.
9   Hevia, *English Lessons*, 26.
10   Rasmussen, *China Trader*, 16.
11   Ristaino, *Port of Last Resort*.
12   On Evelyn Baring, First Earl of Cromer and British proconsul in Egypt, see Roger Owen, *Cromer: Victorian imperialist, Edwardian proconsul* (Oxford: Oxford University Press, 2004). For the British expatriate community in Egypt see Whidden, 'Expatriates in Cosmopolitan Egypt'.
13   For a discussion of the merits and shortcomings of a global approach to imperial history see Ward, 'Transcending the Nation'.

14 Bickers, *Settlers and Expatriates*, 10–11.
15 On the intersection of global and local identities in the contemporary age of globali-sation see Martin Albrow, 'Travelling Beyond Local Cultures', in *Living the Global City: Globalization as a local process* (London: Routledge, 1997), 43–51.

SELECT BIBLIOGRAPHY

Primary sources

Bodleian Library, University of Oxford
MSS. Eng. c. 7285–98   Alfred E. Hippisley papers, 1842–1940

The British Library, London (BL)
Add MS 88932   The papers of Stella Benson
Add MS 52916–52923 Schiff Papers

Foreign Office Library, London
Service lists of the Chinese Customs Service

Houghton Library, Harvard University, Cambridge, MA
b MS Chinese 4   Sir Robert Hart papers
b MS Am 1999–1999.18 Lester Knox Little papers, 1932–64

Imperial War Museum, London (IWM)
86/44/1   Owen D. Gander papers

Library of Congress, Washington, DC (LOC)
MSS84834 Denby Family Papers

The National Archives, Kew (TNA)
CUST 39 Board of Customs and successor: Establishment: Staff Lists
CUST 42 Board of Customs: Other Headquarters Departments: Records
FO 228   Foreign Office: Consulates and Legation, China: General Correspondence
FO 371   Foreign Office: Political Departments: General Correspondence from 1906–66

School of Oriental and African Studies Library, London (SOAS)
MS 380628   Jack F. Blackburn papers, 1927–41
PP MS 69   Bowra papers
PP MS 82   Reginald Follett Codrington Hedgeland papers
PP MS 81   Hugh Gordon Lowder papers

Second Historical Archives of China, Nanjing (SHAC)
Series 679(1)–679(9)   Maritime Customs Service Archive

Thomas Fisher Rare Book Library, University of Toronto
J. O. P. Bland papers, 1863–1945

SELECT BIBLIOGRAPHY

Tianjin Municipal Archives, Tianjin (TMA)
Maritime Customs and Postal Administration archive

Resources created through a collaboration between the Second Historical Archives of China and the Customs Service project team at the University of Bristol and University of Cambridge
Service lists database of employees withdrawn from service
Customs staff decorations, degrees and awards database

Published works

Aitchison, Jean, 'The Chinese Maritime Customs Service in the Transition from the Ch'ing to the Nationalist Era: An examination of the relationship between a Western-style fiscal institution and the Chinese government in the period before the Manchurian incident', unpublished PhD thesis, University of London, 1981.

Anderson, David, *Histories of the Hanged: The dirty war in Kenya and the end of empire* (New York: W. W. Norton, 2005).

Anderson, David M., and David Killingray, eds, *Policing the Empire: Government, authority, and control, 1830–1940* (Manchester: Manchester University Press, 1991).

Anderson, Perry, 'A Belated Encounter: Perry Anderson retraces his father's career in the Chinese Customs Service', *London Review of Books*, 20:15 (1998).

Archer, C. S., *China Servant* (London: Collins, 1946).

Arlington, L. C., *Through the Dragon's Eyes* (London: Constable & Co., 1931).

Arnold, David, *Police Power and Colonial Rule: Madras, 1859–1947* (Oxford: Oxford University Press, 1986).

Atkins, Martyn, *Informal Empire in Crisis: British diplomacy and the Chinese Customs succession, 1927–1929* (Ithaca: East Asia Program, Cornell University, 1995).

Backhouse, E., and J. O. P. Bland, *China under the Empress Dowager: The history of the life and times of Tzu Hsi* (Philadelphia: J. B. Lippincott Co., 1914; first published 1910).

Backhouse, E., and J. O. P. Bland, *Annals & Memoirs of the Court of Peking (from the 16th to the 20th Century)* (Boston: Houghton Mifflin, 1914).

Baines, Dudley, *Emigration from Europe, 1815–1930* (Cambridge: Cambridge University Press, 1995).

Baker, William J., and J. A. Mangan, eds, *Sport in Africa: Essays in social history* (New York: Africana Publishing Co., 1987).

Ballantyne, Tony, and Antoinette M. Burton, eds, *Bodies in Contact: Rethinking colonial encounters in world history* (Durham, NC: Duke University Press, 2005).

Ballhatchet, Kenneth, *Race, Sex, and Class under the Raj: Imperial attitudes and policies and their critics, 1793–1905* (New York: St Martin's Press, 1980).

Bamford, T. W., *Rise of the Public Schools: A study of boys' public boarding schools in England and Wales from 1837 to the present day* (London: Nelson, 1967).

Banister, T. Roger, *The Coastwise Lights of China: An illustrated account of the Chinese Maritime Customs Lights Service* (Shanghai: Statistical Department of the Chinese Maritime Customs Service, 1932).

Barber, Marilyn J., '"Two Homes Now": The return migration of the Fellowship of the Maple Leaf', in *Emigrant Homecomings: The return movement of emigrants, 1600–2000*, edited by Marjory Harper (Manchester: Manchester University Press, 2005), 197–214.

Barlow, Tani, 'Colonialism's Career in Postwar China Studies', in *Formations of Colonial Modernity in East Asia*, edited by Tani Barlow (Durham, NC: Duke University Press, 1997), 373–412.

Bayly, C. A., *Empire and Information: Intelligence gathering and social communication in India, 1780–1870* (Cambridge: Cambridge University Press, 1996).

Bayly, C. A., *The Birth of the Modern World 1780–1914. Global connections and comparisons* (Oxford: Blackwell, 2004)

Bedeski, Robert E., 'China's Wartime State', in *China's Bitter Victory: The war with Japan, 1937–1945*, edited by James Chieh Hsiung and Steven I. Levine (Armonk: M. E. Sharpe, 1992), 33–49.

Berenson, Edward, *Heroes of Empire: Five charismatic men and the conquest of Africa* (Berkeley: University of California Press, 2011).

Bergère, Marie-Claire, '"The Other China": Shanghai from 1919 to 1949', in *Shanghai, Revolution and Development in an Asian Metropolis*, edited by Christopher Howe (Cambridge: Cambridge University Press, 1981), 1–34.

Bergère, Marie-Claire, *Shanghai: China's gateway to modernity* (Stanford: Stanford University Press, 2010).

Best, Antony, *The International History of East Asia, 1900–1968: Trade, ideology and the quest for order* (London: Routledge, 2010).

Bickers, Robert, 'History, Legend and Treaty Port Ideology, 1925–1931', in *Ritual and Diplomacy: The Macartney Mission to China, 1792–1794*, edited by Robert Bickers (London: British Association for Chinese Studies and Wellsweep Press, 1993), 81–92.

Bickers, Robert, 'Shanghailanders: The formation and identity of the British settler community in Shanghai, 1843–1937', *Past and Present*, 159 (1998), 161–211.

Bickers, Robert, *Britain in China: Community, culture and colonialism, 1900–1949* (Manchester: Manchester University Press, 1999).

Bickers, Robert, *Empire Made Me: An Englishman adrift in Shanghai* (London: Allen Lane, 2003).

Bickers, Robert, 'Settlers and Diplomats: The end of British hegemony in the International Settlement, 1937–1945', in *In the Shadow of the Rising Sun: Shanghai under Japanese occupation*, edited by Christian Henriot and Wen-hsin Yeh (Cambridge: Cambridge University Press, 2004), 229–56.

Bickers, Robert, 'Bland, John Otway Percy (1863–1945)', in *The Oxford Dictionary of National Biography*, edited by H. C. G. Matthew and Brian Harrison (Oxford: Oxford University Press, 2004).

Bickers, Robert, 'Purloined Letters: History and the Chinese Maritime Customs Service', *Modern Asian Studies*, 40:3 (2006), 691–723.

Bickers, Robert, 'Anglo-Japanese Relations and Treaty Port China: The case of the Chinese Maritime Customs Service', in *The International History of East Asia, 1900–1968: Trade, ideology and the quest for order*, edited by Antony Best (London: Routledge, 2010), 35–56.

Bickers, Robert, ed., *Settlers and Expatriates: Britons over the seas*, The Oxford History of the British Empire Companion Series (Oxford: Oxford University Press, 2010).

Bickers, Robert, *The Scramble for China: Foreign devils in the Qing Empire, 1832–1914* (London: Allen Lane, 2011).

Bickers, Robert, and Christian Henriot, eds, *New Frontiers: Imperialism's new communities in East Asia, 1842–1953* (Manchester: Manchester University Press, 2000).

Blunt, Alison, '"Land of Our Mothers": Home, identity and nationality for Anglo-Indians in British India, 1919–1947', *History Workshop Journal*, 54 (2002), 49–72.

Bredon, Juliet, *Sir Robert Hart, the Romance of a Great Career: Told by his niece, Juliet Bredon* (London: Hutchinson, 1909).

Bridge, Carl, and Kent Fedorowich, eds, *The British World: Diaspora, culture, and identity* (London: F. Cass, 2003).

Bridge, Carl, and Kent Fedorowich, 'Mapping the British World', *Journal of Imperial and Commonwealth History*, 31:2 (2003), 1–15.

Brooks, Barbara J., *Japan's Imperial Diplomacy: Consuls, treaty ports, and war in China, 1895–1938* (Honolulu: University of Hawai'i Press, 2000).

Brown, Matthew, 'Gregor Macgregor: Clansman, conquistador and coloniser on the fringes of the British Empire', in *Colonial Lives across the British Empire: Imperial careering in the long nineteenth century*, edited by David Lambert and Alan Lester (Cambridge: Cambridge University Press, 2006), 32–57.

Brunero, Donna, *Britain's Imperial Cornerstone in China: The Chinese Maritime Customs Service, 1854–1949* (Abingdon: Routledge, 2006).

Buettner, Elizabeth, *Empire Families: Britons and late imperial India* (Oxford: Oxford University Press, 2004).

Buettner, Elizabeth, '"We Don't Grow Coffee and Bananas in Clapham Junction You Know!": Imperial Britons back home', in *Settlers and Expatriates: Britons over the seas*, edited by Robert Bickers (Oxford: Oxford University Press, 2010), 302–28.

Burton, Antoinette, *After the Imperial Turn: Thinking with and through the nation* (Durham, NC: Duke University Press, 2003).

Butcher, John G., *The British in Malaya, 1880–1941: The social history of a European community in colonial South-East Asia* (Oxford: Oxford University Press, 1979).

Cain, P. J., 'Character and Imperialism: The British financial administration of Egypt, 1878–1914', *Journal of Imperial and Commonwealth History*, 34:2 (2006), 177–200.

Camiscioli, Elisa, 'Reproducing the "French Race": Immigration and pronatalism in early-twentieth-century France', in *Bodies in Contact: Rethinking colonial encounters in world history*, edited by Tony Ballantyne and Antoinette M. Burton (Durham, NC: Duke University Press, 2005), 219–33.

Campbell, Robert Ronald, *James Duncan Campbell* (Cambridge, MA: Harvard University Press, 1970).

Cannadine, David, *The Decline and Fall of the British Aristocracy* (New Haven: Yale University Press, 1990).

Cannadine, David, *Ornamentalism: How the British saw their empire* (Oxford: Oxford University Press, 2001).

Cannon, Isidore Cyril, *Public Success, Private Sorrow: The life and times of Charles Henry Brewitt-Taylor (1857–1938), China Customs commissioner and pioneer translator* (Hong Kong: Hong Kong University Press, 2009).

Caplan, Lionel, *Children of Colonialism: Anglo-Indians in a postcolonial world* (Oxford: Berg, 2001).

Carroll, John M., *Edge of Empires: Chinese elites and British colonials in Hong Kong* (Cambridge, MA: Harvard University Press, 2005).

Carter, James H., *Creating a Chinese Harbin: Nationalism in an international city, 1916–1932* (Ithaca: Cornell University Press, 2002).

Chen Shiqi, *Zhongguo jindai haiguan shi* (History of the modern Chinese Customs) (Beijing: Zhongguo Zhanwang Chubanshe, 2002).

Chen Xiafei, and Han Rongfang, eds, *Archives of China's Imperial Maritime Customs: Confidential correspondence between Robert Hart and James Duncan Campbell, 1874–1907* (Beijing: Foreign Languages Press, 1990).

Chinese Maritime Customs: Staff organisation and control (Shanghai: Statistical Department of the Chinese Maritime Customs Service, 1936).

Clancy-Smith, Julia Ann, and Frances Gouda, eds, *Domesticating the Empire: Race, gender, and family life in French and Dutch colonialism* (Charlottesville: University Press of Virginia, 1998).

Clausen, Søren, and Stig Thøgersen, eds, *The Making of a Chinese City: History and historiography in Harbin* (Armonk: M. E. Sharpe, 1995).

Clifford, Nicholas, 'Sir Frederick Maze and the Chinese Maritime Customs, 1937–41', *The Journal of Modern History*, 37:1 (1965), 18–34.

Clifford, Nicholas, *Spoilt Children of Empire: Westerners in Shanghai and the Chinese revolution of the 1920s* (Hanover: University Press of New England, 1991).

Coates, P. D., *The China Consuls: British consular officers, 1843–1943* (Oxford: Oxford University Press, 1988.

Cochran, Sherman, ed., *Inventing Nanjing Road: Commercial culture in Shanghai, 1900–1945* (Ithaca: Cornell East Asia Program, 1999).

Cohen, Paul, *Discovering History in China: American historical writing on the recent Chinese past* (New York: Columbia University Press, 1984).

Cohen, Paul, *History in Three Keys: The Boxers as event, experience, and myth* (New York: Columbia University Press, 1997).

Constantine, Stephen, 'British Emigration to the Empire-Commonwealth since 1880: From overseas settlement to diaspora?' *Journal of Imperial and Commonwealth History*, 31:2 (2003), 16–35.

Cook's Guide to Peking (London: Thomas Cook & Son, 1924).

Cooper, Frederick, 'Networks, Moral Discourse, and History', in *Intervention and Transnationalism in Africa: Global-local networks of power*, edited by Thomas Callaghy, Ronald Kassimir and Robert Latham (Cambridge: Cambridge University Press, 2001), 23–46.

Cooper, Frederick, *Colonialism in Question: Theory, knowledge, history* (Berkeley: University of California Press, 2005).

Cooper, Frederick, and Ann Laura Stoler, eds, *Tensions of Empire: Colonial cultures in a bourgeois world* (Berkeley: University of California Press, 1997).

Cornet, Christine, 'The Bumpy End of the French Concession and French Influence in Shanghai, 1937–1946', in *In the Shadow of the Rising Sun: Shanghai under Japanese occupation*, edited by Christian Henriot and Wen-hsin Yeh (Cambridge: Cambridge University Press, 2004), 257–76.

Croly, Herbert David, *Willard Straight* (New York: Macmillan, 1924).

Croskey, Julian, *The Shen's Pigtail, and Other Cues of Anglo-China Life* (New York: G. P. Putnam's Sons, 1894).

Croskey, Julian, *The Chest of Opium* (London: Neville Beeman, 1896).

Croskey, Julian, *'The S. G.': A romance of Peking* (Brooklyn: Mason, 1900).

Curtin, Philip D., *Death by Migration: Europe's encounter with the tropical world in the nineteenth century* (Cambridge: Cambridge University Press, 1989).

Darwin, John, *The Empire Project: The rise and fall of the British world-system, 1830–1970* (Cambridge: Cambridge University Press, 2009).

Davidoff, Leonore, and Catherine Hall, *Family Fortunes: Men and women of the English middle class, 1780–1850* (Chicago: University of Chicago Press, 1987).

Davin, Anna, 'Imperialism and Motherhood', in *Tensions of Empire: Colonial cultures in a bourgeois world*, edited by Frederick Cooper and Ann Laura Stoler (Berkeley: University of California Press, 1997), 87–151.

De Quincey, Thomas, *China: A revised reprint of articles from 'Titan'* (Edinburgh: J. Hogg, 1857).

Dean, Britten, 'British Informal Empire: The case of China', *Journal of Imperial and Commonwealth History*, 14:1 (1976), 64–81.

Dickens, Charles, 'The Great Exhibition and the Little One', *Household Words: A Weekly Journal*, 3:5 (July 1851), 356–60.

Dickinson, G. Lowes, *Letters from a Chinese Official: Being an Eastern view of Western civilization* (Garden City: Doubleday, 1915; 1st edition 1901).

Dillon, Edward J., 'The Chinese Wolf and the European Lamb', *The Contemporary Review*, 79 (1901), 1–31.

Dirks, Nicholas B., *Castes of Mind: Colonialism and the making of modern India* (Princeton: Princeton University Press, 2001).

Documents Illustrative of the Origin, Development and Activities of the Chinese Customs Service 7 vols (Shanghai: Statistical Department of the Inspectorate General of Customs, 1936–40).

Dong, Stella, *Shanghai: The rise and fall of a decadent city* (New York: William Morrow, 2000).

Douglas, Robert K., *Society in China*, 2nd ed. (London: A. D. Innes & Co., 1894).

Drage, Charles, *Servants of the Dragon Thone: Being the lives of Edward and Cecil Bowra* (London: Peter Dawnay, 1966).

Duara, Prasenjit, *Sovereignty and Authenticity: Manchukuo and the East Asian modern* (Lanham: Rowman and Littlefield, 2003).

Duus, Peter, Ramon Hawley Myers and Mark R. Peattie, eds, *The Japanese Informal Empire in China, 1895–1937* (Princeton: Princeton University Press, 1989).

Eastman, Lloyd E., *The Abortive Revolution: China under Nationalist rule, 1927–1937* (Cambridge, MA: Council on East Asian Studies, Harvard University, 1990).

Eberhard-Bréard, Andrea, 'Robert Hart and China's Statistical Revolution', *Modern Asian Studies*, 40:3 (2006), 605–29.

Endicott, Stephen Lyon, *Diplomacy and Enterprise: British China policy, 1933–1937* (Vancouver: University of British Columbia Press, 1975).

Esherick, Joseph, 'Harvard on China: The apologetics of imperialism', *Bulletin of Concerned Asian Scholars*, 4 (1972), 9–16.

Fairbank, John K. 'The Definition of the Foreign Inspector's Status (1854–55): A chapter in the early history of the Inspectorate of Customs at Shanghai', *Nankai Social and Economic Quarterly*, 9:1 (1936), 129–32.

Fairbank, John K., 'Synarchy under the Treaties', in *Chinese Thought and Institutions*, edited by John K. Fairbank (Chicago: University of Chicago Press, 1957), 204–31.

Fairbank, John K., 'A Preliminary Framework', in *The Chinese World Order: Traditional China's foreign relations*, edited by John King Fairbank (Cambridge, MA: Harvard University Press, 1968), 1–19.

Fairbank, John K., *Trade and Diplomacy on the China Coast: The opening of the treaty ports, 1842–1854* (Stanford, CA: Stanford University Press, 1969).

Fairbank, John K., Katherine Frost Bruner and Elizabeth MacLeod Matheson, eds, *The I. G. in Peking: Letters of Robert Hart, Chinese Maritime Customs, 1868–1907* (Cambridge, MA: Belknap Press of Harvard University Press, 1975).

Fairbank, John King, Martha Henderson Coolidge and Richard J. Smith, *H. B. Morse, Customs commissioner and historian of China* (Lexington: University Press of Kentucky, 1995).

Feuerwerker, Albert, *The Foreign Establishment in China in the Early Twentieth Century* (Ann Arbor: Center for Chinese Studies, University of Michigan, 1976).

Finnane, Antonia, *Far from Where?: Jewish Journeys from Shanghai to Australia* (Carlton, Vic.: Melbourne University Press, 1999).

French, Paul, *Through the Looking Glass: China's foreign journalists from Opium Wars to Mao* (Hong Kong: Hong Kong University Press, 2009).

Gordon, C. A., ed., *An Epitome of the Reports of the Medical Officers to the Chinese Imperial Maritime Customs Service, from 1871 to 1882* (London: Baillière, Tindall & Cox, 1884).

Gould, Ed., *The Lighthouse Philosopher: The adventures of Bill Scott* (Saanichton, BC: Hancock House, 1976).

Grant, Joy, *Stella Benson: A biography* (London: Macmillan, 1987).

Hall, Catherine, ed., *Cultures of Empire: Colonizers in Britain and the Empire in the nineteenth and twentieth centuries* (New York: Routledge, 2000).

Hall, Catherine, *Civilising Subjects: Metropole and colony in the English imagination, 1830–1867* (Cambridge: Polity, 2002).

Hall, Catherine, and Sonya O. Rose, eds, *At Home with the Empire: Metropolitan culture and the imperial world* (Chicago: University of Chicago Press, 2006).

Han Kuo-huang, 'J. A. Van Aalst and His Chinese Music', *Asian Music*, 19:2 (1988), 127–30.

Harling, Philip, *The Waning of 'Old Corruption': The politics of economical reform in Britain, 1779–1846* (Oxford: Clarendon Press, 1996).

Harper, Marjory, *Emigrant Homecomings: The return movement of emigrants, 1600–2000* (Manchester: Manchester University Press, 2005).

Harper, Marjory, and Stephen Constantine, *Migration and Empire*, The Oxford History of the British Empire Companion Series (Oxford: Oxford University Press, 2010).

Hart, Robert, *These from the Land of Sinim: Essays on the Chinese question*, 2nd ed. (London: Chapman & Hall, 1903).

Hart, Robert, Katherine Frost Bruner, John King Fairbank and Richard J. Smith, *Entering China's Service: Robert Hart's journals, 1854–1863* (Cambridge, MA: Council on East Asian Studies, Harvard University Press, 1986).

Hart, Robert, Richard J. Smith, John King Fairbank and Katherine Frost Bruner, *Robert Hart and China's Early Modernization: His journals, 1863–1866* (Cambridge, MA: Harvard University Press, 1991).

Harumi Goto-Shibata, *Japan and Britain in Shanghai, 1925–31* (Basingstoke: Macmillan, 1995).

Haynes, Douglas, *Imperial Medicine: Patrick Manson and the conquest of tropical disease* (Philadelphia: University of Pennsylvania Press, 2001).

Henriot, Christian, *Shanghai, 1927–1937: Municipal power, locality, and modernization* (Berkeley: University of California Press, 1993).

Henriot, Christian, and Wen-hsin Yeh, eds, *In the Shadow of the Rising Sun: Shanghai under Japanese occupation* (Cambridge: Cambridge University Press, 2004).

Hevia, James, *English Lessons: The pedagogy of imperialism in nineteenth-century China* (Durham, NC: Duke University Press, 2003).

Hirth, Friedrich, *The Ancient History of China, to the End of the Ch'ou Dynasty* (Freeport, NY: Books for Libraries Press, 1969; first pub. 1908).

Hooper, Beverley, *China Stands Up: Ending the Western presence, 1948–50* (London: Allen & Unwin, 1986).

Hopkins, A. G., ed., *Globalization in World History* (New York: W. W. Norton & Co., 2002).

Horowitz, Richard, 'Politics, Power and the Chinese Maritime Customs Service: The Qing restoration and the ascent of Robert Hart', *Modern Asian Studies*, 40:3 (2006), 549–81.

Howe, Christopher, *Shanghai, Revolution and Development in an Asian Metropolis* (Cambridge: Cambridge University Press, 1981).

Hyam, Ronald, *Empire and Sexuality: The British experience* (Manchester: Manchester University Press, 1990).

Johnson, George M., 'Stella Benson (6 January 1892–6 December 1933)', in *British Short Fiction Writers, 1915–1945. Dictionary of Literary Biography Vol. 162*, edited by John H. Rogers (Detroit: Gale Research, 1996), 22–31.

Kennedy, Dane, *Islands of White: Settler society and culture in Kenya and Southern Rhodesia, 1890–1939* (Durham, NC: Duke University Press, 1987).

Kennedy, Dane, *The Magic Mountains: Hill stations and the British Raj* (Berkeley: University of California Press, 1996).

Killingray, David, Margarette Lincoln and Nigel Rigby, eds, *Maritime Empires: British imperial maritime trade in the nineteenth century* (Woodbridge: Boydell Press, 2004).

King, Frank H. H., 'The Boxer Indemnity – "Nothing but Bad"', *Modern Asian Studies*, 40:3 (2006), 663–89.

King, Paul, *In the Chinese Customs Service: A personal record of forty-seven years* (London: T. F. Unwin, 1924).

King, Veronica and Paul, *The Commissioner's Dilemma* (London: Heath Cranton, 1932).

Kirk-Greene, Anthony, 'Imperial Administration and the Athletic Imperative: The case of the district officer in Africa', in *Sport in Africa: Essays in social history*, edited by William J. Baker and J. A. Mangan (New York: Africana Pub. Co., 1987), 81–113.

Kirk-Greene, Anthony, *On Crown Service: A history of HM colonial and overseas civil services, 1837–1997* (London: I. B. Tauris, 1999).

Kirk-Greene, Anthony, *Britain's Imperial Administrators, 1858–1966* (New York: St Martin's Press, 2000).

Kirk-Greene, Anthony, '"Not quite a gentleman": The desk diaries of the Assistant Private Secretary (Appointments) to the Secretary of State for the Colonies, 1899–1915', *English Historical Review*, 472 (2002), 622–33.

Kirk-Greene, Anthony, *Symbol of Authority: The British district officer in Africa* (London: I. B. Tauris, 2006).

Ladds, Catherine, '"The Life Career of Us All": Germans and Britons in the Chinese Maritime Customs Service, 1854–1917', *Berliner China-Hefte: Chinese History and Society*, 33 (2008), 34–53.

Ladds, Catherine, '"Youthful, Likely Men, Able to Read, Write and Count": Joining the foreign staff of the Chinese Customs Service, 1854–1927', *Journal of Imperial and Commonwealth History*, 36:2 (2008), 227–42.

Laidlaw, Zoë, *Colonial Connections, 1815–45: Patronage, the information revolution and colonial government* (Manchester: Manchester University Press, 2005).

Laidlaw, Zoë, 'Richard Bourke: Irish liberalism tempered by empire', in *Colonial Lives across the British Empire: Imperial careering in the long nineteenth century*, edited by David Lambert and Alan Lester (Cambridge: Cambridge University Press, 2006), 113–44.

Lambert, David, and Alan Lester, eds, *Colonial Lives across the British Empire: Imperial careering in the long nineteenth century* (Cambridge: Cambridge University Press, 2006).

Lester, Alan, *Imperial Networks: Creating identities in nineteenth-century South Africa and Britain* (London: Routledge, 2001).

Lester, Alan, 'British Settler Discourse and the Circuits of Empire', *History Workshop Journal*, 54 (2002), 24–48.

Lethbridge, Henry J., *Hong Kong, Stability and Change: A collection of essays* (Hong Kong: Oxford University Press, 1978).

Levine, Philippa, ed., *Gender and Empire*, The Oxford History of the British Empire Companion Series (Oxford: Oxford University Press, 2004).

Levine, Philippa, 'Sexuality, Gender, and Empire', in *Gender and Empire*, edited by Philippa Levine (Oxford: Oxford University Press, 2004), 134–55.

Li, Lan and Wildy, Deidre, 'A New Discovery and Its Significance: The statutory declarations made by Sir Robert Hart concerning his secret domestic life in nineteenth-century China', *Journal of the Hong Kong Branch of the Royal Asiatic Society*, 43 (2003), 63–87.

Lu Hanchao, *Beyond the Neon Lights: Everyday Shanghai in the early twentieth century* (Berkeley: University of California Press, 1999).

MacKenzie, John, 'Hunting in Eastern and Central Africa in the Late Nineteenth Century, with Special Reference to Zimbabwe', in *Sport in Africa: Essays in social history*, edited by William J. Baker and J. A. Mangan (New York: Africana Pub. Co., 1987), 172–95.

Mackerras, Colin, *Western Images of China* (Hong Kong: Oxford University Press, 1991).

Macpherson, Kerrie L., *A Wilderness of Marshes: The origins of public health in Shanghai, 1843–93* (Hong Kong: Oxford University Press, 1987).

Magee, Gary B., and Andrew S. Thompson, 'The Global and Local: Explaining migrant remittance flows in the English-speaking world, 1880–1914', *The Journal of Economic History*, 66:1 (2006), 177–202.

Magee, Gary B., and Andrew S. Thompson, *Empire and Globalisation: Networks of people, goods and capital in the British world, c. 1850–1914* (Cambridge: Cambridge University Press, 2010).

Mangan, J. A., *'Benefits Bestowed'?: Education and British imperialism* (Manchester: Manchester University Press, 1988).

Mangan, J. A., *The Games Ethic and Imperialism: Aspects of the diffusion of an ideal* (London: F. Cass, 1998).

Marshall, P. J., 'Britain and China in the Late Eighteenth Century', in *Ritual & Diplomacy: The Macartney Mission to China, 1792–1794*, edited by Robert Bickers (London: Wellsweep, 1993), 11–29.

Mason, Charles, *The Chinese Confessions of Charles Welsh Mason* (London: Grant Richards, 1924).

Maugham, W. Somerset, *On a Chinese Screen* (London: Vintage, 2000; 1st edition 1922).

Maugham, W. Somerset, *The Travel Books* (London: Heinemann, 1955).

McCulloch, Jock, 'Empire and Violence, 1900–1939', in *Gender and Empire*, edited by Philippa Levine (Oxford: Oxford University Press, 2004), 220–39.

McDevitt, Patrick F., *'May the Best Man Win': Sport, masculinity, and nationalism in Great Britain and the empire, 1880–1935* (Basingstoke: Palgrave Macmillan, 2004).

McDevitt, Patrick F., 'Muscular Catholicism: Nationalism, masculinity, and Gaelic team sports, 1884–1916', in *Bodies in Contact: Rethinking colonial encounters in world history*, edited by Tony Ballantyne and Antoinette M. Burton (Durham, NC: Duke University Press, 2005), 201–18.

McKenzie, Kirsten, *Scandal in the Colonies: Sydney and Cape Town, 1820–1850* (Carlton, Vic.: Melbourne University Press, 2004).

Meng Yue, *Shanghai and the Edges of Empires* (Minneapolis: University of Minnesota Press, 2006).

Michie, Alexander, *The Englishman in China During the Victorian Era as Illustrated in the Career of Sir Rutherford Alcock* (Taipei: Ch'eng-Wen Pub. Co., 1966; first published 1900).

Miners, Norman, *Hong Kong under Imperial Rule, 1912–1941* (Oxford: Oxford University Press, 1987).

Miners, Norman, 'The Localisation of the Hong Kong Police Force, 1842–1947', *Journal of Imperial and Commonwealth History*, 18:3 (1990), 296–315.

Mitter, Rana, *A Bitter Revolution: China's struggle with the modern world* (Oxford: Oxford University Press, 2004).

Morse, Hosea Ballou, *The International Relations of the Chinese Empire* (Taipei: Ch'eng-Wen Pub. Co., 1971; first published 1910–17).

Muller, Gregor, *Colonial Cambodia's 'Bad Frenchmen': The rise of French rule and the life of Thomas Caraman, 1840–1887* (London: Routledge, 2006).

Munn, Christopher, *Anglo-China: Chinese people and British rule in Hong Kong, 1841–1880* (Hong Kong: Hong Kong University Press, 2009).

New, Christopher, *Shanghai: A novel* (New York: Summit Books, 1985).

Ogborn, Miles, *Global Lives: Britain and the world, 1550–1800* (Cambridge: Cambridge University Press, 2008).

O'Leary, Richard, 'Robert Hart in China: The significance of his Irish roots', *Modern Asian Studies*, 40:3 (2006), 538–604.

Osterhammel, Jürgen, 'Semi-Colonialism and Informal Empire in Twentieth-Century China: Towards a framework of analysis', in *Imperialism and After: Continuities and discontinuities*, edited by Wolfgang J. Mommsen and Jürgen Osterhammel (London: HarperCollins, 1986), 290–314.

Paisley, Fiona, 'Childhood and Race: Growing up in the empire', in *Gender and Empire*, edited by Philippa Levine (Oxford: Oxford University Press, 2004), 240–59.

Paul, Kathleen, 'Communities of Britishness: Migration in the last gasp of empire', in *British Culture and the End of Empire*, edited by Stuart Ward (Manchester: Manchester University Press, 2001), 180–217.

Pedersen, Jean Elisabeth. '"Special Customs": Paternity suits and citizenship in France and the colonies, 1870–1912', in *Domesticating the Empire: Race, gender, and family life in French and Dutch colonialism*, edited by Julia Ann Clancy-Smith and Frances Gouda (Charlottesville: University Press of Virginia, 1998), 43–64.

Perkin, Harold, *The Rise of Professional Society: England since 1880* (London: Routledge, 2002).

Perry, Elizabeth J., *Shanghai on Strike: The politics of Chinese labor* (Stanford: Stanford University Press, 1993).

Platt, D. C. M., *The Cinderella Service: British consuls since 1825* (Harlow: Longman, 1971).

Potter, Simon J., 'Webs, Networks, and Systems: Globalization and the media in the nineteenth- and twentieth-century British Empire', *Journal of British Studies*, 46:3 (2007), 621–46.

Provisional Instructions for the Guidance of the In-Door Staff (Shanghai: Statistical Department of the Inspectorate General, 1877).

Putnam Weale, B. L., *Indiscreet Letters from Peking* (New York: Arno Press, 1970).

Qu Tongzu, *Local Government in China under the Ch'ing* (Cambridge, MA: Harvard University Press, 1962).

Rasmussen, A. H., *China Trader* (New York: Crowell, 1954).

Rasmussen, A. H., *Return to the Sea* (London: Constable, 1956).

Rasmussen, A. H., *Sea Fever* (London: Constable, 1952).

Richards, Eric, 'Running Home from Australia: Intercontinental mobility and migrant expectations in the nineteenth century', in *Emigrant Homecomings: The return movement of emigrants, 1600–2000*, edited by Marjory Harper (Manchester: Manchester University Press, 2005), 77–104.

Ristaino, Marcia, *Port of Last Resort: The diaspora communities of Shanghai* (Stanford: Stanford University Press, 2001).

Rogaski, Ruth, *Hygienic Modernity: Meanings of health and disease in treaty-port China* (Berkeley: University of California Press, 2004).

Rowe, William T., *China's Last Empire: The great Qing* (Cambridge, MA: Belknap Press, 2009).

Schrecker, John E., *Imperialism and Chinese Nationalism: Germany in Shantung* (Cambridge, MA: Harvard University Press, 1971).

Scidmore, Eliza, *China, the Long-Lived Empire* (New York: The Century Co., 1900).

Scully, Eileen, *Bargaining with the State from Afar: American citizenship in treaty port China, 1844–1942* (New York: Columbia University Press, 2001).

Sinclair, Georgina, *At the End of the Line: Colonial policing and the imperial endgame* (Manchester: Manchester University Press, 2006).

Sinha, Mrinalini, 'Britishness, Clubbability, and the Colonial Public Sphere', in *Bodies in Contact: Rethinking colonial encounters in world history*, edited by Tony Ballantyne and Antoinette M. Burton (Durham, NC: Duke University Press, 2005), 183–200.

Spence, Jonathan D., *To Change China: Western advisers in China, 1620–1960* (New York: Penguin Books, 2002. First pub. 1969).

Stoler, Ann Laura, *Carnal Knowledge and Imperial Power: Race and the intimate in colonial rule* (Berkeley: University of California Press, 2002).

Strahan, Lachlan, *Australia's China: Changing perceptions from the 1930s to the 1990s* (Cambridge: Cambridge University Press, 1996).

Strauss, Julia C., *Strong Institutions in Weak Polities: State Building in Republican China, 1927–1940* (Oxford: Oxford University Press, 1998).

Thomas, Nicholas, *Colonialism's Culture: Anthropology, travel, and government* (Princeton: Princeton University Press, 1994).

Thomas, Nicholas, and Richard Eves, *Bad Colonists: The South Seas Letters of Vernon Lee Walker and Louis Becke* (Durham, NC: Duke University Press, 1999).

Thompson, Andrew S., *The Empire Strikes Back?: The impact of imperialism on Britain from the mid-nineteenth century* (Harlow: Pearson Longman, 2005).

Trumbull, George R., *An Empire of Facts: Colonial power, cultural knowledge, and Islam in Algeria, 1870–1914* (Cambridge: Cambridge University Press, 2009).

Tyler, William Ferdinand, *Pulling Strings in China* (London: Constable & Co., 1929).

Van de Ven, Hans, 'Robert Hart and Gustav Detring During the Boxer Rebellion', *Modern Asian Studies*, 40:3 (2006), 631–62.

Van de Ven, Hans, *War and Nationalism in China, 1925–1945* (London: RoutledgeCurzon, 2003).

Vertovec, Steven, and Robin Cohen, eds, *Conceiving Cosmopolitanism: Theory, context and practice* (Oxford: Oxford University Press, 2002).

Wakeman Jr, Frederic, *Strangers at the Gate: Social disorder in South China, 1839–1861* (Berkeley: University of California Press, 1966).

Wakeman, Jr, Frederic, 'Hanjian (Traitor)!: Collaboration and retribution in wartime Shanghai', in *Becoming Chinese: Passages to modernity and beyond*, edited by Wen-hsin Yeh (Berkeley: University of California Press, 2000), 298–341.

Wakeman Jr, Frederic, 'Shanghai Smuggling', in *In the Shadow of the Rising Sun: Shanghai under Japanese occupation*, edited by Christian Henriot and Wen-hsin Yeh (Cambridge: Cambridge University Press, 2004), 116–55.

Wakeman Jr, Frederic, and Wen-hsin Yeh, eds, *Shanghai Sojourners* (Berkeley: Institute of East Asian Studies, University of California, 1992).

Ward, Stuart, ed., *British Culture and the End of Empire* (Manchester: Manchester University Press, 2001).

Ward, Stuart, 'Transcending the Nation: A global imperial history?' in *After the Imperial Turn: Thinking with and through the nation*, edited by Antoinette Burton (Durham, NC: Duke University Press, 2003), 44–56.

Wasserstrom, Jeffrey N., *Student Protests in Twentieth-Century China: The view from Shanghai* (Stanford: Stanford University Press, 1991).

Wildenthal, Lora, 'Race, Gender, and Citizenship in the German Colonial Empire', in *Tensions of Empire: Colonial cultures in a bourgeois world*, edited by Frederick Cooper and Ann Laura Stoler (Berkeley: University of California Press, 1997), 263–83.

Wilkinson, W. H., *'Where Chinese Drive.' English student-life at Peking* (London: W. H. Allen & Co., 1885).

Witchard, Anne Veronica, *Thomas Burke's Dark Chinoiserie: Limehouse Nights and the queer spell of Chinatown* (Farnham: Ashgate, 2009).

Wood, Frances, *No Dogs and Not Many Chinese: Treaty port life in China, 1843–1943* (London: John Murray, 2000).

Woolf, Stuart, 'Statistics and the Modern State', *Comparative Studies in History and Society*, 31:3 (1989), 588–604.

Worcester, G. R. G., *The Junkman Smiles* (London: Chatto and Windus, 1959).

Wright, Stanley Fowler, *The Origin and Development of the Chinese Customs Service, 1843–1911* (Shanghai: privately circulated, 1936).

Wright, Stanley Fowler, *China's Struggle for Tariff Autonomy, 1843–1938* (Shanghai: Kelly & Walsh, 1938).

Wright, Stanley Fowler, *Hart and the Chinese Customs* (Belfast: W. Mullan, 1950).

Yeh, Wen-hsin, *Becoming Chinese: Passages to modernity and beyond* (Berkeley: University of California Press, 2000).

Yeh, Wen-hsin, 'Shanghai Modernity: Commerce and culture in a republican city', *The China Quarterly*, 150 (1997), 375–94.

Yeh, Wen-hsin, *Shanghai Splendor: Economic sentiments and the making of modern China, 1843–1949* (Berkeley: University of California Press, 2007).

Zarrow, Peter, *China in War and Revolution, 1895–1949* (London: Routledge, 2005).

Zelin, Madeleine, *The Magistrate's Tael: Rationalizing fiscal reform in eighteenth-century Ch'ing China* (Berkeley: University of California Press, 1984).

INDEX

Note: page numbers in *italic* refer to figures and tables

Lightning Source UK Ltd.
Milton Keynes UK
UKOW06f1230220316

270663UK00003B/7/P

9 781784 993702